Oxford Sketchbook

Editorial Director: Timothy Auger
Assistant Editor: Pasha Siraj
Designer: Yolande Lim
Production Manager: Sin Kam Cheong

First published in 2005 by
Archipelago Press,
an imprint of
Editions Didier Millet
121 Telok Ayer Street, #03-01
Singapore 068590
www.edmbooks.com

Reprinted 2012, 2014

Colour separation by
Colourscan Co. Pte Ltd, Singapore
Printed by Tien Wah Press, Singapore

ISBN 978-981-4155-05-2

Printed on 160gsm Modigliani Neve

Artist's Acknowledgments

Oxford was a city I had sketched a number of times whilst completing a series of architectural cards, before I was asked to do this sketchbook by my friend Didier Millet, the French publisher. Didier had discovered the splendour of Oxford's buildings whilst visiting England for a wedding in the nearby Cotswolds.

My thanks must go to Tim Auger, my editor, who with his enthusiasm and knowledge of Oxford, having studied at Christ Church, has helped me find places I might have missed. And Roger White, my writer, who was at Wadham, has written a wonderfully incisive text with much praise for the city, but also with a critical eye.

I am also indebted to Roger and Heidi Chalfont and Ali and Boyd Gunnell for their hospitality whilst I was working in Oxford; and to Judi and Mike Brown, who live in the city, for their help. I should like to express my gratitude to Ros Carter, whose ex-editorial skills have kept my handwritten notes in order. And finally thanks are due to Jayne Norris for her arrangements and hospitality when I stayed in Singapore for the final stages in the preparation of the book.

Oxford is indeed a 'City of Dreaming Spires' and its 'Town and Gown' architecture is a sight to behold when walking its streets or sketching its buildings.

I have tried to do it justice in my own small way.

Graham Byfield

Oxford Sketchbook

Watercolours by Graham Byfield

Text by Roger White

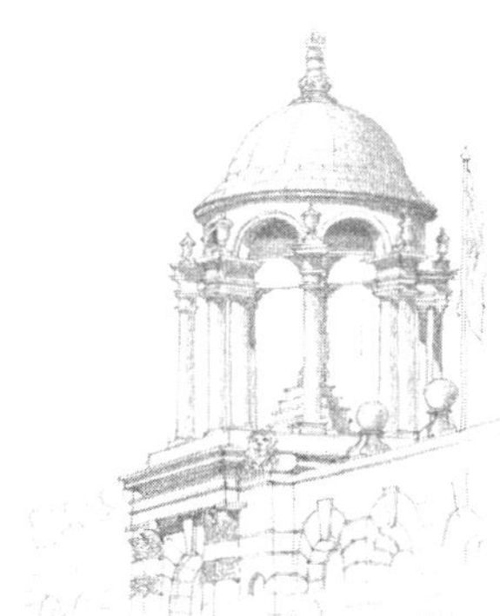

edm EDITIONS DIDIER MILLET

Contents

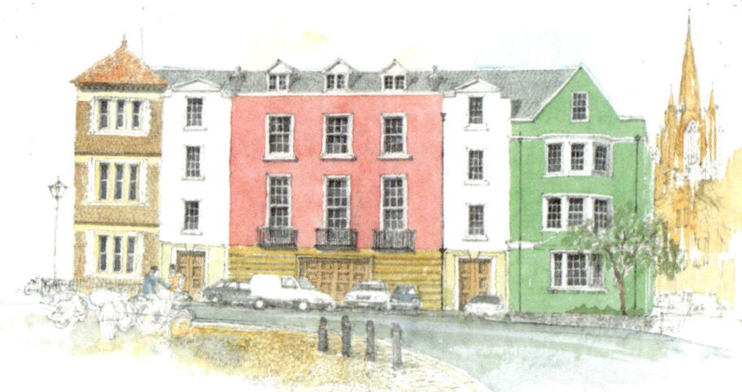

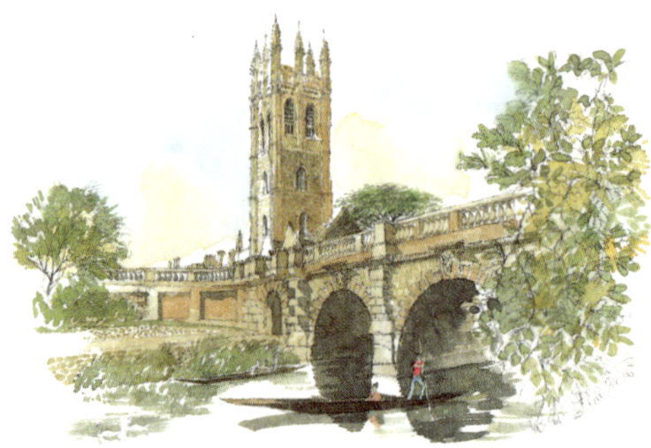

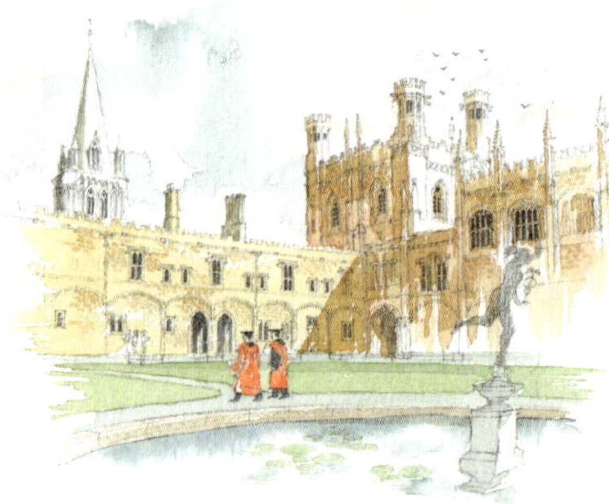

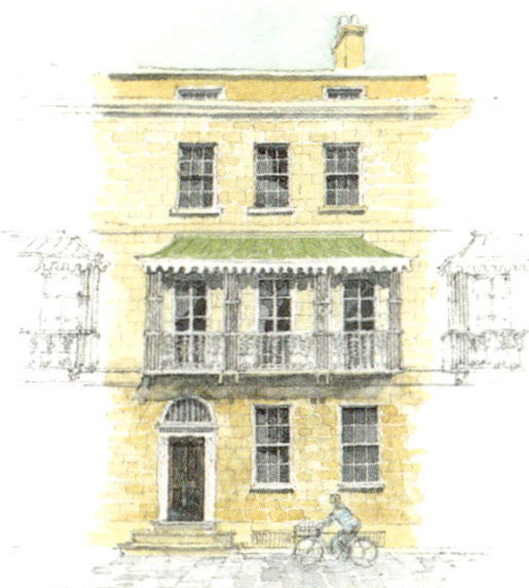

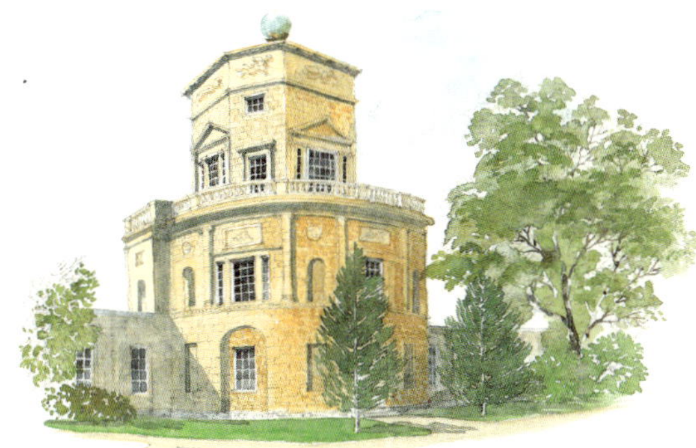

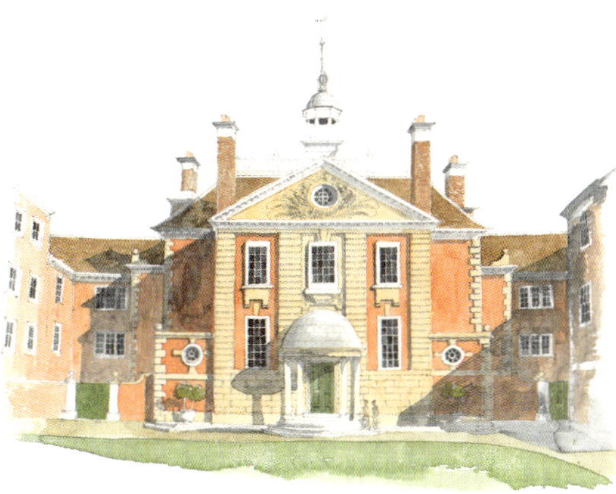

Introduction

The Victorian writer Matthew Arnold famously called Oxford a 'city of dreaming spires', 'home of lost causes', 'whispering from her towers the last enchantments of the Middle Age'. The poet Keats thought it the finest city in the world. At the other extreme the socialist prime minister Ramsay MacDonald dismissed the University as 'a painted lady, from which Labour has nothing to expect', and a more recent wag has referred to it as 'the Latin Quarter of Cowley', in reference to the enormous car-manufacturing eastern suburbs. The truth is that any generalisation about Oxford, even the most generally accepted one concerning its physical beauty, is liable to be flawed, because it is simply too full of contradictions and anomalies. Yes, of course it is beautiful, but there is plenty of ugliness too. Yes, it is guilty of self-regarding smugness, but it also engages in perennial soul-searching and breast-beating. Yes, compared to many other universities it is rich, and some of its colleges are very rich indeed; but compared to some comparable American institutions it is by no means rich, and a number of Oxford colleges teeter chronically on the brink of extinction for lack of funds.

Until a century ago Oxford must indeed have struck approaching travellers as a kind of golden mirage, its justly celebrated skyline of towers, spires, domes and turrets rising from its lush setting of water meadows and hills, uncomprised by industrialisation or unsightly suburbs. The vision that inspired Matthew Arnold can still be recaptured in the views across Christ Church Meadows from the south or Port Meadow from the west, but otherwise twentieth century development wraps thickly around the historic core and ensures a tedious crawl in from the encircling bypass. Even the preservation of the skyline - arguably the city's most precious single asset - was a close-run thing, with the erection of an ugly and intrusive tower block for the Department of Engineering in 1960 prompting the city council to impose an essential height limit on new buildings. And here are two more Oxford contradictions: almost all the buildings for which the city is famous and visited are the creation of the University and colleges, yet given a free hand the University would certainly have proceeded to blight the place with hideous new blocks even more than it has actually been allowed to; and the restraining brake which has spared us this is applied by the same city council which has itself been responsible for some of Oxford's most unattractive developments.

When we think of Oxford we think, of course, of the University and colleges. Historically, Oxford originated as a modest market town into which a federation of colleges has progressively intruded, an academic cuckoo in a civic nest. The tension between 'Town' and 'Gown' goes a very long way back and persists today, if more peacefully than before. Its most extreme manifestation was the St Scholastica's Day riot of 1355, when a pub brawl escalated into a massacre in which more than sixty students are said to have been killed and several chaplains scalped. The expiatory procession imposed on the townspeople by the King continued until 1825. Massacres apart, it is not hard to sympathise with the townspeople, for Oxford had been functioning quite happily as a centre for commerce and communications long before the first student appeared in the 12th century. It is not, despite what the street plan of the historic centre may suggest, a town of Roman origin, though some sort of river crossing over the Thames may have existed then. A Saxon town, first mentioned in 912, developed on raised ground to the north of the river; its main north-south and east-west streets crossed at right-angles at what is

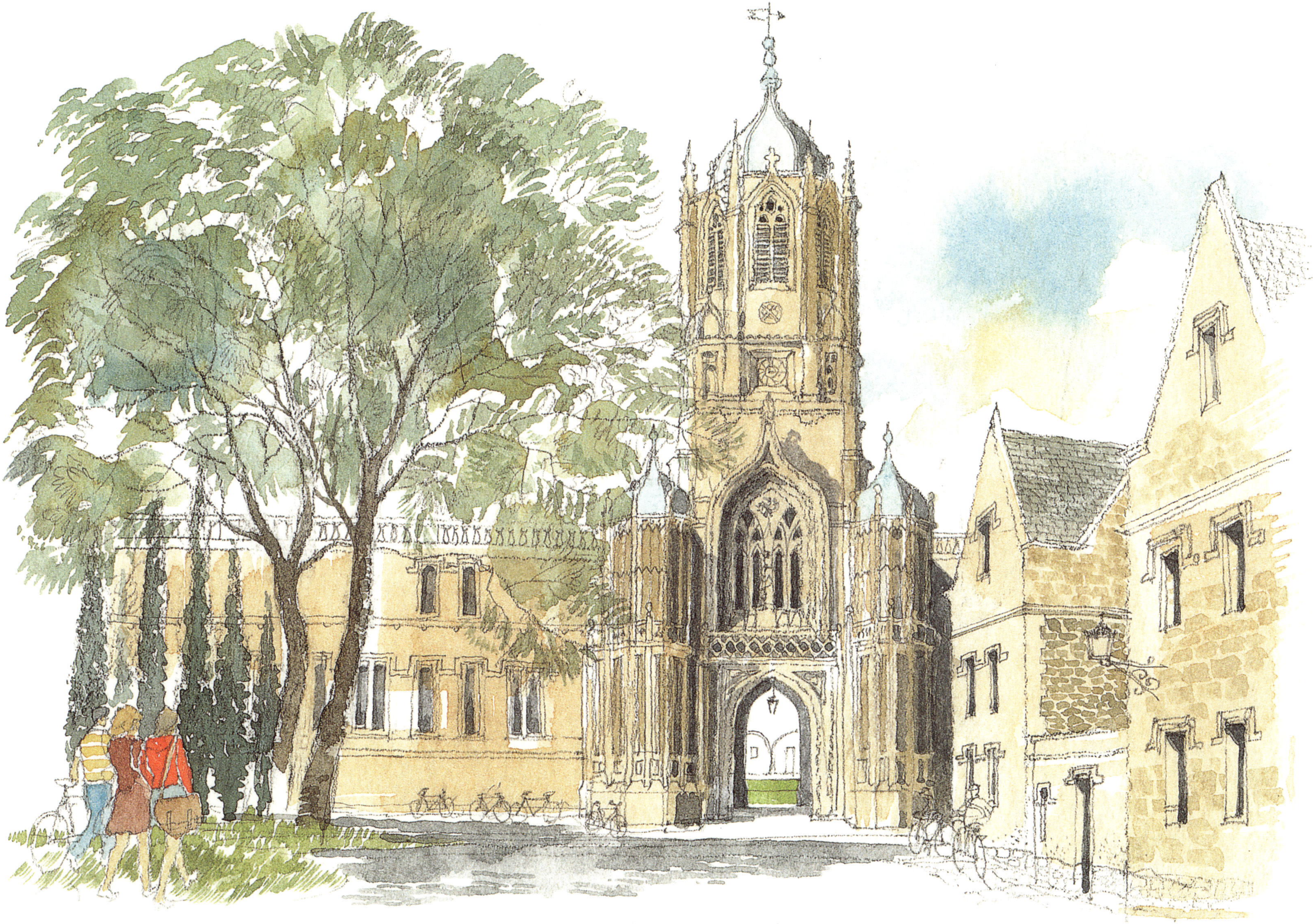

Tom Tower, Christ Church, the magnificent entrance to Oxford's grandest college. The upper half is Sir Christopher Wren's brilliant completion of Cardinal Wolsey's unfinished gate tower.

now Carfax, and still form the bones of central Oxford's layout. The new settlement may have been associated with the nunnery said to have been founded in the early 8th century by the Saxon princess St Frideswide, whose virtue was miraculously saved when an over-ardent princely suitor was struck by lightning. In any case it stood on the frontier between the kingdoms of Mercia and Wessex, at what increasingly became a nodal point for communications - first by water and road, and later by canal and railway. By the time of Doomsday Book Oxford had already seen several historic events (notably the murder of King Edmund Ironside and the burning of all the resident Danes within St Frideswide's nunnery) and had acquired a ring of protective walls. The Normans recognised its strategic significance by raising a castle on the west side, and Henry I built the palace of Beaumont outside the walls to the north where the romantic Richard the Lionheart was born.

Although King Alfred was subsequently alleged to have been the founder of the University (and indeed in 1381, in order to win a lawsuit, University College forged documents to prove its foundation by Alfred in 872), it was not actually until some time in the 12th century that Oxford became a meeting place for scholars. Exactly why is not known; some say it was because the various monasteries that had been established in and around the town developed an educational dimension, others that the monasteries were attracted to Oxford by the presence of the scholars. It may also be that war with France in the late 12th and early 13th centuries prevented clever young men from travelling to study at the university of Paris. In any event, by 1190 civil and canon law were being taught, and the curriculum then expanded to include theology and the liberal arts. By the early 13th century between 200 and 300 students and seventy teachers are recorded in Oxford, and in 1214 a chancellor was appointed, thus recognising the university as a corporate entity for the first time.

Student numbers expanded quite rapidly, but to begin with they lived mainly in privately-run 'academic halls', really glorified lodging houses run by principals licensed by the University. A typical example might comprise a hall for dining and lectures, a kitchen, a block in which the students lived five to a room, and maybe a row of shops to generate income. These halls, of which there may have been as many

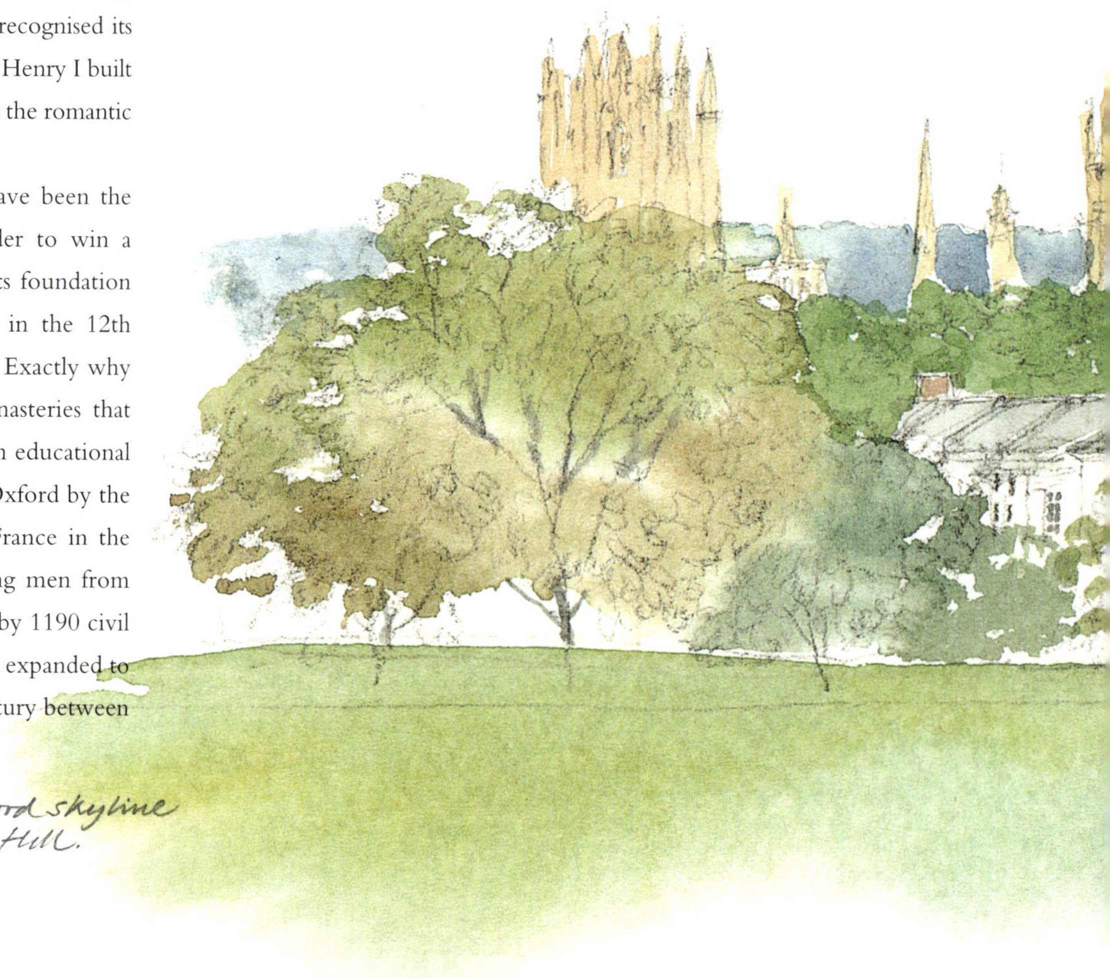

The celebrated Oxford skyline from Headington Hill.

as a hundred by the beginning of the 14th century, were gradually superseded by colleges, so that today only St Edmund Hall remains as a reminder - and even that has been a college since 1957. The colleges differed not so much in function as in size and wealth, since they tended to be founded and endowed by rich individuals, and all had a chapel. Since a major factor in their foundation was the growing need to educate a literate government bureaucracy, and since medieval civil servants were predominantly priests, the founders were often kings, queens, or senior clerics (although Balliol College was founded by John of Balliol as a penance for kidnapping the Bishop of Durham). Merton College, for instance, which has a good claim to be the oldest, was founded in 1262 by Walter de Merton, a priest who rose to be Chancellor of England and Bishop of Rochester.

Thus began the process whereby the academic cuckoo insinuated itself into the centre of Oxford, as rich benefactors bought up land and property from the townspeople, clearing the existing buildings to put up their own. Over the ensuing centuries the colleges gradually proliferated and expanded, so that by the 18th century virtually the whole eastern

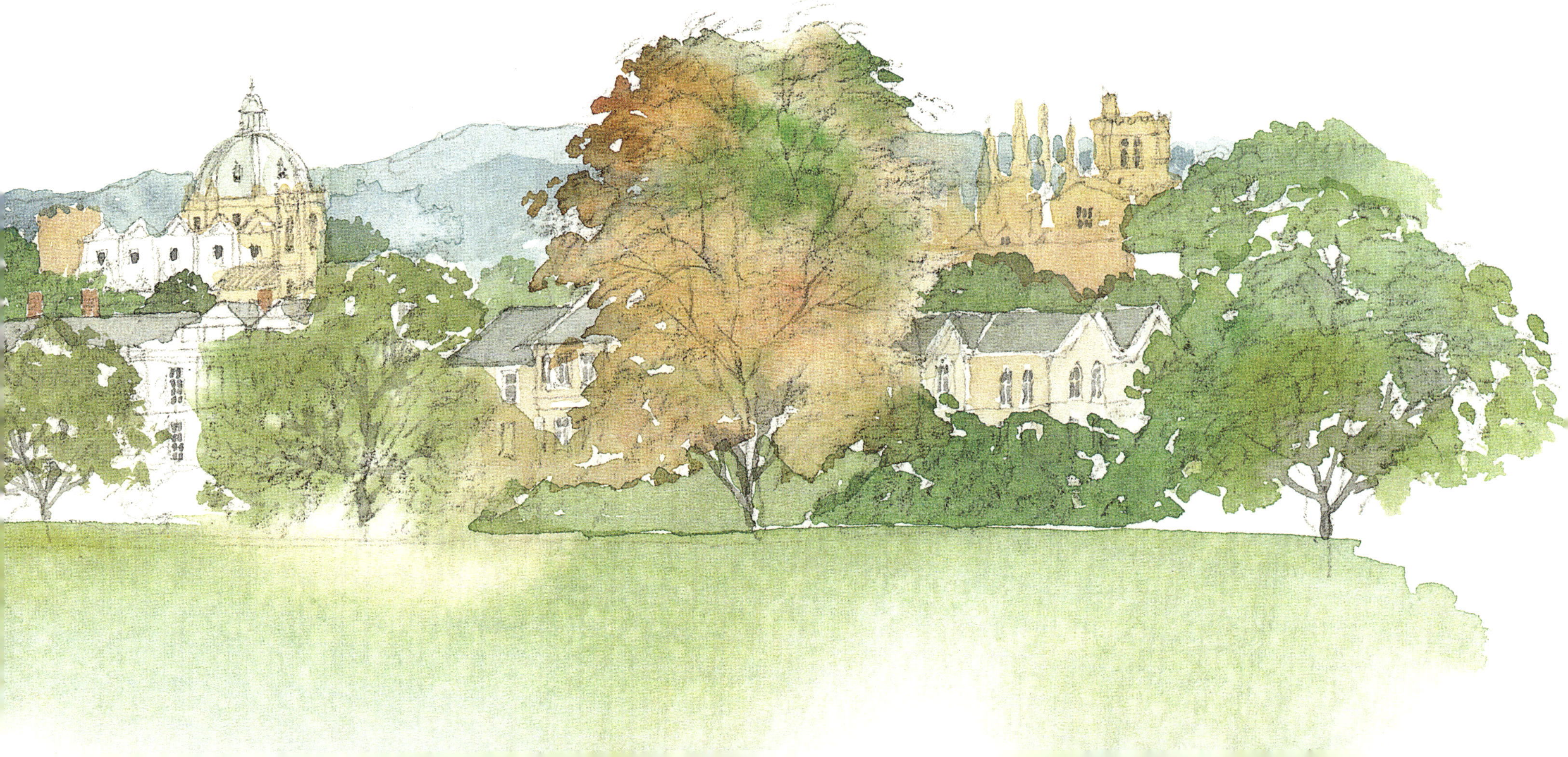

The choir of St Frideswides Priory, now England's smallest ancient cathedral.

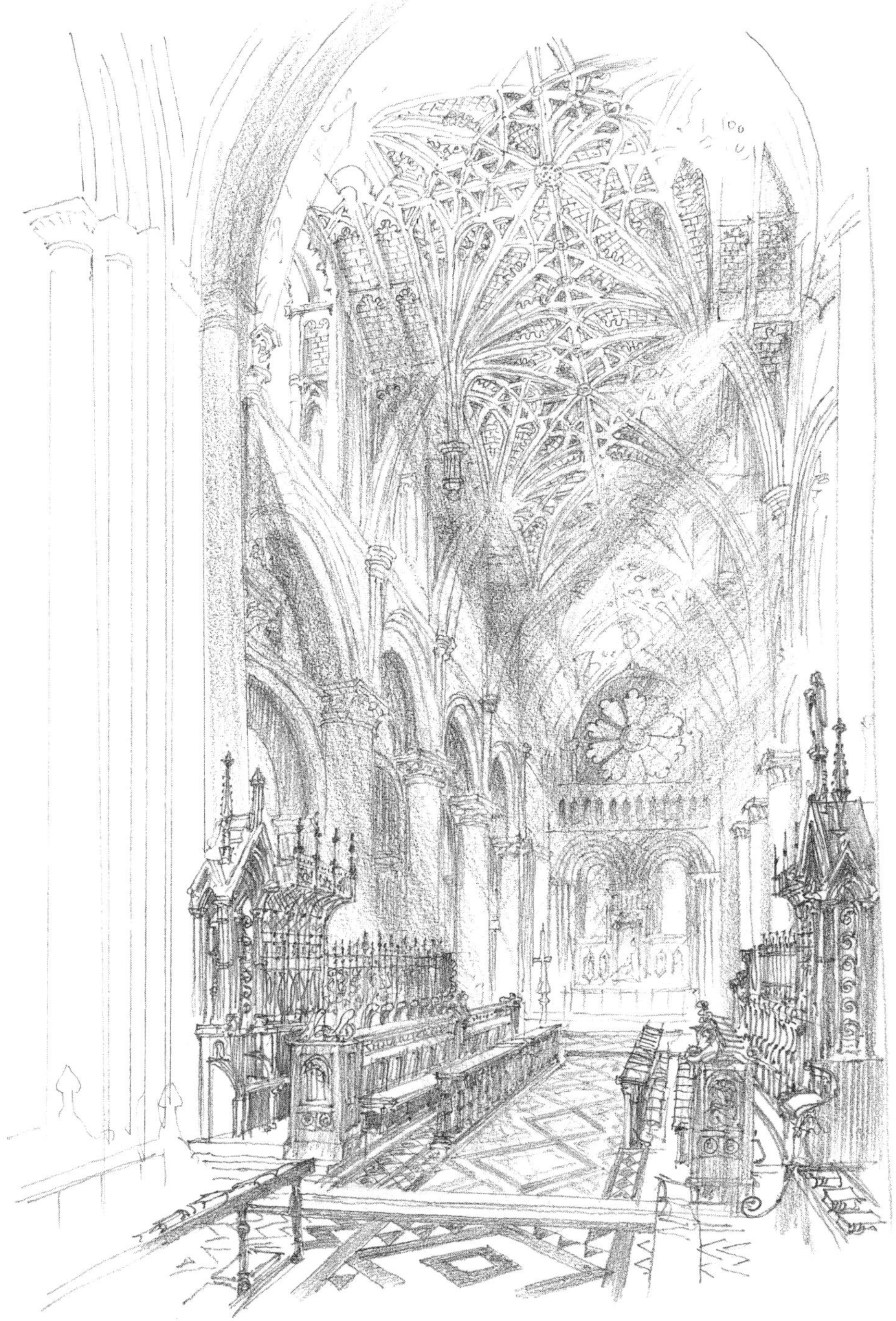

half of the centre was given over to college or university buildings - a trend that still continues. In the High Street (or The High, as it is always known) domestic frontages still exist but they are outnumbered and overshadowed. As recently as 1937 a whole block of attractively picturesque houses was demolished to make way for the lumpish New Bodleian Library. Nowadays such demolition would be unthinkable, but as space grows shorter many colleges are taking over houses on the perimeter of their city-centre sites and converting them discreetly into student rooms, so that what look from the street to be houses for private individuals are in reality nothing of the kind. Still, the continuing juxtaposition of such domestic frontages, generally small-scale and picturesquely irregular, with the grander and more symmetrical college façades, is crucial to the visual appeal of Oxford's streets.

The 14th century was a particularly propitious time to found a college, for economic decline and the ravages of the Black Death had caused depopulation and the freeing up of land in the centre. New College, founded by William of Wykeham, Bishop of Winchester, in 1372 (though he had been buying up land for the previous ten years), took advantage of the situation to occupy an unprecedentedly spacious site in the north-east corner of the town, bounded on north and east by the town walls. It was much the biggest foundation to date, with seventy inmates, and for the first time some of these were undergraduates; and whereas previous colleges had been built in an ad hoc way with no particular overall plan, New College introduced the idea of grouping its buildings around a quadrangle. Like all colleges (but unlike the academic halls), it had not only a dining hall and lodgings for the inmates but also a library and a chapel. Coming less than two decades after the St Scholastica's Day

The Inner Quad of Jesus College. Founded in 1571, past students have been T.E. Lawrence and Harold Wilson. In 1974 it was the first men's college to admit women to study.

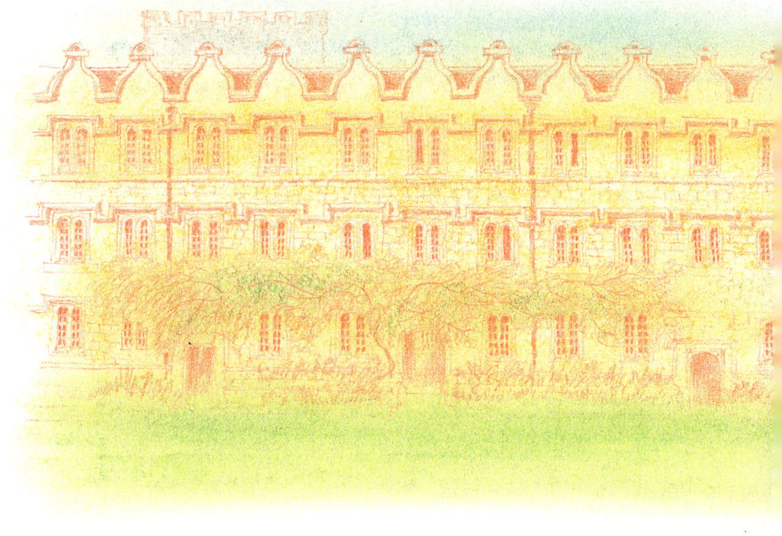

massacre, access was controlled by a gatehouse with a very stout door, and the whole complex was turned defensively in upon itself.

This was to be the pattern for subsequent college building, and it resulted in a feature very characteristic of Oxford: a constellation of essentially private domains, protected by high stone walls, battlements, spiked railings and watchful porters. Within these defences, colleges may be unexpectedly, disconcertingly spacious, like New College, St John's or Trinity, often with a glorious garden and even, in the case of Magdalen, a deer park; or they may be intricately small-scale, like Brasenose, Lincoln or Oriel. Even a college as vast and imposing as Christ Church juxtaposes the grand with the intimate: who, having first traversed Tom Quad, the university's largest quadrangle, could predict the tiny medieval cloister tucked invisibly alongside the college chapel - which also happens to double as England's smallest ancient cathedral? The same is true of the townscape as a whole. Despite the grandeur of its set-pieces, the special quality of Oxford lies at least as much in its narrow alleys and hidden corners, like the passage that burrows through from Holywell Street, past the tiny Turf Tavern, beneath the louring medieval town walls and out again into New College Lane - which is itself a sequence of right-angle bends, running between high stone walls overhung with wisteria.

Until the Reformation of the 1530s all Oxford's scholars were clerics in holy orders (today's academic robes are a distant reminder of that) and the University was technically an ecclesiastical body operating under canon rather than civil law, responsible ultimately to the Pope. A number of colleges were in fact founded to provide a higher education to high-flying monks from specific orders and monasteries - Canterbury College, for instance, was an adjunct of Canterbury Cathedral Priory, whose name lives on in Canterbury Quad of Christ Church. The present Worcester College was formerly Gloucester College and, uniquely, drew monks from several different Benedictine monasteries; in amongst its present predominantly Georgian buildings is a 15th-century range with the coats of arms of those monasteries over the doors. All Souls College was founded in 1438 by the then Archbishop of Canterbury, Henry Chichele, to train secular (i.e. non-monastic) clergy and ecclesiastical lawyers, while Magdalen, in addition to its complement of graduates and undergraduates, had a grammar school for the education of choristers and the sons of townspeople.

The Reformation brought an abrupt and traumatic change to the whole basis of Oxford's academic existence. It is true that the colleges escaped with their fabrics largely unscathed; after all the country still needed clergy, albeit they would no longer be Catholic, and the government certainly needed administrators, so it was obviously in the national interest that they should continue to function. After being suppressed, therefore, they were refounded as secular institutions, while the monastic colleges too were refounded under new names - St Bernard's became St John's, Durham College became Trinity, and so on. All the same, much damage was done to chapels, with the destruction of sculptures and stained glass considered idolatrous, and priceless books and religious manuscripts were burned. The college most dramatically affected was the one just then in the process of being set up by Cardinal Wolsey, which he had intended should be much the biggest and grandest at either Oxford or Cambridge. With typical high-handedness Wolsey had closed

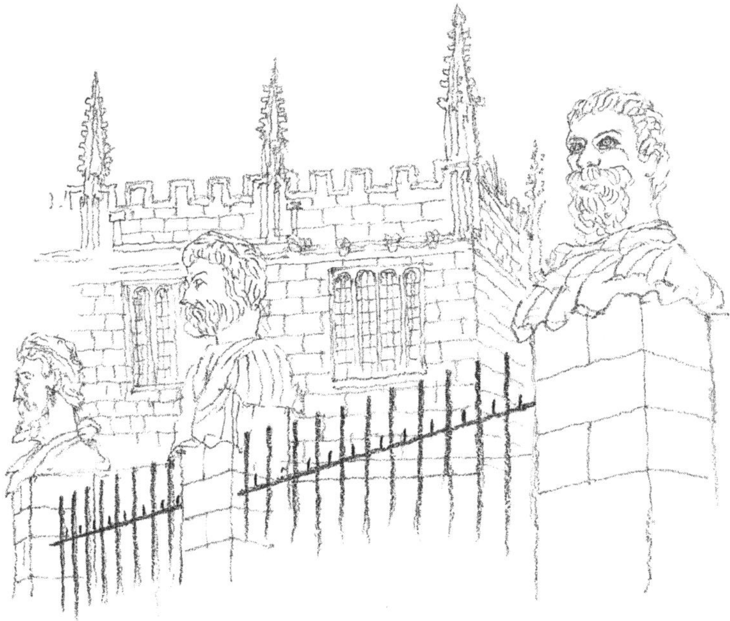

The so-called 'Emperors' Heads' in Broad Street, re-carved in 1972.

down the ancient priory of St Frideswide to make way for his new foundation, which was to be called 'Cardinal College'. By the time of his disgrace in 1529 the enormous hall had been completed, but although Henry VIII adopted the college as his own, renaming it Christ Church, the proposed chapel on a par with that at King's College, Cambridge was abandoned in favour of reusing the priory church, and the fan-vaulted cloister around the main quadrangle was left unfinished.

One of the greatest changes resulting from the Reformation was to the composition of University membership. Medieval students were poor clerics who were expected to share a monastic existence in unheated rooms. By Elizabeth I's reign, although roughly half were still youths from relatively humble backgrounds who needed a university education as a prerequisite to becoming clergymen or schoolmasters, the other half were from the middle or upper classes. They were financed by their parents and they expected rather more in the way of creature comforts - at the very least, a fireplace in their room. So from now on residential blocks were made a little less austere, although they continued to use the medieval plan of groups of rooms opening off staircases, which is still the standard Oxford arrangement today. As for the Fellows, they were still required to be celibate clerics, but for the first time the heads of colleges were allowed to marry, and their wives were likewise not prepared to put up with medieval discomfort.

Meanwhile the University too had been acquiring its own stock of increasingly fine buildings. As a rather nebulous entity it had no endowments, unlike the colleges, and to begin with it held its lectures mainly in rented property in the area between the north town wall and the church of St Mary the Virgin on the High Street. This area has ever since been the symbolic heart of the University. At first, meetings of its governing body (known as Convocation) and disciplinary body (the Chancellor's Court) were held in the church itself, but in the 1320s an addition was made to the north side of the church specifically for this purpose, with a very modest room for the University's small collection of books and manuscripts above. A century later, with the help of benefactions, the University was able to embark on a much more ambitious building for the holding of theology lectures, known as the Divinity School; as finally completed in 1483, it was given a fabulously complex and delicate stone vault which makes it one of the most beautiful medieval rooms in Europe.

By that stage it had been decided to add an extra floor to contain the library donated in 1444 by Duke Humphrey of Gloucester, younger son of Henry V; from this grew the great library known as the Bodleian, called after Sir Thomas Bodley who reorganised and expanded it at the beginning of the 17th century to take account of the vast increase in the publication of printed books (Duke Humphrey's, of course, would have been largely hand-written). One of Bodley's coups was to reach an agreement with the Stationers' Company in London that Oxford should receive a free copy of every book printed by the company's members, thus inaugurating its status as a copyright library and ensuring a permanent and perpetual storage headache. Duke Humphrey (as the original 15th-century upper library is known) was enlarged modestly, and at the same time a whole new quadrangle was tacked on to accommodate all the different University faculties or schools - hence the name 'Schools Quadrangle'. Even though the faculties have long since moved out to more spacious accommodation, their names are still lettered above the doors that led to them.

The political turbulence of the mid-17th century by no means passed Oxford by - on the contrary, although the townspeople on the whole inclined to support Parliament, the University (by now very firmly established as top dog in town) showed its general conservatism and in particular its belief in High Church Anglicanism by aligning firmly with the King. For the first years of the Civil War Oxford became the royalist capital, with Charles I staying in Christ Church and his wife Henrietta Maria in Merton College, and a door was cut in an intervening wall to enable them to visit each other without going out into the street. Munitions were stored in New College's bell tower, a drawbridge was installed over the River Cherwell alongside Magdalen College, outer defensive ditches were dug, and the town acquired its own mint. Surprisingly, Oxford escaped a bruising siege; its surrender was negotiated in 1646 after the king's incognito departure and there was remarkably little damage apart from the demolition of most of the medieval castle.

The period that followed the Civil War, and particularly the Restoration of the monarchy in 1660, was from an intellectual point of view one of the most remarkable in Oxford's history. The Ashmolean Museum (the University's museum of the fine arts) has a brilliant bust in the Bernini manner of that quintessential Oxford Restoration intellect, Sir Christopher Wren - undergraduate at Wadham College in the 1650s, subsequently Fellow of All Souls (where the elaborate sundial he designed can still be seen) and, from 1661, the University's Savilian Professor of Astronomy. He was part of a circle of scientifically-minded young men which revolved around John Wilkins, Warden of Wadham, and although he was of course to carve his name in history primarily as architect of the rebuilt City of London, he inevitably left his mark on the way Oxford looked.

One of his first commissions as an architect was to produce a scheme for a building to house the University's ceremonies. The University has always been keen on its ceremonial, and degree days are still a great

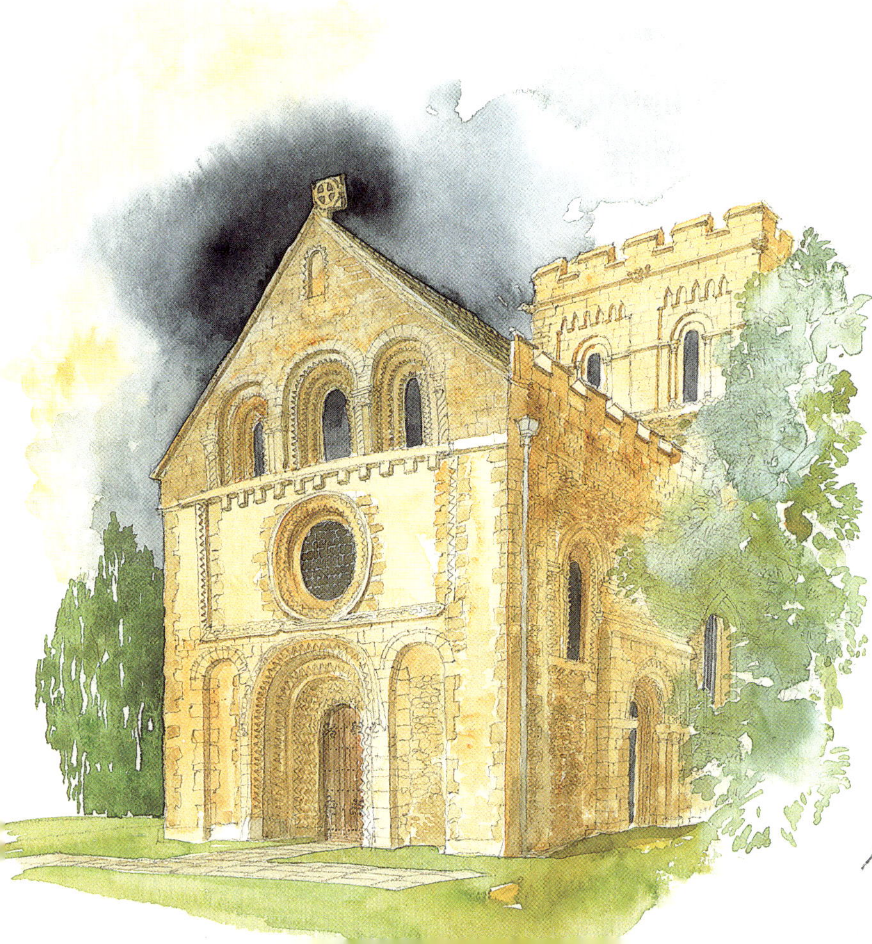

Iffley, in the southern suburbs, has one of England's finest Norman village churches.

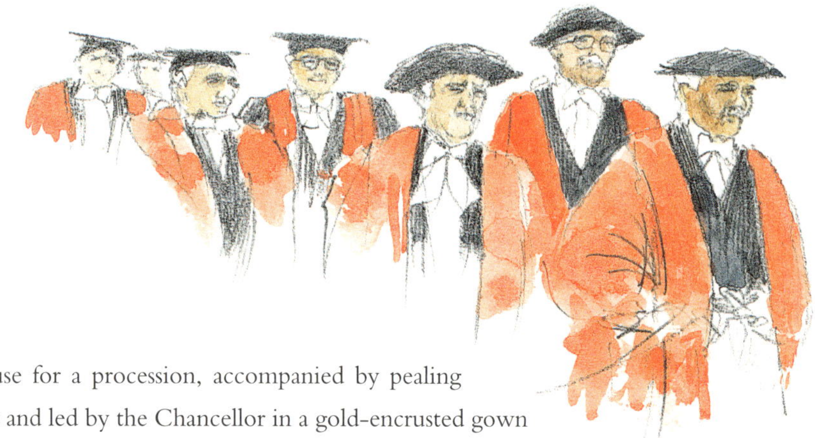

The Encaenia annual ceremony takes place in June. University members in full regalia parade through the streets on the way to the Sheldonian Theatre for a ceremony in latin at which honorary degrees are bestowed.

excuse for a procession, accompanied by pealing bells and led by the Chancellor in a gold-encrusted gown remarkably similar to that of the Speaker of the House of Commons. The annual Encaenia ceremony, at which honorary degrees are awarded to the accompaniment of Latin speeches, is immediately followed by an event called 'Lord Crewe's Benefaction' in the great North Quad at All Souls, at which some hundred or so individuals in colourful doctoral robes consume large quantities of strawberries and cream washed down by champagne. Wren's contribution to the University's self-esteem was the Sheldonian Theatre, a strange D-plan auditorium based on an antique Roman theatre - an excusably immature design, but still the first at Oxford to be entirely classical in its architectural vocabulary.

Oxford had been slow to adjust to the innovations of the Renaissance, and prior to Wren this had produced some pretty odd Gothic/Classical hybrids. A good example is Canterbury Quad at St John's of the 1630s, which combines Renaissance arcades fit for 15th- century Florence, 16th-century Mannerist centrepieces, and battlemented Tudor Gothic elevations that could have been built at any time in the two centuries prior to their actual erection - and still manages to be a very beautiful space. The chapel and library at Brasenose College, finished the year that Wren designed the Sheldonian (1663), likewise combine Gothic and Classical in a disconcerting way. The Gothic lingered so long in Oxford that builders had scarcely abandoned it as their stock-in-trade before architects were reviving it again. Wren was the first, designing a remarkable octagonal tower (known as Tom Tower after Great Tom, the medieval bell that hangs within it) over Cardinal Wolsey's unfinished gateway to Christ Church and - though he would have preferred to do it classical - employing Gothic because anything else would have jarred. His one-time assistant Nicholas Hawksmoor adopted the same consciously contextual approach when he designed a new Gothic quad for All Souls in 1715. Hawksmoor, if anything a greater architect than Wren, loved Oxford and its skyline, and did more than any man before him to stamp his personality on both. He would have done more, but his fantastical schemes for college after college were mostly shelved as too expensive and impractical. Still, the extraordinary Gothic twin towers of All Souls are his, as are the beefily Baroque Clarendon Building and the bones of Queen's College's grandiloquent front quad.

Most of important of all, perhaps, he conceived the idea of a new square to act as a focus or forum for the University. Radcliffe Square, that exercise in townscape so perfect that it seems to resemble an extremely grand stage set, owes its existence to Hawksmoor, who also had the brilliant (if characteristically impractical) idea of mooring a great domed library in its centre. The Radcliffe Camera, as the library is known, was actually designed by James Gibbs on the basis of Hawksmoor's original idea (the University, with typical inertia, had taken twenty years to acquire the necessary land, by which time the architect was dead), and it is probably Oxford's best claim to a building of world class. Like the Square, it is named after the enormously rich doctor whose fortune was later to pay for the Radcliffe Infirmary and the Radcliffe Observatory.

After the intellectual ferment of the Restoration period, the 18th century was undoubtedly an era of what one writer has called 'gouty slumber'. Too many Fellows simply marked time while waiting for a well-paid college living (that is, a country parish of which there were hundreds in the gift of the various colleges) to become available.

Three quarters of undergraduates were now drawn from the gentry and aristocracy, fee-paying gentlemen-commoners who saw this as an opportunity to spend three years having a damned good time, and often as not left without a degree. Even more than their Tudor predecessors they expected to be housed in comfort, with the kind of panelled rooms they would have experienced at home. The net result was that, if not much work got done, the colleges did at least milk their wealthy Old Boys for donations to finance handsome new buildings. Paradoxically this was perhaps above all the age of the library, despite the apparently limited use to which their contents were put. In addition to the Radcliffe Camera, superbly gracious examples went up at Queen's, All Souls, Christ Church, Worcester and Oriel. The Codrington Library at All Souls was paid for by an alumnus who had become a rich sugar-planter in Barbados; his marble statue presides over the vast, cool interior, improbably clad as a Roman soldier. Most of these great rooms contain collections of such value that they tend to be maintained as museum pieces, empty of readers, while the real reading goes on elsewhere in more mundane working libraries.

For much the same reason, the libraries are among the many Oxford jewels that remain frustratingly invisible to the average visitor, along with the almost equally impressive array of college halls. The third element in the essential triumvirate of college buildings, the chapel, is usually more accessible, though opening times remain so completely variable as to be unpredictable. The grandest, inevitably is that at Christ Church, which has the unique distinction of being the only one to double as a cathedral. Throughout the Middle Ages Oxford was part of an enormous diocese whose cathedral was over a hundred miles away at Lincoln. Henry VIII carved out a new diocese from this and originally intended its cathedral to be the abbey church of Oseney, on Oxford's western fringe, whose monastery he had just closed down. For whatever reason he decided instead to designate the ex-priory church of St Frideswide, less than half the length of Oseney but more central. One result of this anomalous arrangement is that while the cathedral of course has a bishop, it is run by a Dean who is also head of the college in which it sits. Despite its modest size the interior is crowded with aesthetic incident, including a gorgeous late-Gothic vault, the somewhat battered shrine of St Frideswide, and a superb run of Pre-Raphaelite stained glass by William Morris and Edward Burne-Jones.

Next in scale come the medieval chapels of Merton, New College, All Souls and Magdalen, more characteristic of Oxford in their T-plan - that is to say, they consist only of choir and transepts. At both Merton and New College it was originally intended to adopt the more usual cruciform plan, but having paused before embarking on the nave it was realised that in fact the building worked perfectly well without one, since there were no external parishioners and the college inmates could all sit, monk-like, at facing stalls in the choir. By the time All Souls chapel was begun in 1438 the T-plan seemed the obvious solution and

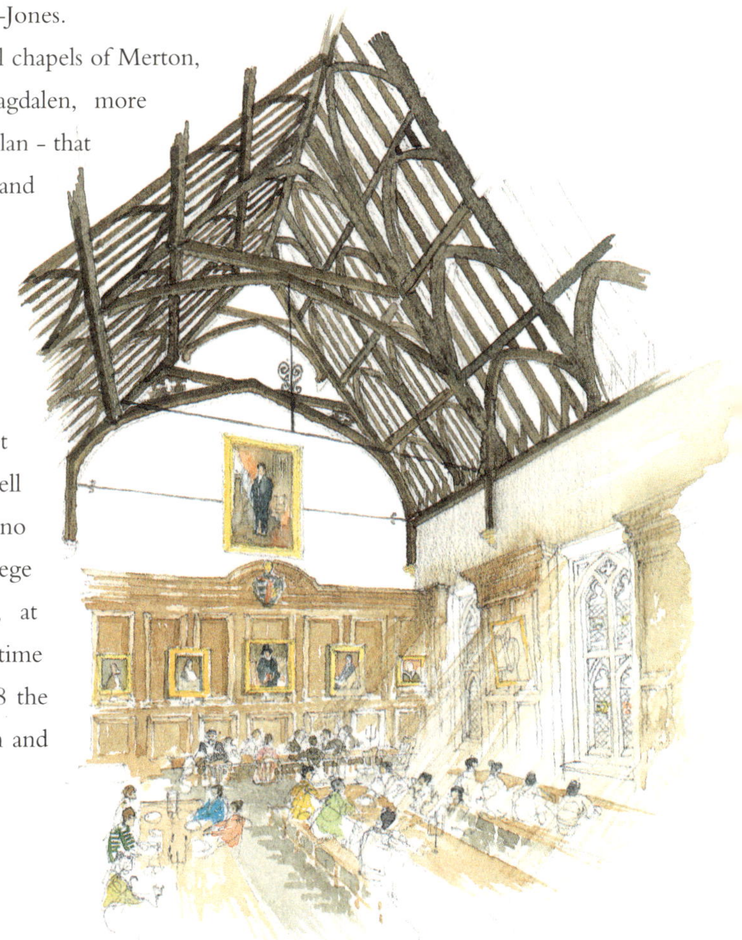

Lincoln College Hall. It has the oldest surviving 15th-century roof in Oxford, and is quite small and intimate compared with some of the grander halls.

so it remained into the 17th century, an Oxford peculiarity. Though the times, and the inmates, became progressively more secular, chapel building and rebuilding continued through the 18th and 19th centuries. Trinity boasts one of the most sumptuous late 17th century ecclesiastical interiors in the country, complete with Oxford's only specimens by that ultimate virtuoso of woodcarving, Grinling Gibbons.

In the 19th century Oxford regained both its intellectual edge and its enthusiasm for religion, becoming a hotbed of religious ferment. The Wesley brothers had in fact launched Methodism in Oxford (John Wesley was a Fellow of Lincoln College), but their main achievements were to be elsewhere. But in the 1840s three Oxford clergymen, John Keble, Edward Pusey and John Newman launched the Anglo-Catholic

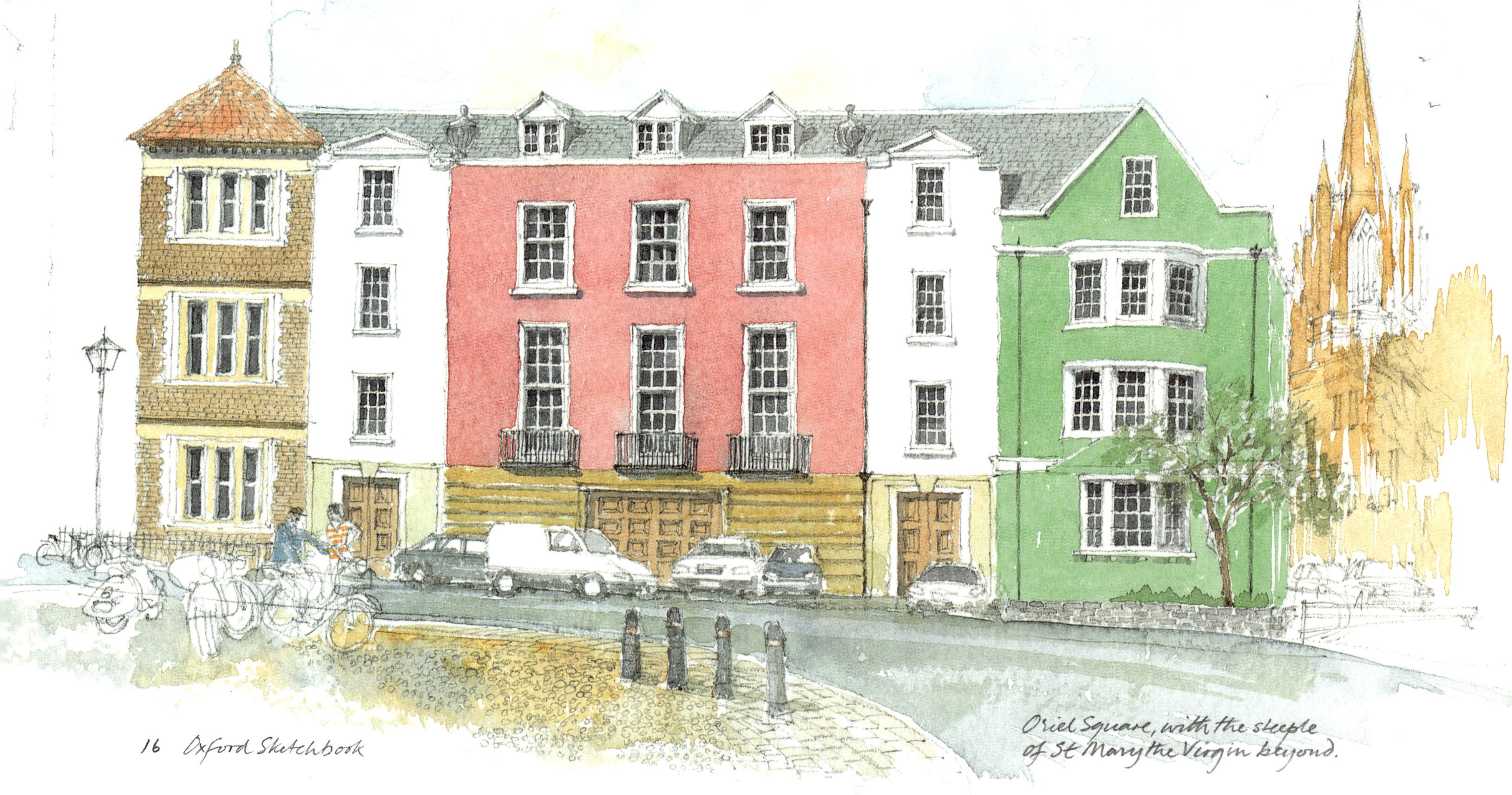

Oriel Square, with the steeple of St Mary the Virgin beyond.

Martyrs' Memorial, St Giles.

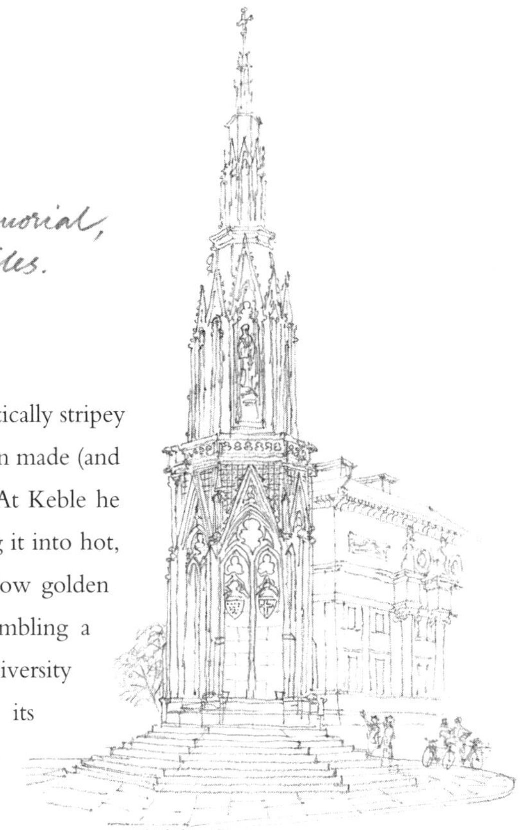

'Oxford Movement', or Tractarianism as it was known on account of the numerous tracts and pamphlets it generated. Newman, whose sermons packed out St Mary's Church, left the city after being denounced as a papist by several bishops, and in 1845 dismayed his friends by converting to Catholicism. Oxford remained an Anglo-Catholic stronghold, however, and Keble College (begun 1868) was a Tractarian monument, as were St Edward's School, Pusey House and the Cowley Fathers - the latter the first new English monastic community since the Reformation. At much the same time that the Anglo-Catholics were launching their movement, those of a more Low Church persuasion were pointedly financing the erection of the Martyrs' Memorial at the bottom end of St Giles (1841-2), a commemoration of the fact that Archbishop Cranmer, and Bishops Latimer and Ridley, had been burnt at the stake as heretics in 1556, just around the corner on Broad Street (a granite cross in the road marks the exact spot). Mansfield College (1887-9), a new foundation specifically for nonconformists, was another symbolic riposte to the Tractarians.

By the time Keble was designed by William Butterfield, Gothic had long been back in the architectural ascendant. The Martyrs' Memorial is a copy of a late 14th century Eleanor Cross, and there are plenty of buildings of the period which are more or less careful copies of medieval styles thought to be at home in Oxford. There were other Victorian architects, however, who wanted something more gutsily original. GG Scott replaced Exeter College's medieval chapel with something modelled on the Sainte-Chapelle in Paris, very fine of its kind but utterly at variance with Oxford tradition. At Worcester College William Burges gave the cool neoclassical chapel interior a High Victorian makeover of the fruitiest kind, ornate and richly-coloured. Butterfield's characteristically stripey chapel at Balliol proved so unpopular that offers were soon made (and declined) to pay for a more conventional replacement. At Keble he took his love of polychromy a stage further by translating it into hot, patterned, red brick, unprecedented in this city of mellow golden stone; the chapel has been unkindly described as resembling a dinosaur in a Fair Isle sweater. Like the new scientific University Museum across the road (1855-60), which behind its Venetian Gothic façade has a glass roof supported on cast-iron columns, it was an emphatic statement of the belief that Oxford and its architecture must move forwards rather than backwards, even at the risk of ugliness.

These were decades of greater upheaval than the city had seen since the Reformation. In 1790 it had been connected to the country's canal network, and the tentative beginnings of industrialisation were continued by the arrival of the railways in the 1850s (fierce objections by the University fortunately meant that the tracks were built on the less attractive west side of town, rather than alongside Magdalen Bridge). In an age of reforming zeal, the University could not escape indefinitely. As a result not only was it made more accessible to middle-class undergraduates, especially to those who wanted a career in the professions or in the expanding home and colonial civil services, but Fellowships too were opened up to competition, non-Anglicans were allowed as students, the curriculum was dramatically expanded, and there even began to be talk of admitting women in some limited form. An Act of 1887 at last allowed Fellows to marry, which was a spur to the development of the fields to the north of the city for substantial family houses. Leafy middle-

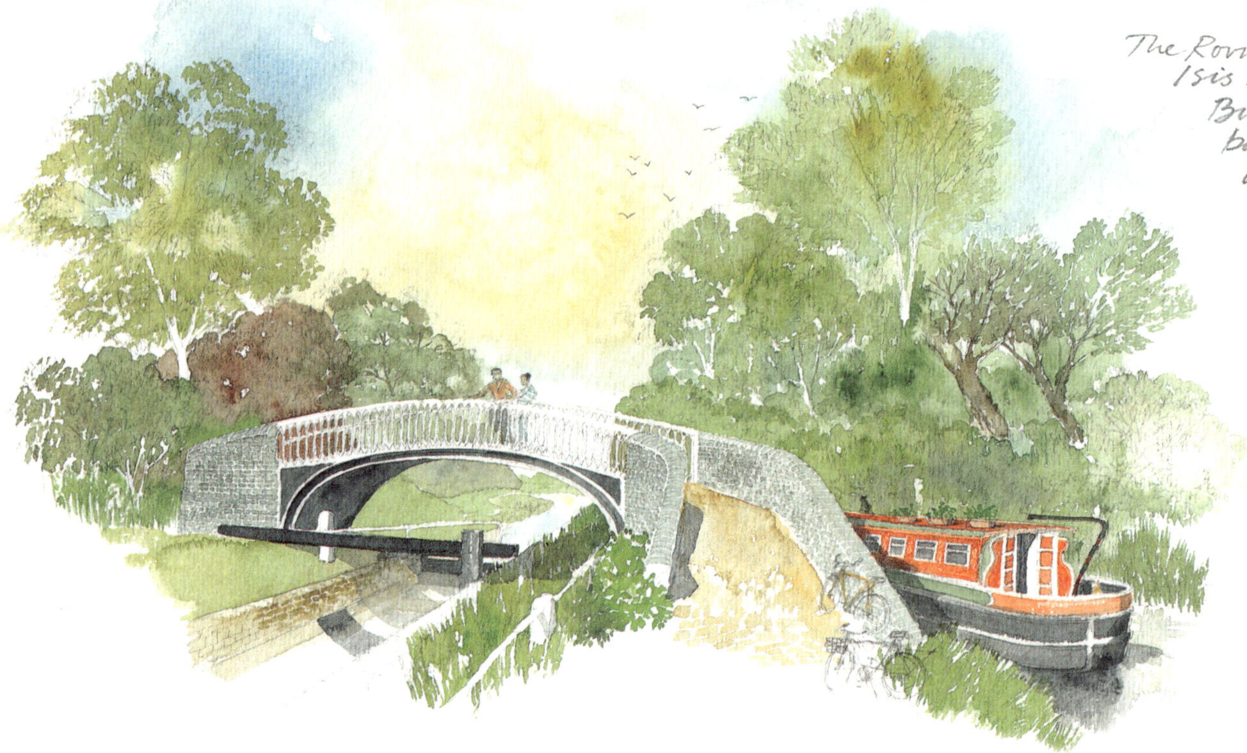

The Roving Bridge at the Isis Lock on the Oxford Canal. Built in 1796 to carry coal barges to Oxford, the canal is used today by colourful narrow boats and pleasure craft.

class North Oxford was a great social success and a textbook piece of suburban planning, in contrast to the much more cramped working class housing that was simultaneously growing up to the east and west of the historic centre. In North Oxford too are found several of the women's colleges, notably Lady Margaret Hall and Somerville, which were both founded in 1878/9 although neither achieved full college status until 1960. They began modestly on their spacious suburban sites, gradually adding buildings in a deliberately domestic, non-collegiate manner which it was thought would feel less intimidating to sensitive young ladies.

In 1910, when Edwardian Oxford still basked in the warm sunshine of Empire and it seemed that, despite all the evident changes of the past century, the city and University would somehow always remain fundamentally the same, an apparently small event took place which was indeed to effect a transformation. This was the opening of a small industrial premises at the corner of the eminently picturesque streets of Holywell and Longwall, just across the road from the medieval wall enclosing the Magdalen deer park. The proprietor was the young William Morris (not to be confused with the Victorian designer), a manufacturer of bicycles and motor cars. His first bull-nosed Morris car was assembled here two years later, followed in 1913 by the start of mass-production out on the eastern edge of the city at Cowley. In a relatively short time Oxford became a major industrial centre and huge new working class suburbs mushroomed, enveloping previously distinct villages like Iffley and Headington and linking them with the centre. By 1925 over 40 per cent of all British cars were being produced here, and the population soared accordingly.

It cannot be pretended that such development has added much to the sum of Oxford's beauties, although Lord Nuffield (as Morris became) did endeavour to make amends for - as some saw it - doing so much to ruin its setting, by funding a new college for postgraduate research. Sited on the unlovely west flank of the old centre, on the site of the former canal basin, Nuffield College adopted a curiously old-fashioned style for 1949, being designed at the founder's insistence in Cotswold Gothic, which he thought was more in the Oxford tradition than Classical, let alone something modern. Until at least the 1960s Oxford's preferred styles were indeed highly traditional, whether watered-down Gothic or neo-Georgian. This was no doubt partly because nervous college building committees were unsure what to make of the manifestations of Modernism going up outside Oxford, and partly because they genuinely felt that they owed it to Oxford's distinguished architectural past to go for styles and materials that would 'fit in'. So the decision to build an entirely new college, St Catherine's, to a minimalist Modern design by a Danish architect came as a considerable shock to the system. Nothing about it was remotely in the Oxford tradition - not the style, nor the materials (yellow brick, concrete, plate glass), nor the plan (detached parallel blocks set around wind-swept open spaces). In the year of its completion, 1964, a leading critic memorably described it as 'the best motel in Oxford'.

At least it could be said in defence of St Catherine's that it was sufficiently away from other buildings as not to impinge visually. The real challenge came when progressive architects were asked to add new buildings immediately alongside old ones, a challenge to which they have risen with pretty mixed success in the past forty years. Most of the early successes were scored by the firm of Powell & Moya, who at Brasenose in 1959, Christ Church (1964-7) and Corpus Christi (1969) showed that infills in a frankly modern idiom could not only be ingenious but also neighbourly. Equally there have been some disasters; Queen's College's Florey Building (mercifully invisible from the historic centre), an amphitheatre clad in shiny red tile and floor-to-ceiling plate glass, has proved a sociological and maintenance nightmare. The new accommodation block shoe-horned into St Edmund Hall's cramped site rears its crude roofline painfully into views down the High Street. Not surprisingly, perhaps, some colleges have retreated gratefully into the arms of more traditional architects, with very varied results - Magdalen has opted for further watered-down Cotswold Gothic as recently as 1999, Merton College for constipated neo-Tudor and Linacre for stripped Jacobean, while Victorian Gothic Manchester College went inexplicably for Toytown neo-Georgian. On the other hand the admittedly very rich St John's College has shown with two successive new buildings that with good materials, sensitive architects - and a big budget - great things can be achieved. Since 2001 travellers arriving in Oxford by train have been greeted by a monumental façade of striped brick piers topped by a copper-clad ziggurat, which is the new Said Business School. One of the most satisfying new buildings in town is the Rothermere American Institute (2001), whose elegant façade nods towards the Tudor oriels of the adjoining Mansfield College library but makes it quite clear that it is not interested in tame pastiche.

Variously characterised as a 'hot bed of cold feet', and a place where people nail their colours to the fence, Oxford has long ago mastered the art of seeming to remain stationary while actually being in a state of continual change and evolution. The late 20th century saw the proliferation of postgraduates, of new research institutes and new subjects, and the metamorphosis of single-sex colleges into mixed colleges, all without civilisation as Oxford knows it coming to a premature end. It remains one of the world's great nurseries of aspiring politicians, who hone their debating skills at the Union; it is no accident that every post-war Prime Minister except Callaghan and Major has been a product of the university - which nevertheless demonstrated its independence by refusing to award the customary honorary degree to Mrs Thatcher. It has also at last, in the shape of a former Rhodes Scholar, Bill Clinton, produced a President of the United States, as well as innumerable politicians of developing nations.

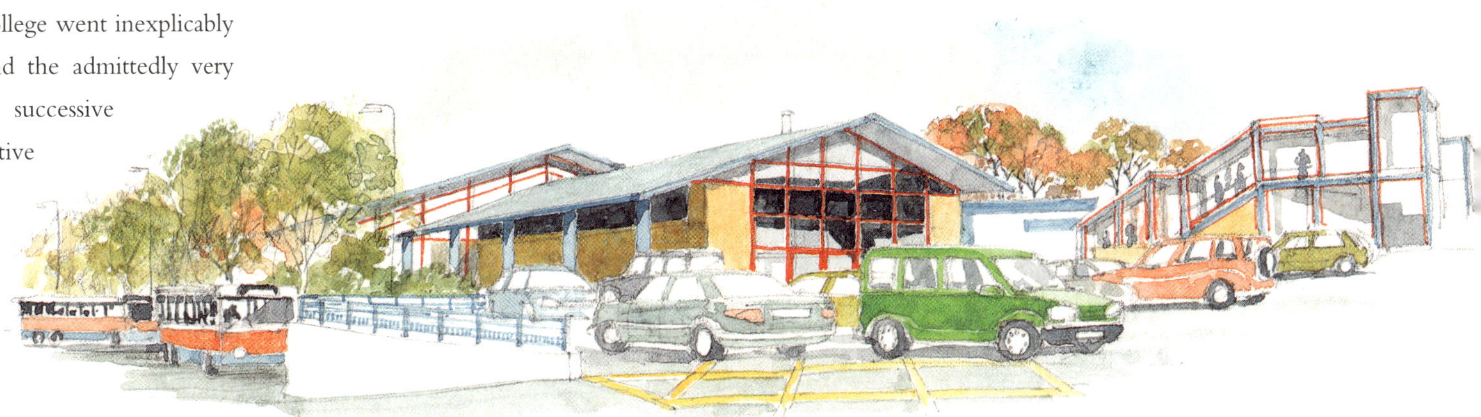

Oxford's modern railway station is, for many visitors, their first introduction to the city.

Oxford's Centre

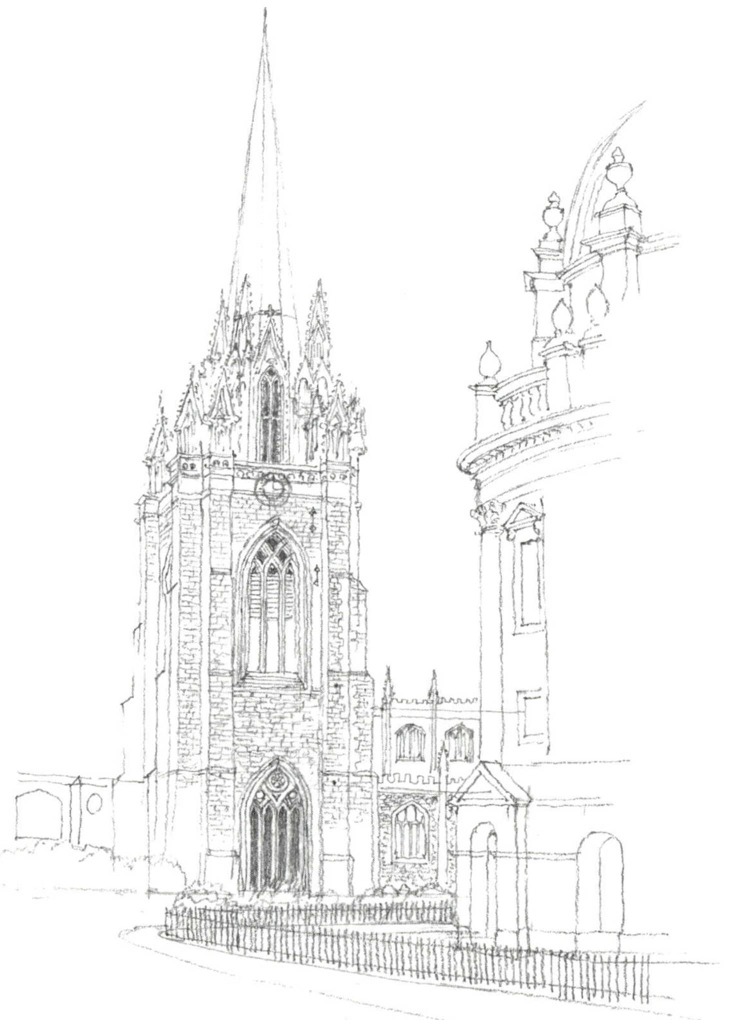

The story - possibly apocryphal - is often told of bewildered tourists standing somewhere in the middle of Oxford and asking, 'but where is the University?'. The answer, with such a diffuse organism, could be 'nowhere and everywhere'. The entire centre of the city has been colonised by college and university buildings, and if they have a centre as such it is surely the area bounded on the south by the High Street ('the High'), on the west by Cornmarket, and on the east by the River Cherwell; the northern boundary is more difficult to establish. The focus of the University is Radcliffe Square, undoubtedly one of the great public spaces of Europe, enclosed by a succession of magnificent frontages and dominated by the serene circular bulk of the Radcliffe Camera. Defining the north side is the Bodleian Library, with its incalculable wealth of books and manuscripts, and beyond it the Sheldonian Theatre, the imposing setting for degree ceremonies.

Elsewhere, for instance on the High or Broad Street ('the Broad'), the grand buildings are juxtaposed with more humble domestic frontages, Town intermingled with Gown to their mutual architectural advantage. These spacious thoroughfares are contrasted with narrower streets and lanes that curve or twist, such as Holywell Street or New College Lane. Stone alternates with painted plaster, or more occasionally brick and half-timber, to create an almost invariably pleasing visual medley. Trees rising above high walls hint at inaccessible gardens, and everywhere the vertical accents of towers, spires and turrets punctuate the vistas. This is townscape at its most satisfying. At the eastern end of the High the bell tower of Magdalen College, in an architectural fanfare, announces one of the world's handsomest urban sequences to travellers crossing the adjoining bridge into the city.

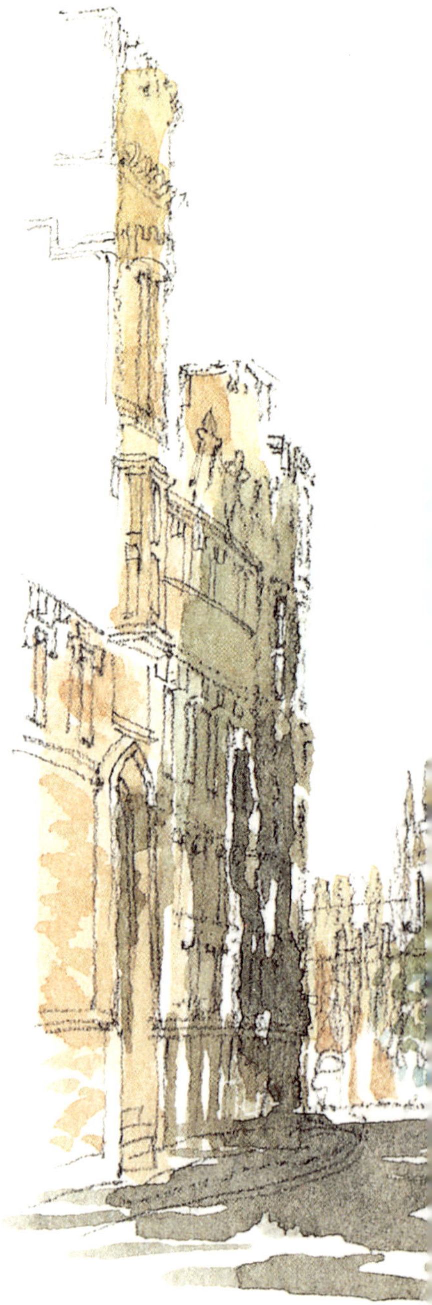

Radcliffe Square is the university's focus and forum.

The High is one of the world's great streets, lined with a mixture of grand and modest buildings, and with the All Souls College sycamore tree providing a green punctuation mark at exactly the right point on the street's gentle curve.

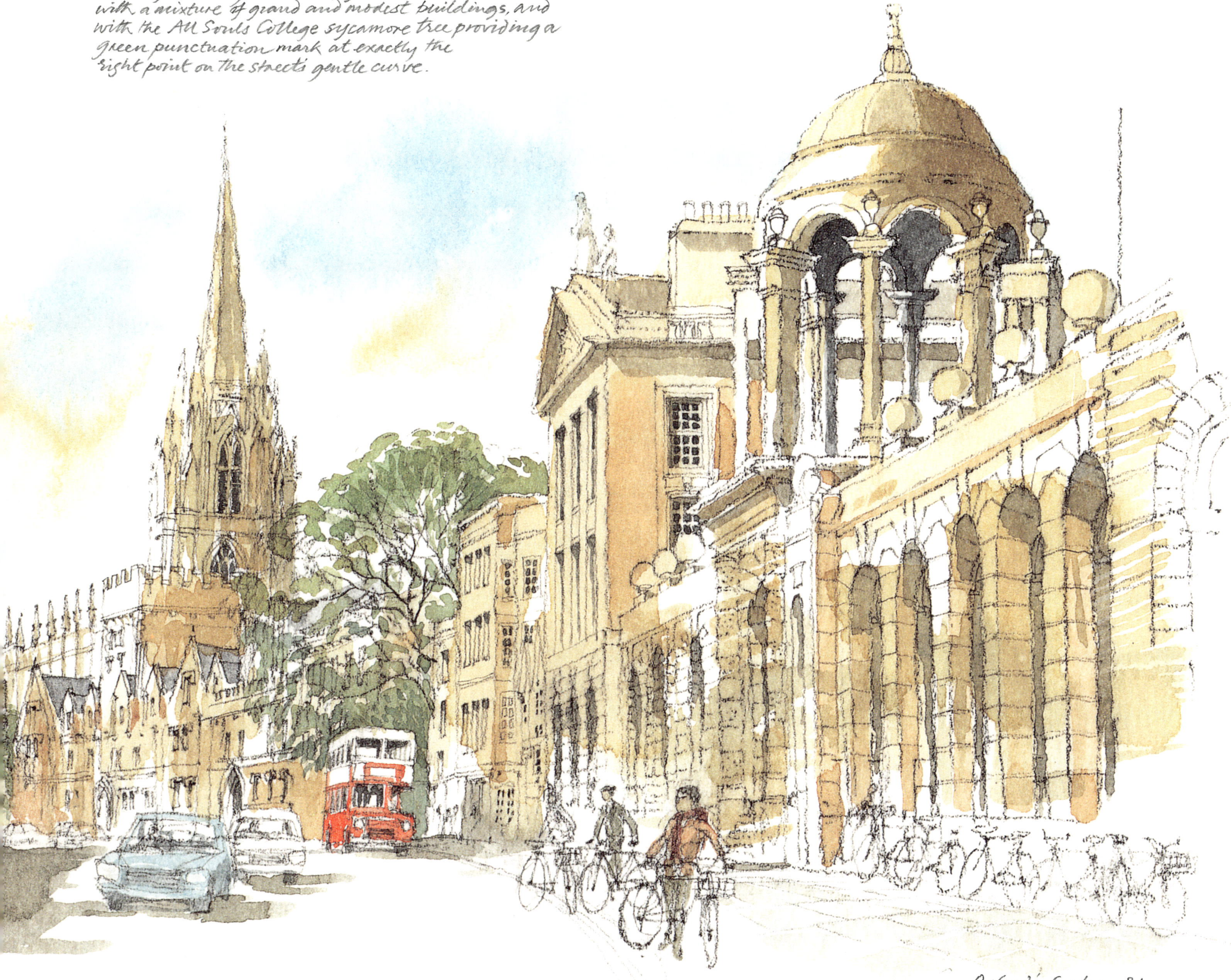

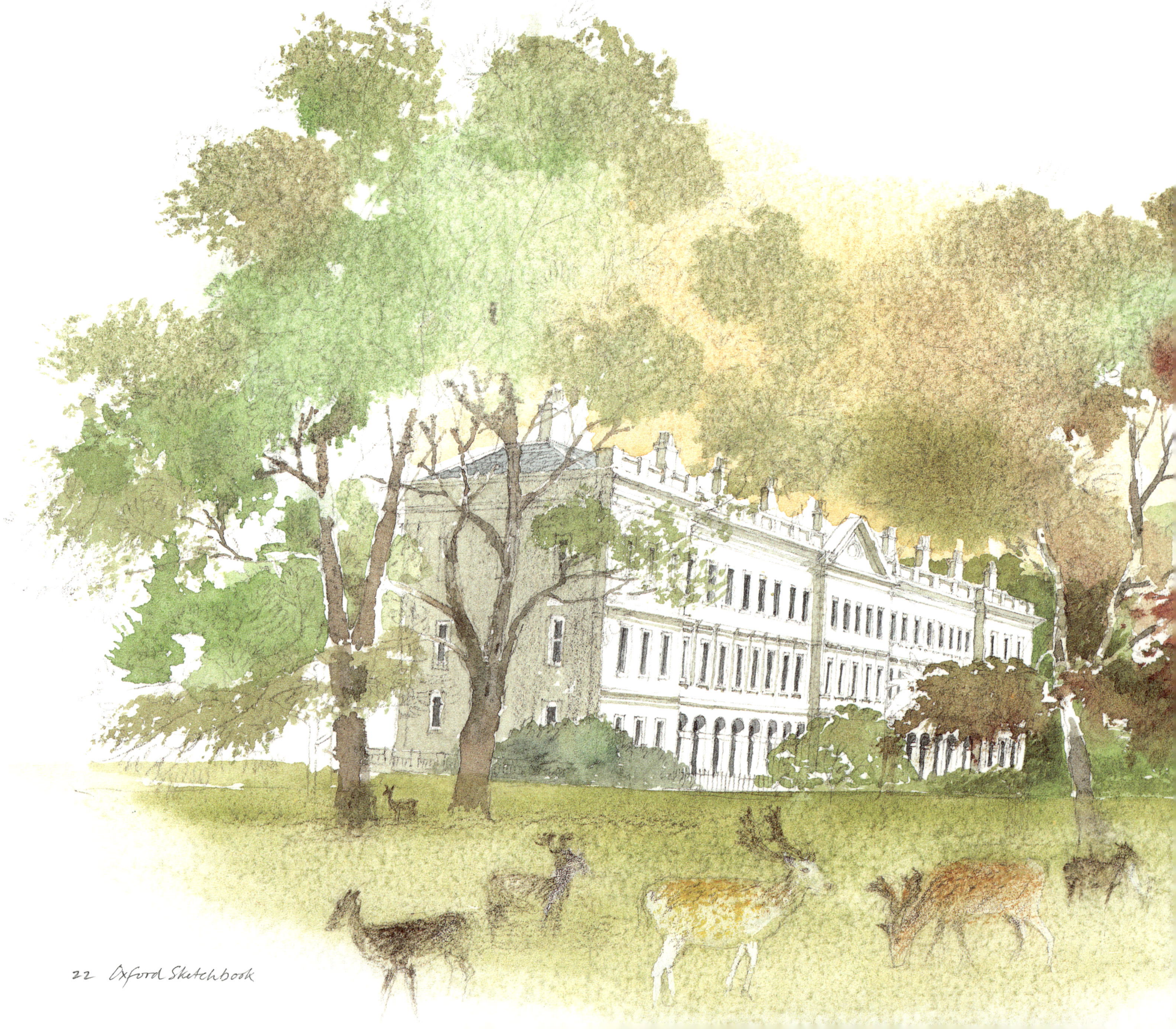

Magdalen is perhaps Oxford's most romantic college, occupying a uniquely spacious site that is bounded on one side by the River Cherwell. The New Building (left), an unfinished fragment of an ambitious Palladian scheme to rebuild the medieval college, overlooks the city's only deer park.

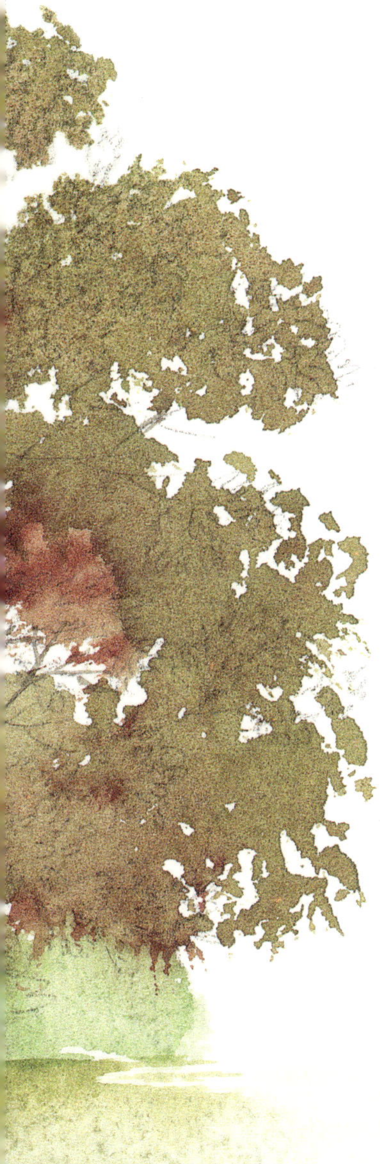

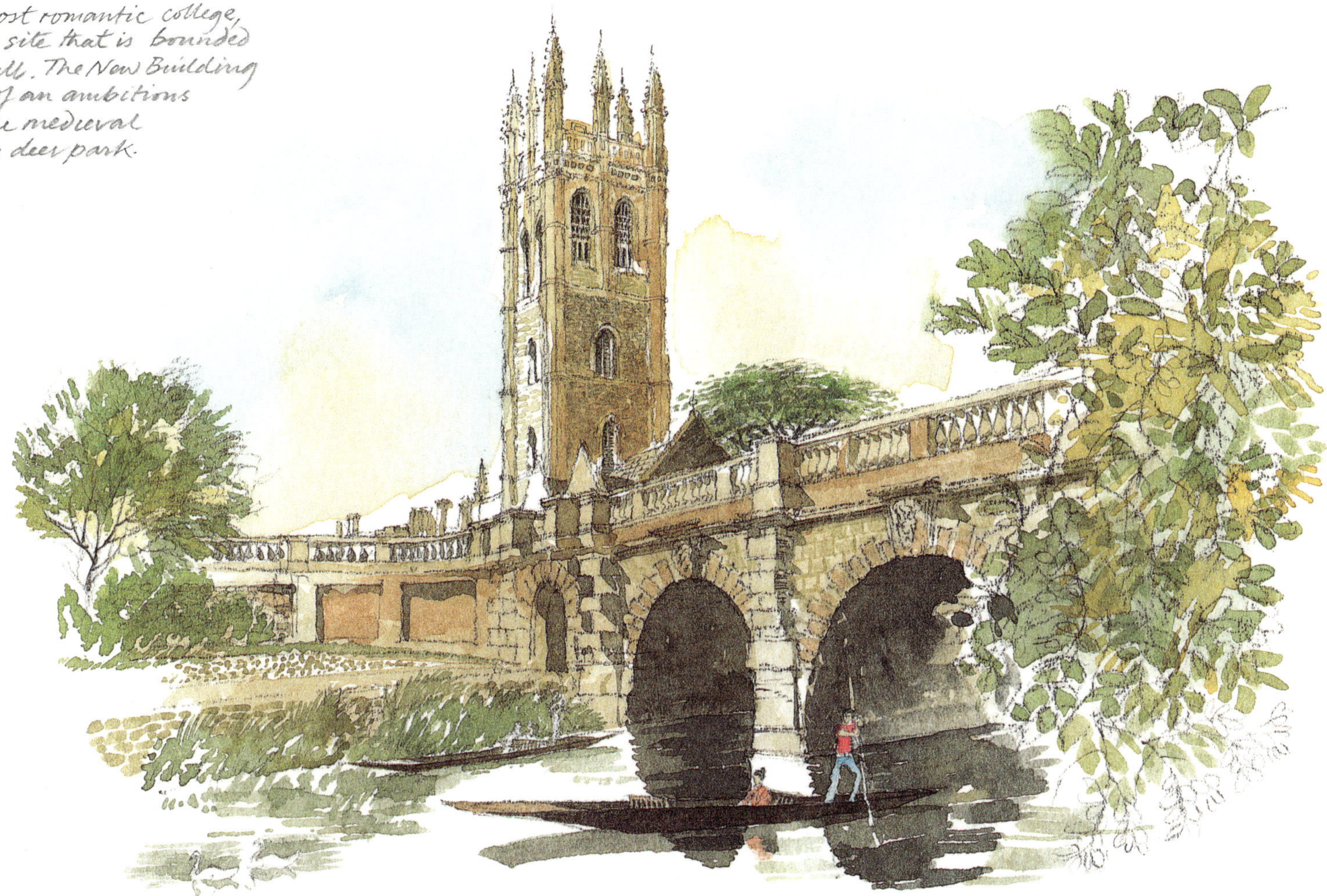

The soaring 15th-century bell tower dominates the eastern end of The High, adjoining Magdalen Bridge, built in the 1770s.

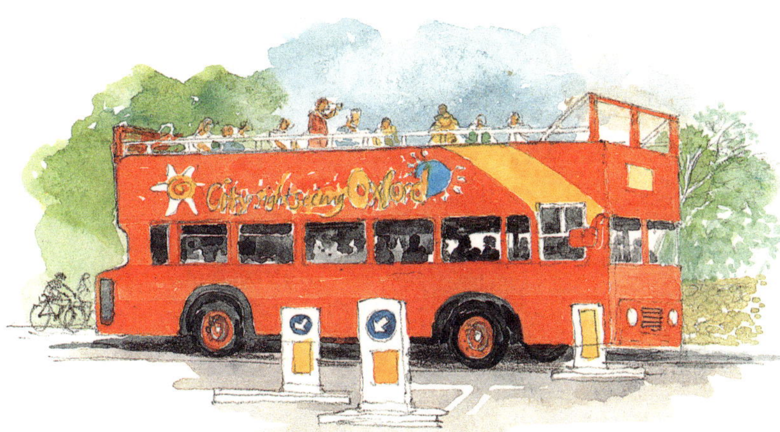

Open-top bus on a sightseeing tour. The 'official' tour of the city.

Magdalen's late-medieval core is arranged around a cloister, with the hall and chapel along one side. Both Oscar Wilde and the future King Edward VIII had rooms overlooking the cloister. Poet Laureate John Betjeman was also at the college.

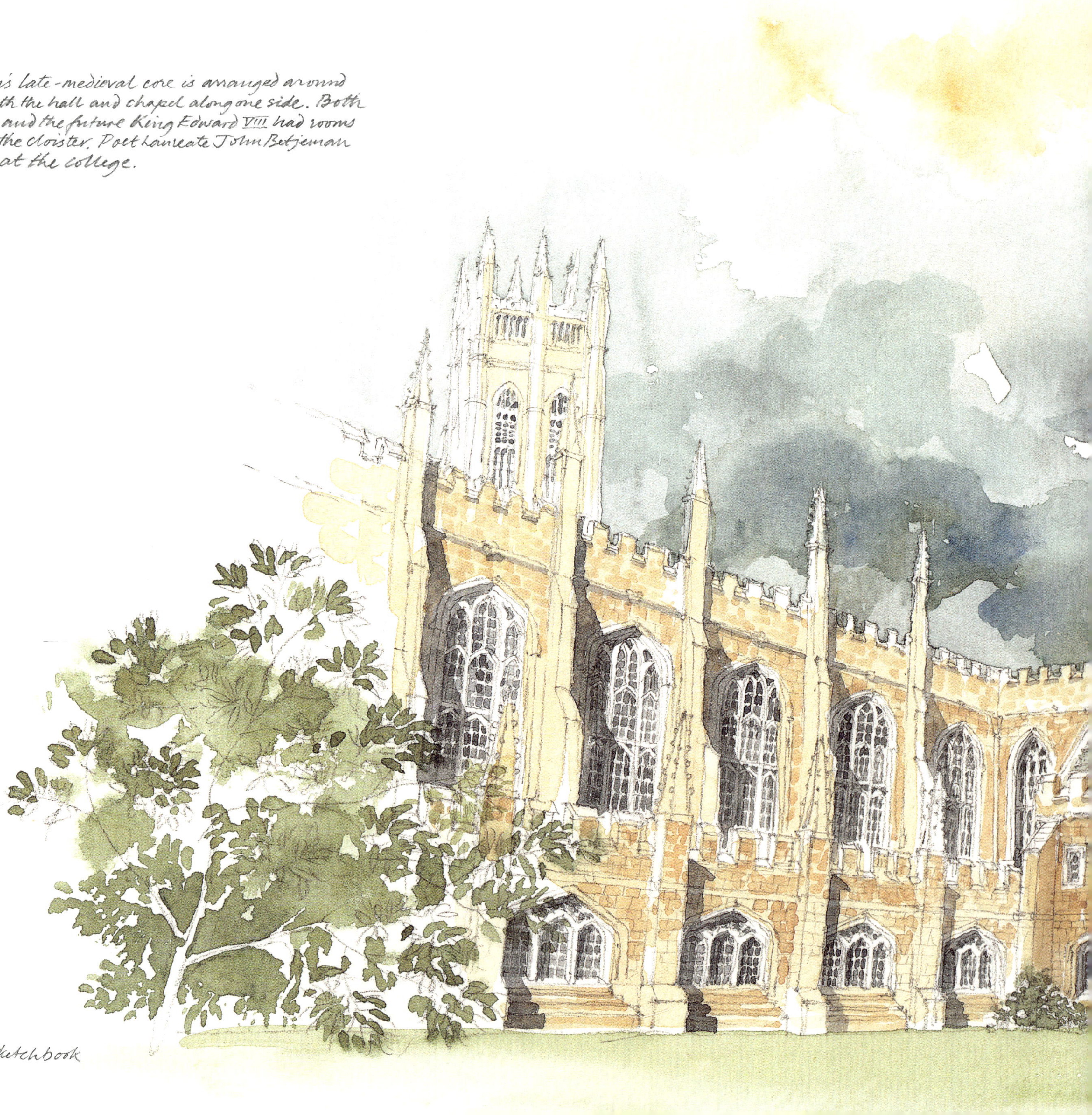

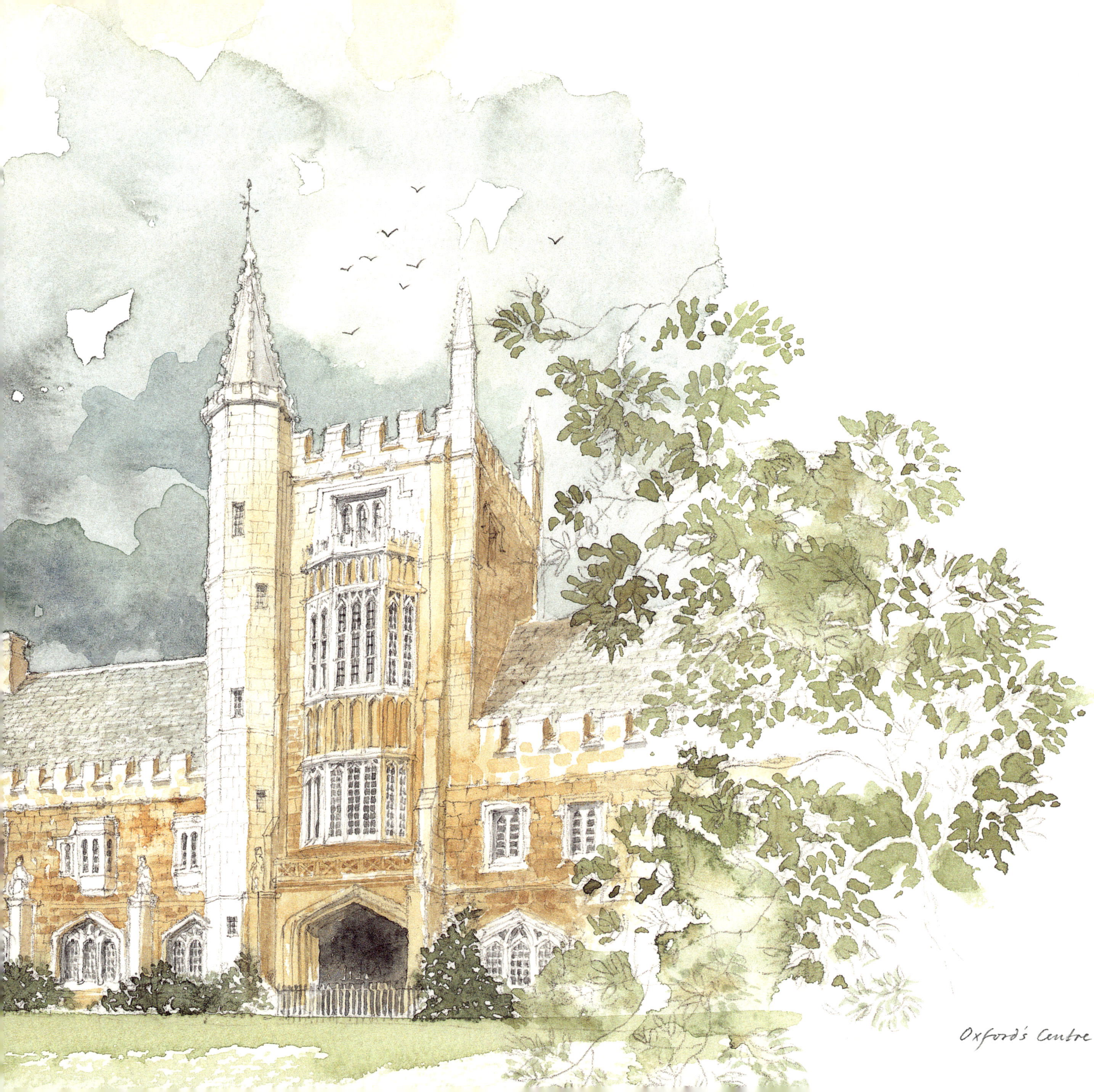

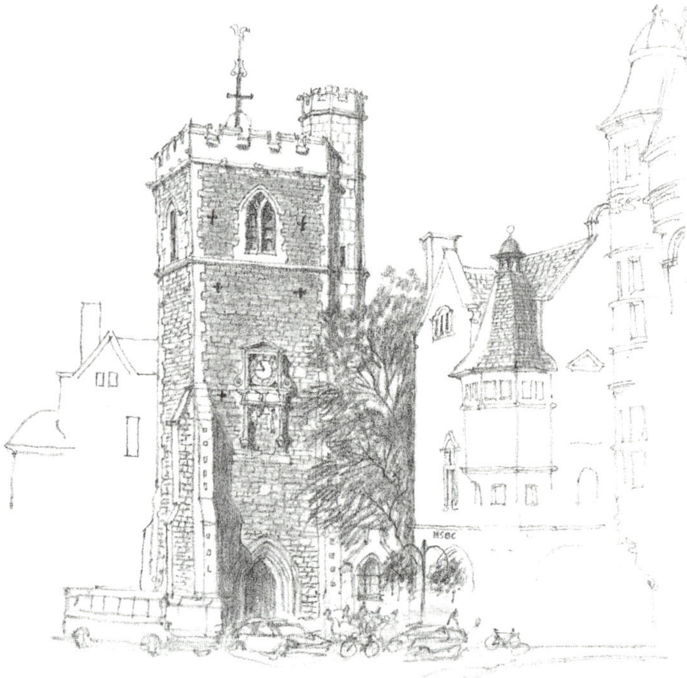

Carfax, centre of the Saxon town, is still the focus of the 'Town' part of Oxford.

A detail of the baroque porch to St Mary the Virgin.

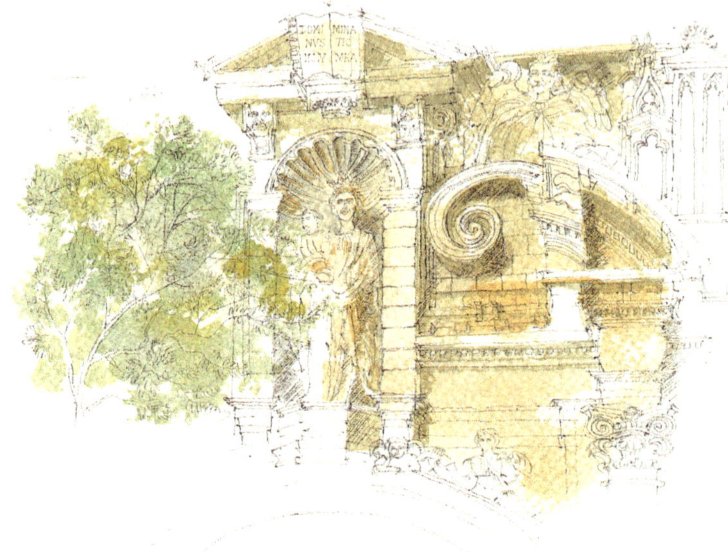

The Mitre is a relic of the centuries when Oxford was a great coaching centre, and up to forty stage coaches trundled down The High every day.

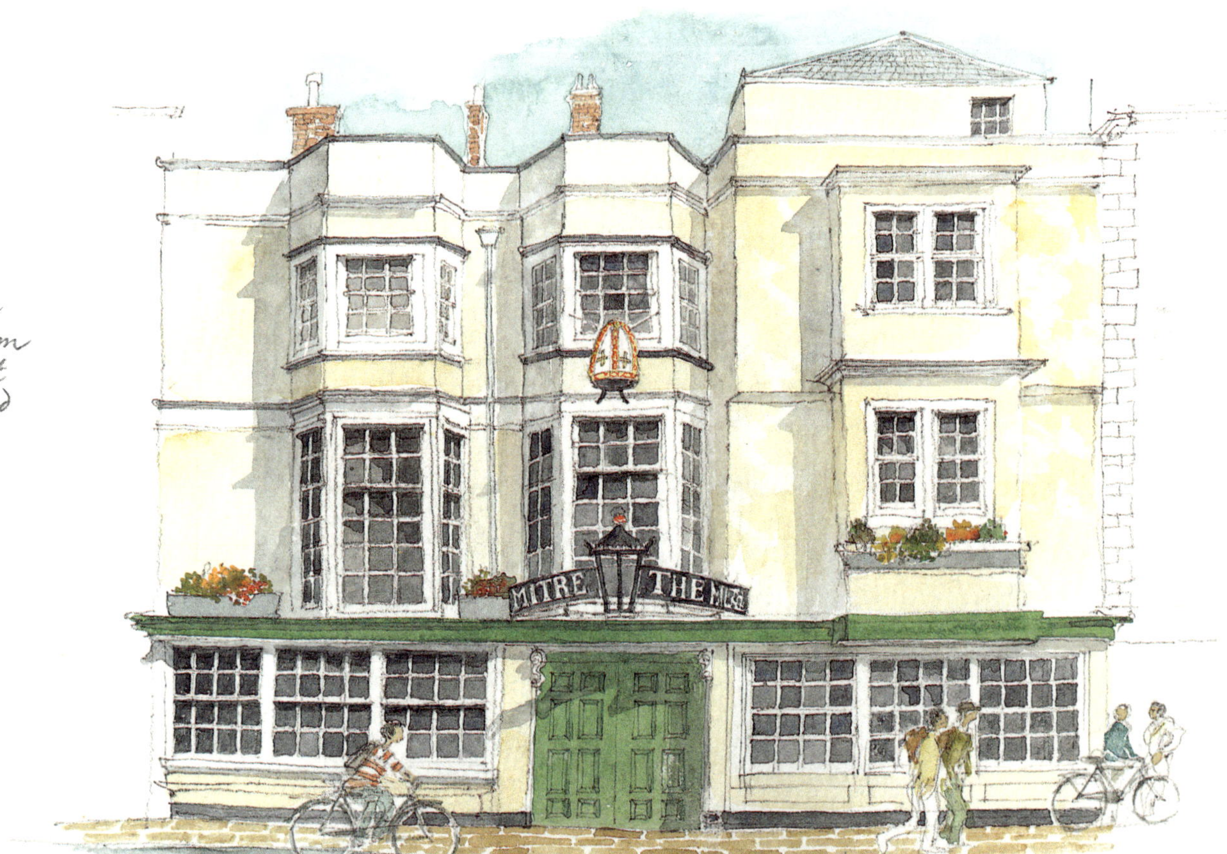

All Saints Church was rebuilt in the early 18th century.
On the right is the High Street frontage
of Brasenose College.

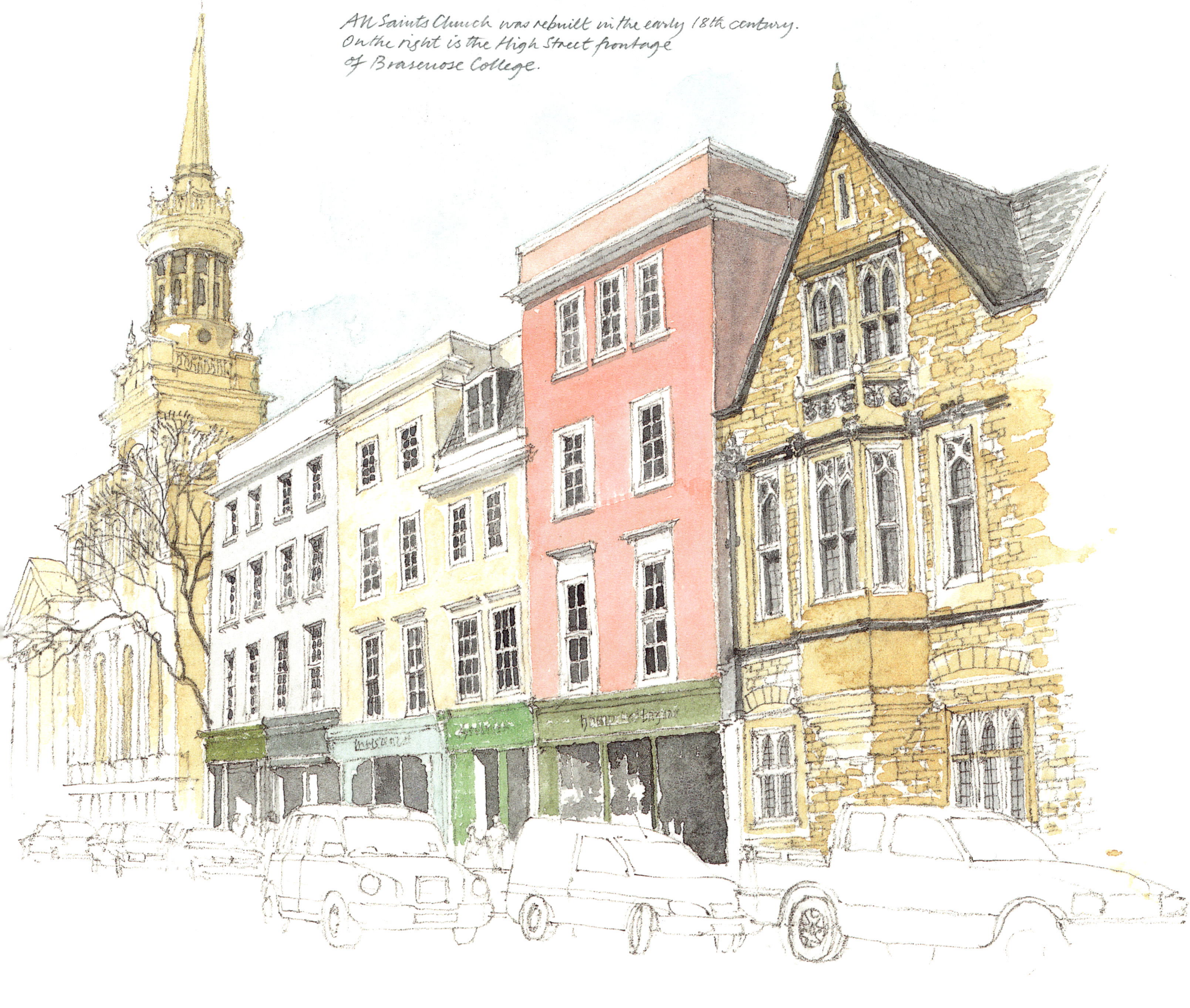

Although the Queen's College was founded in 1340, most of it was rebuilt in the early 18th century to create Oxford's grandest quadrangle. Formal dinner in the hall is traditionally heralded by a fanfare on a silver trumpet.

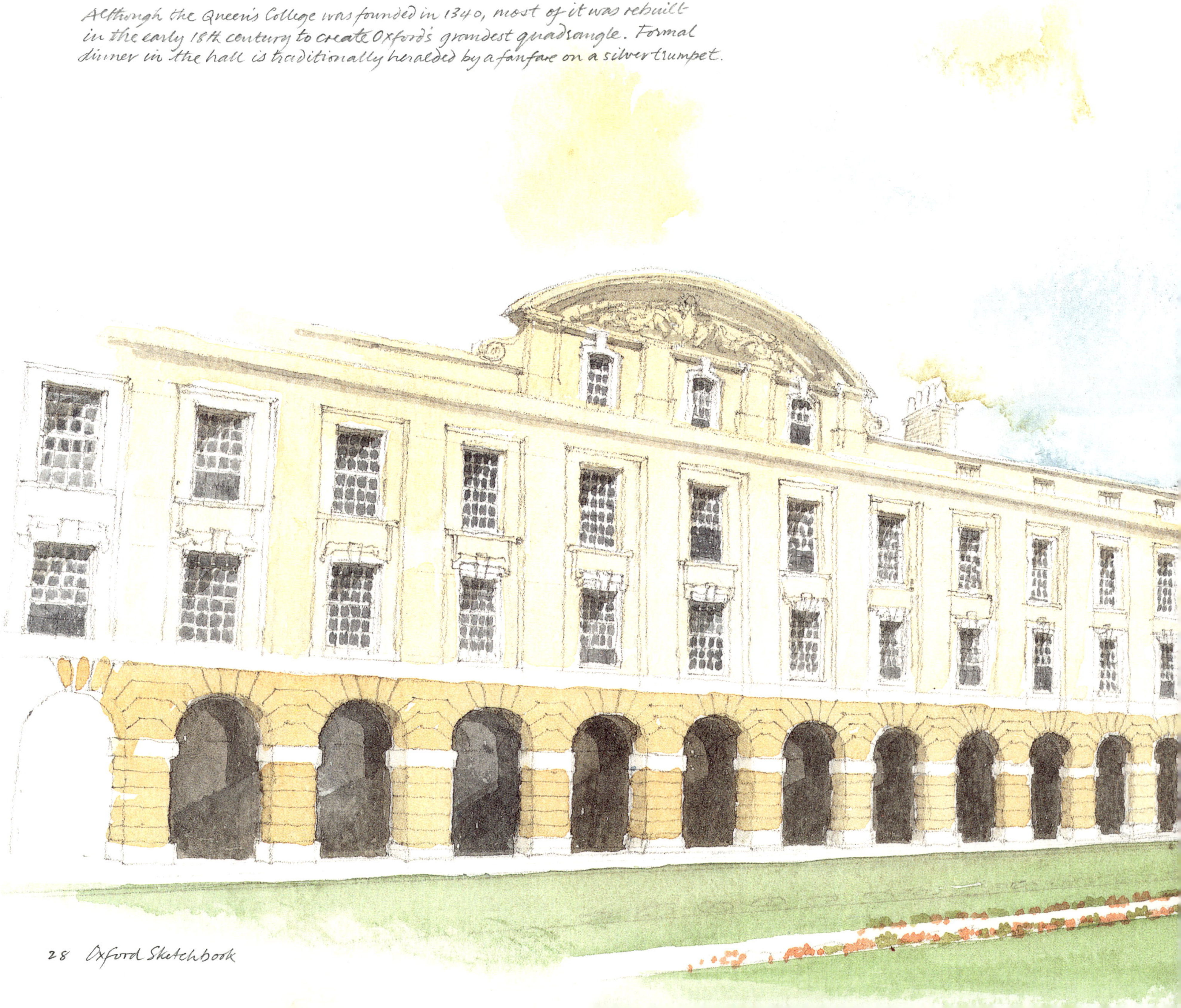

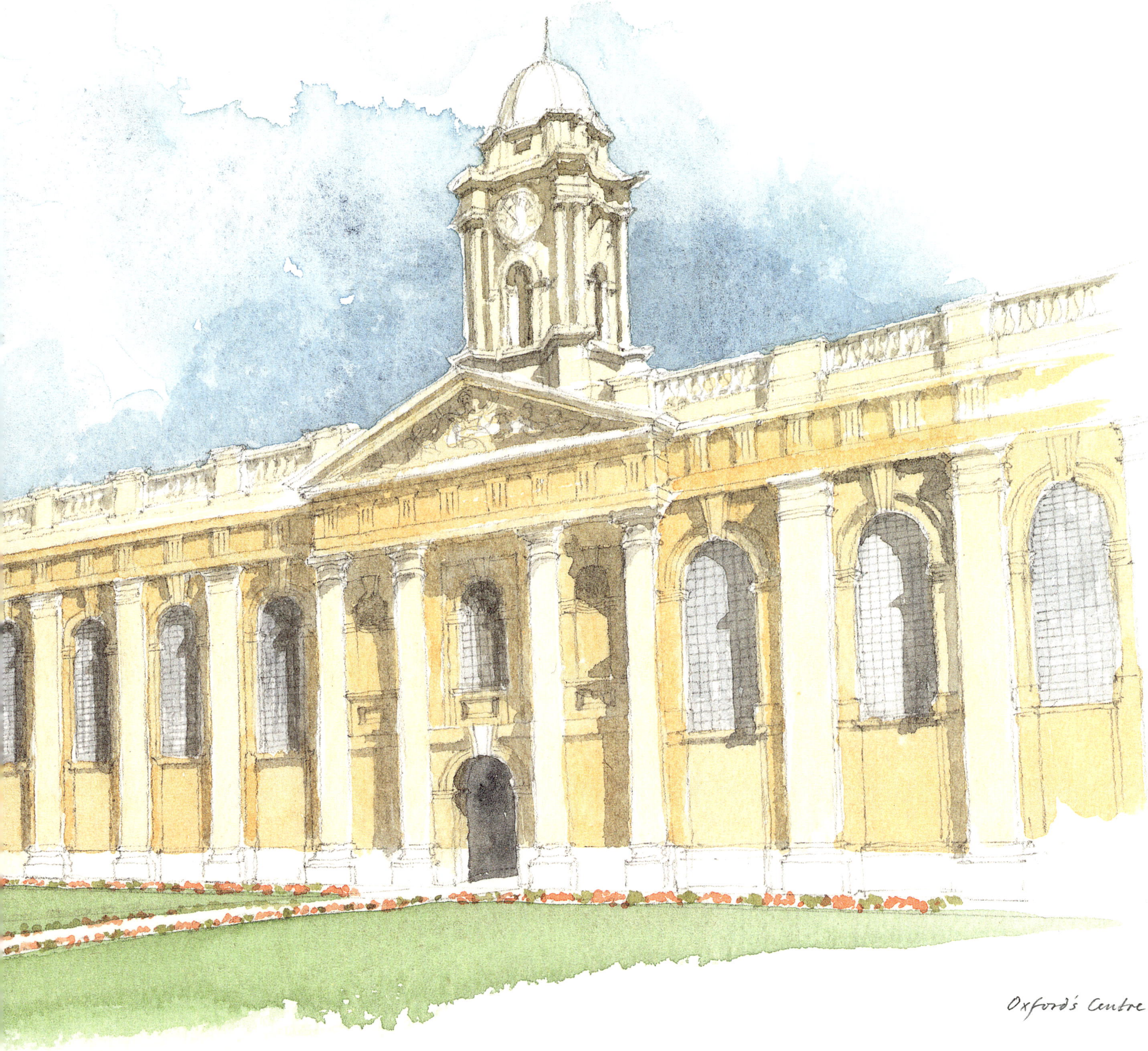

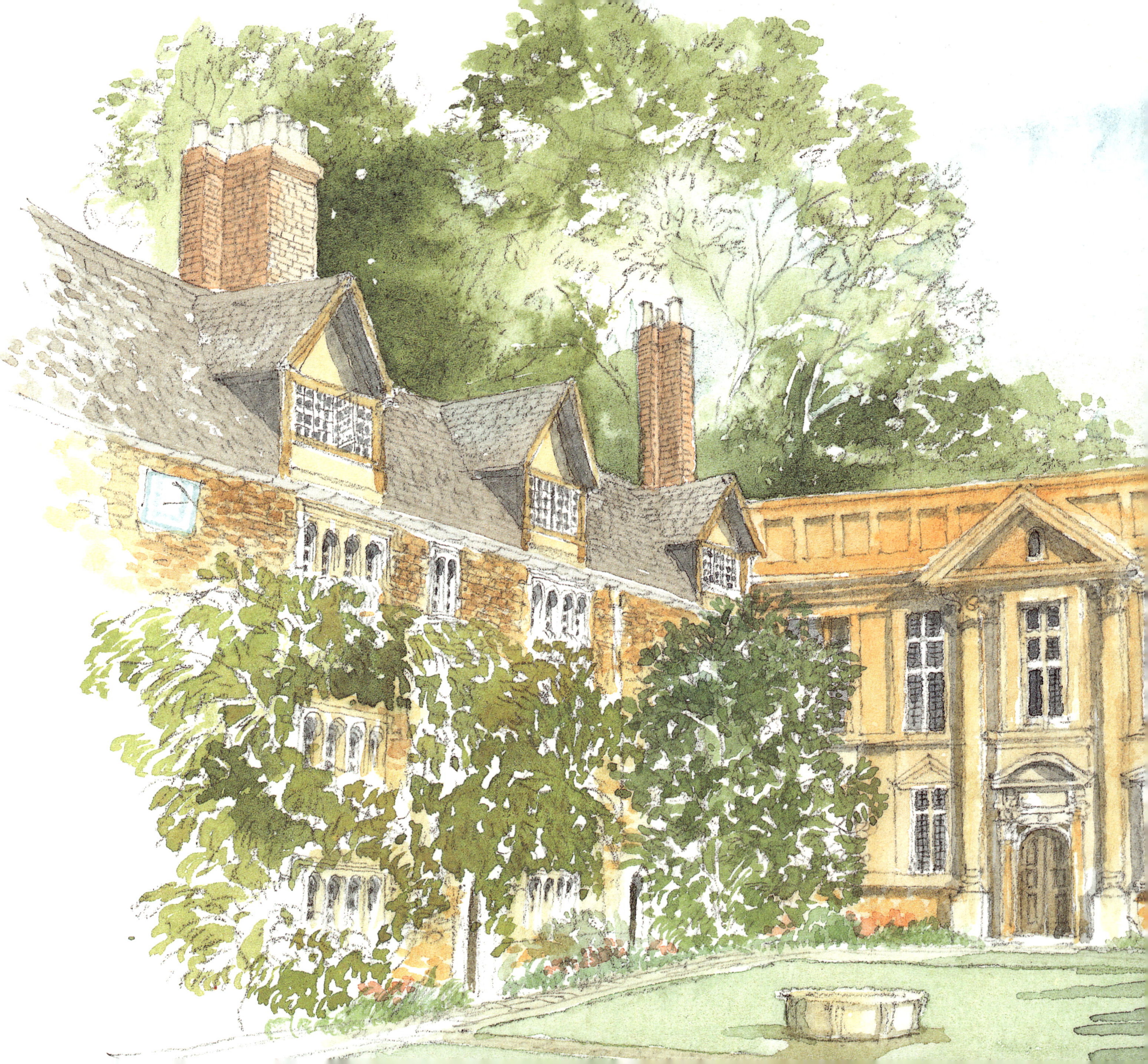

The intimate Front Quad at St Edmund's Hall (usually known as Teddy Hall) is one of Oxford's most charming. The canopy over the door to the former library is supported on piles of carved stone books.

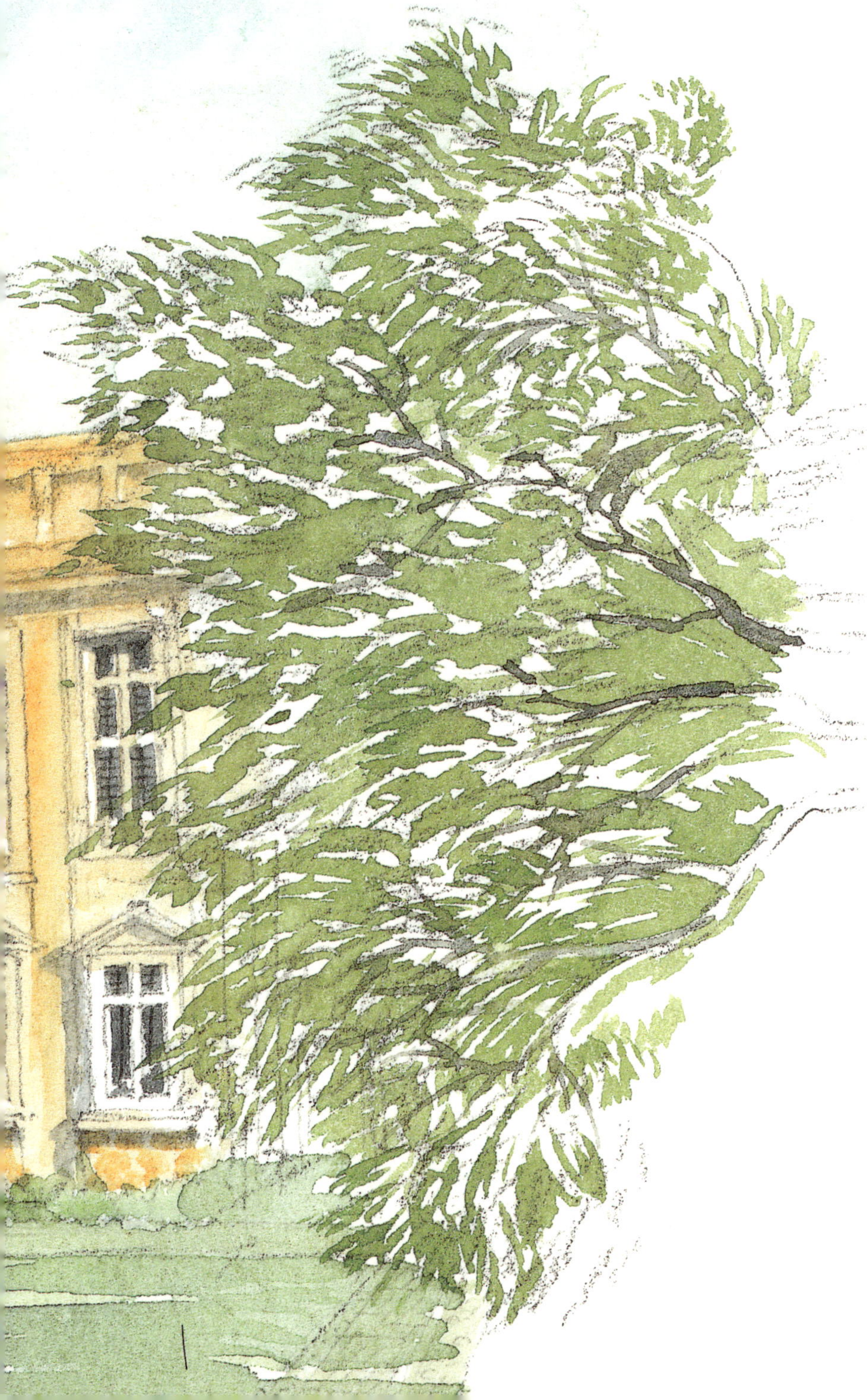

Oxford University cycling club is the oldest in Britain. Some of the dons' ancient bikes contrast with the modern mountain bike which a lot of the students use. It is thought there are about 20,000 cyclists on the streets of the city each day.

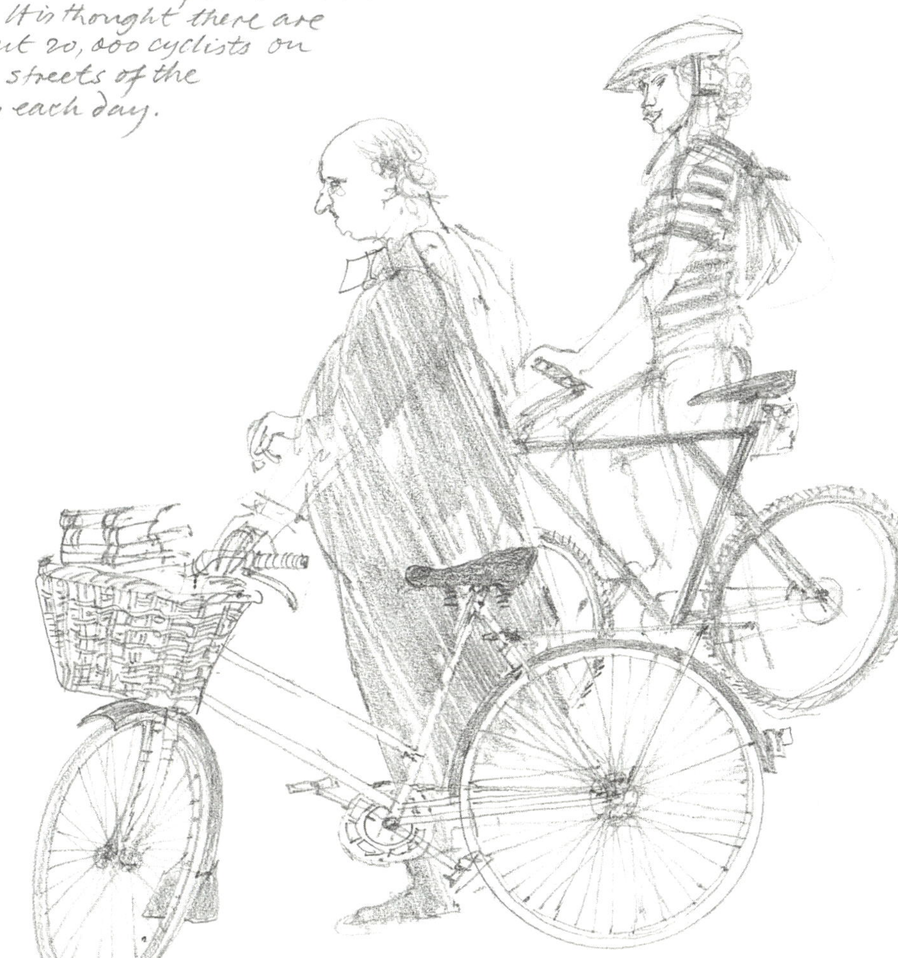

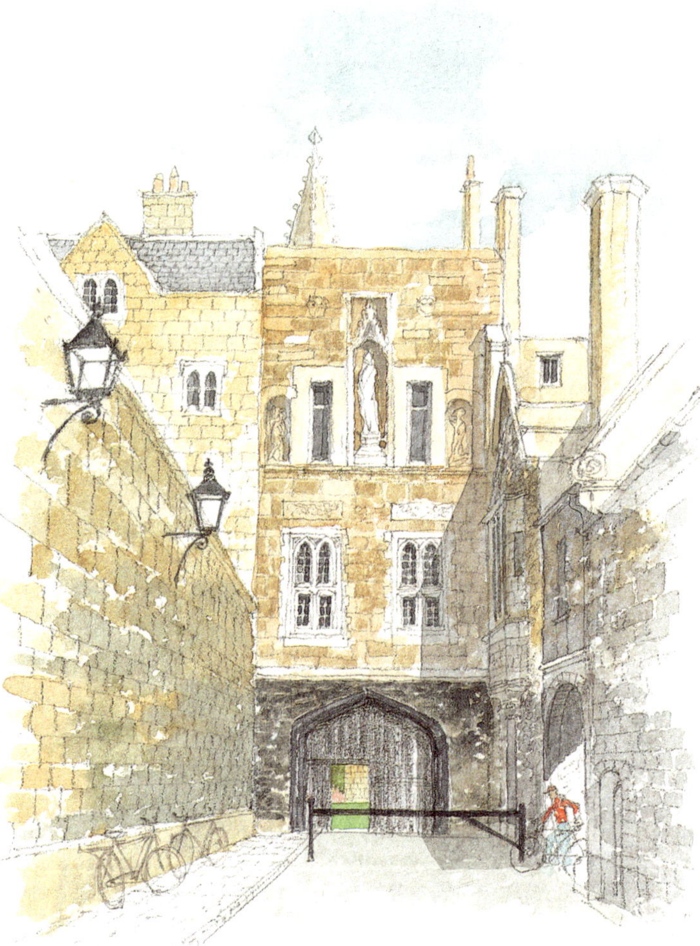

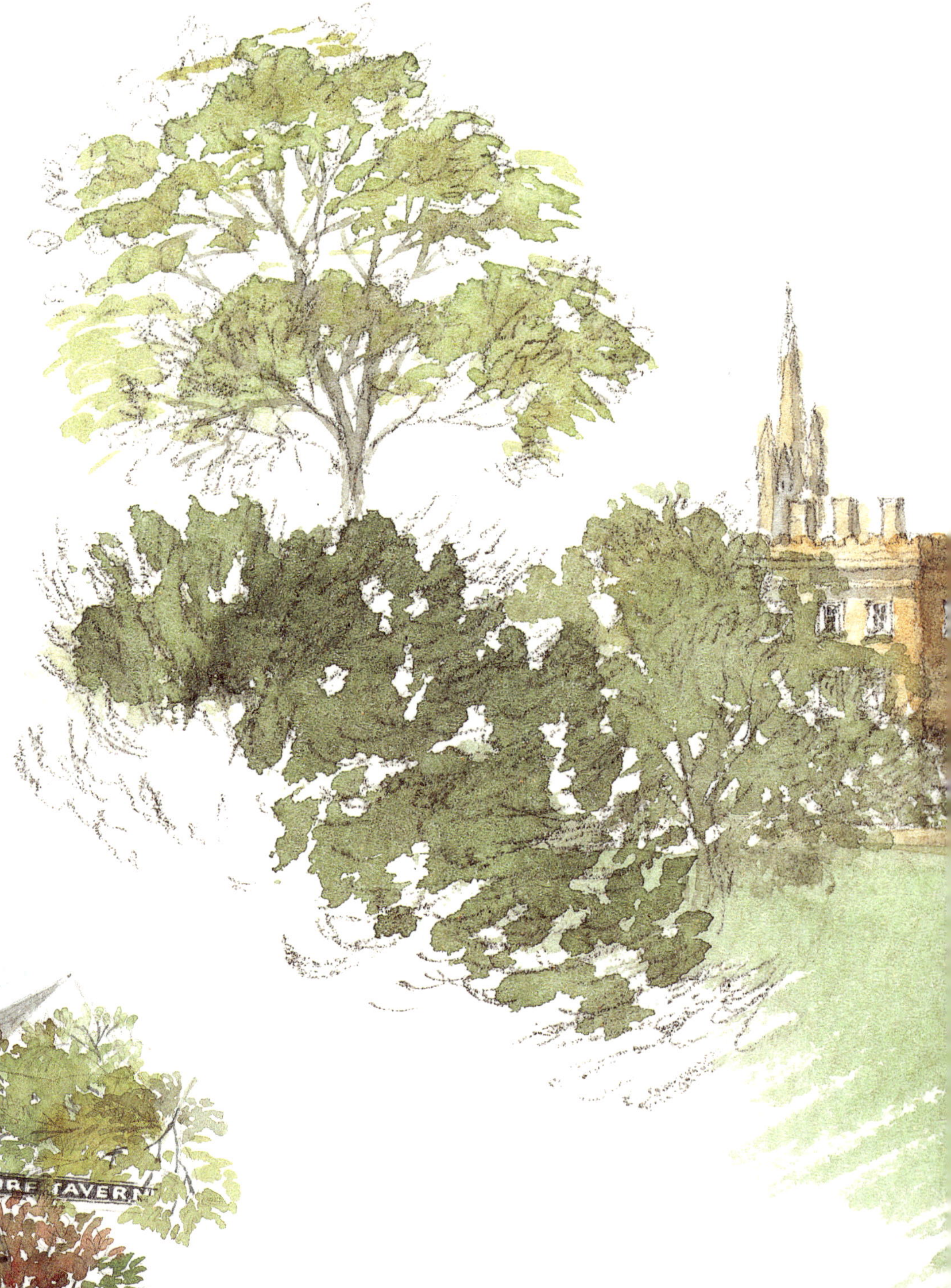

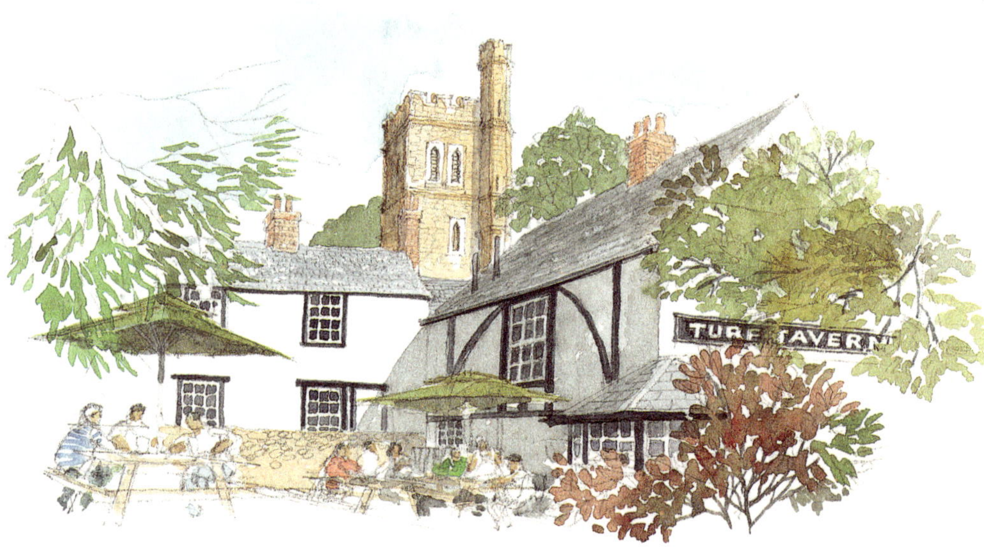
TAVERN

New College was 'new' in 1379, when it was founded by William of Wykeham, Bishop of Winchester; he believed its purpose should be to produce 'men of great learning, fruitful to the church of God, and to the King and Realm'. The original entrance was through a defensible gate tower (top left) and the spacious site was enclosed on two sides by the existing city walls, beneath which nestles the Turf Tavern. The New College garden is one of Oxford's finest.

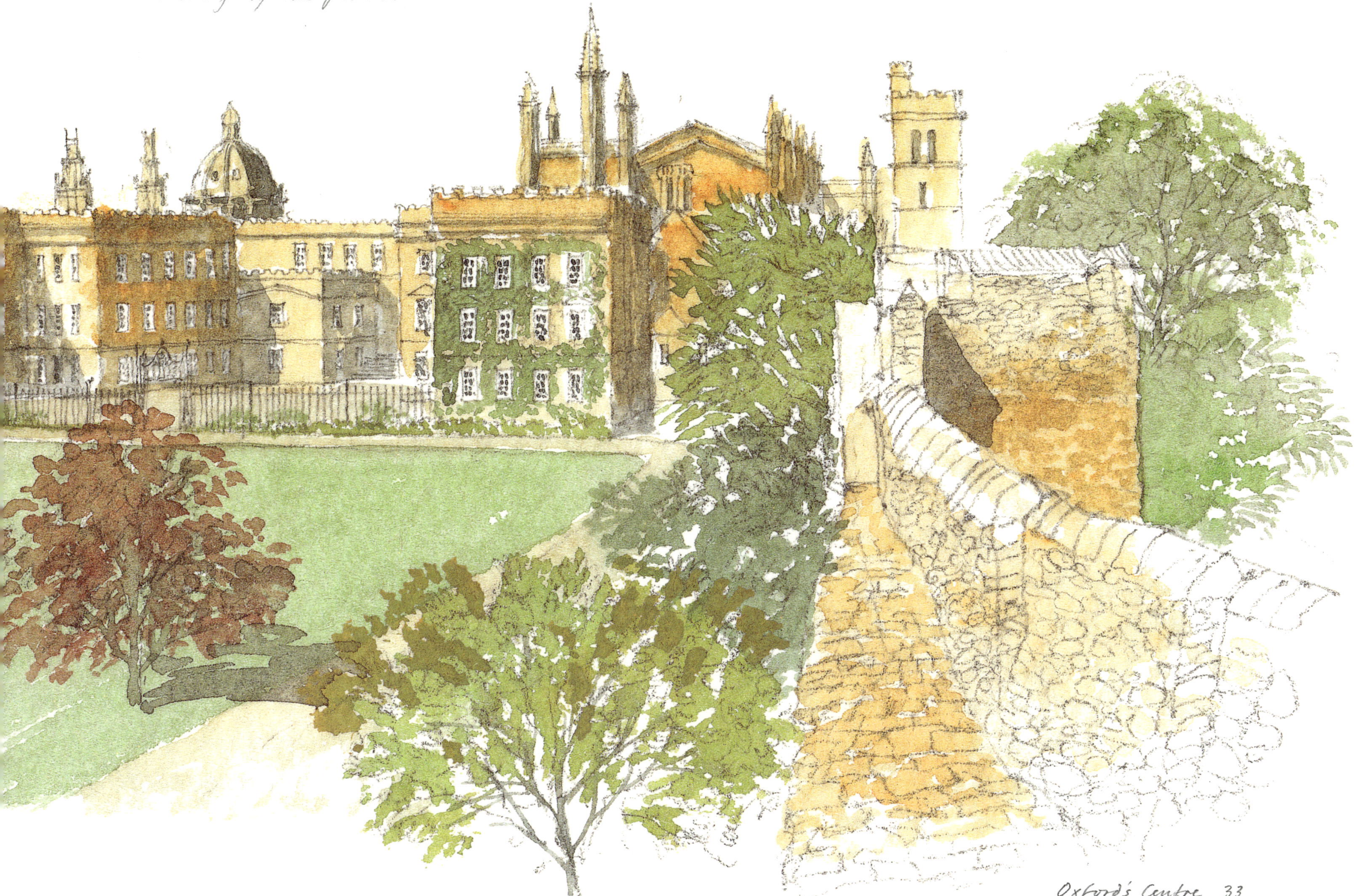

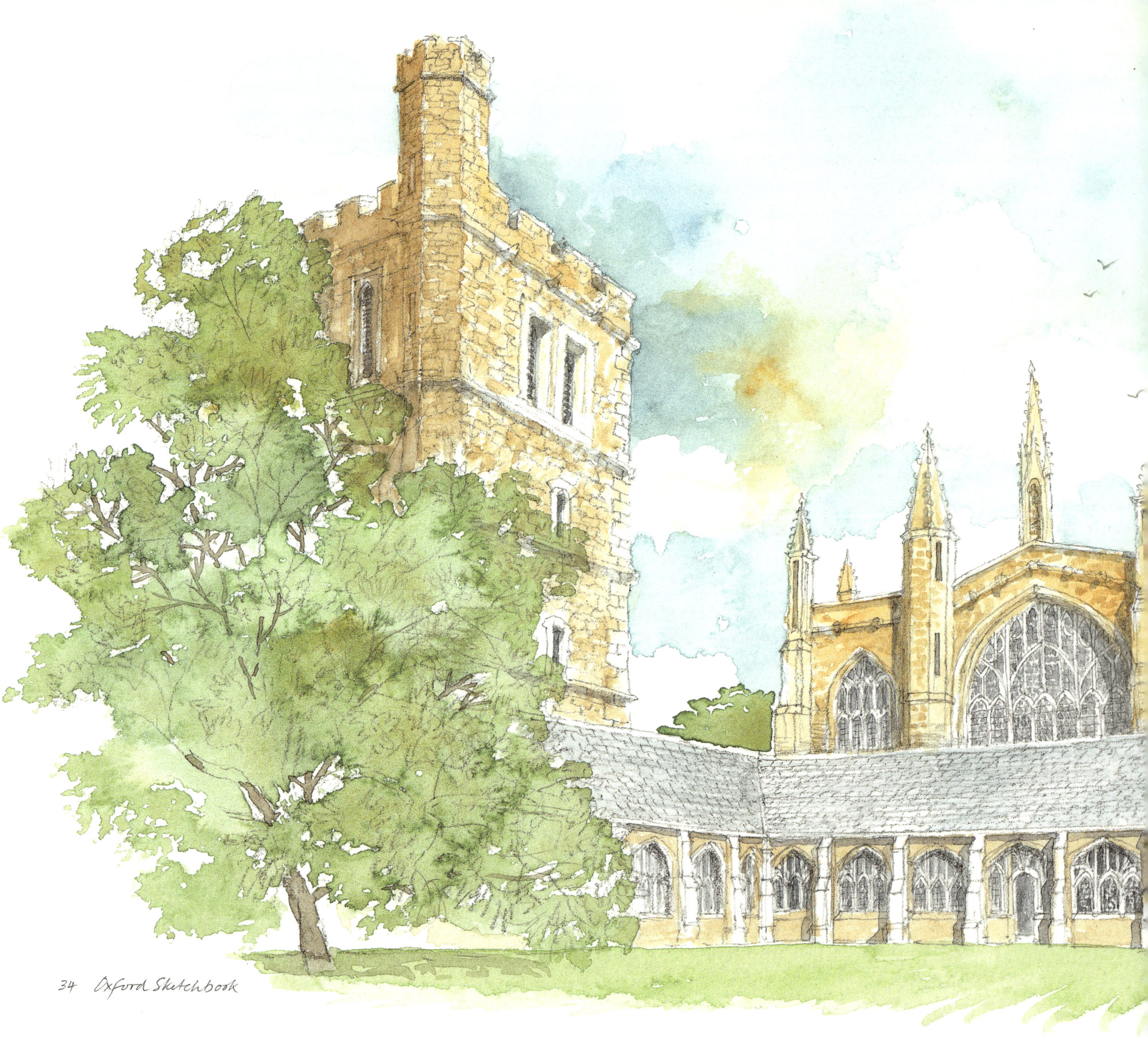

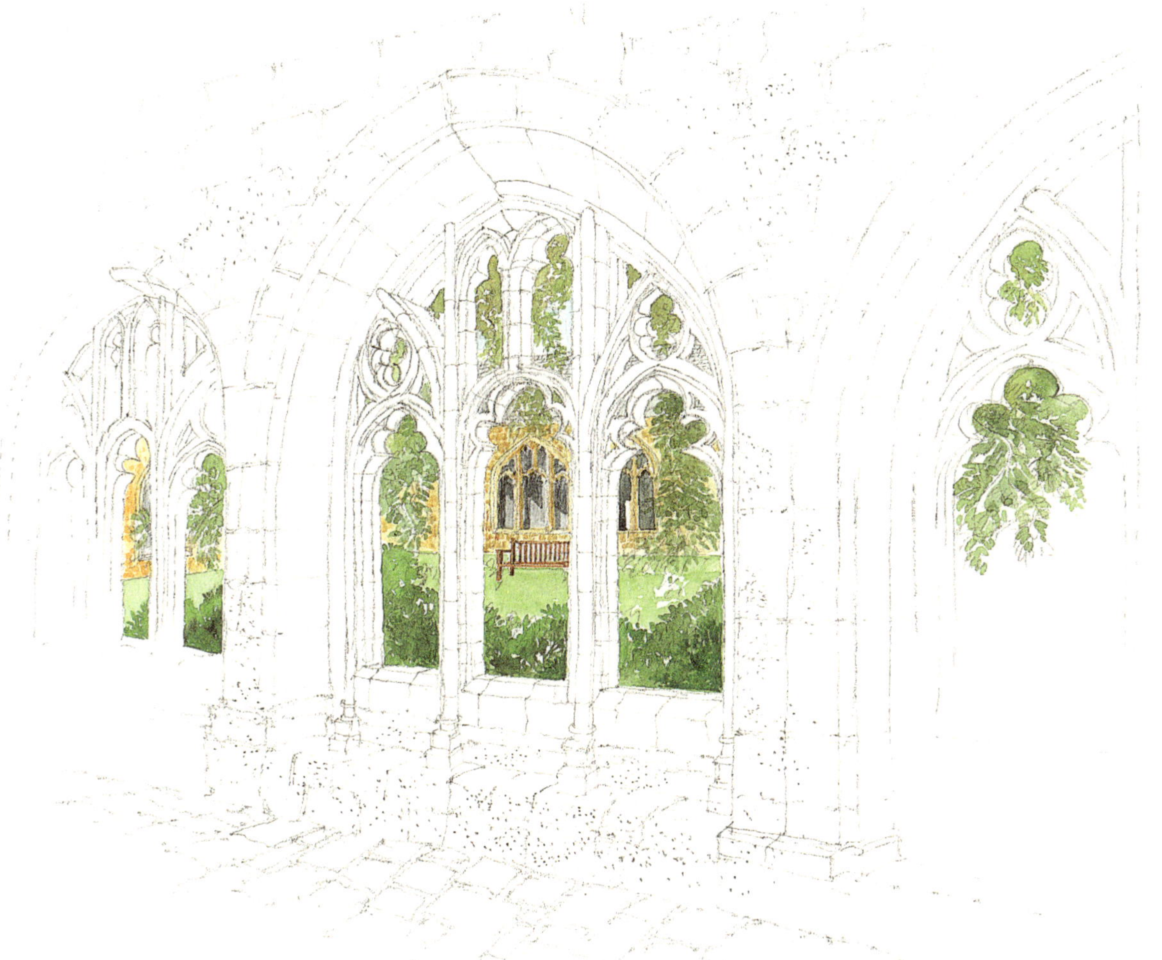

The sequestered cloister recaptures better than anywhere else the early monastic character of Oxford's colleges.

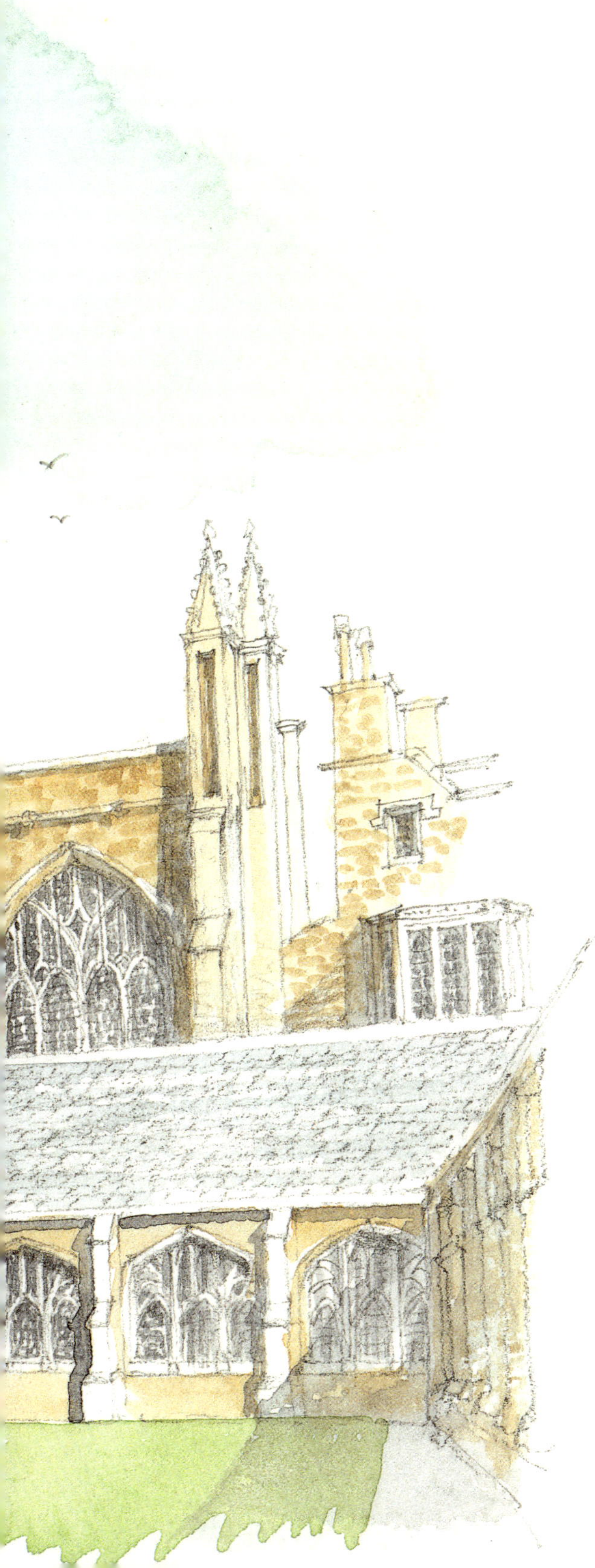

Above New College's cloister rise the bell tower and the chapel. The treasures of the latter include William of Wykeham's ornate crozier, a painting by El Greco, and a powerful sculpture by Epstein.

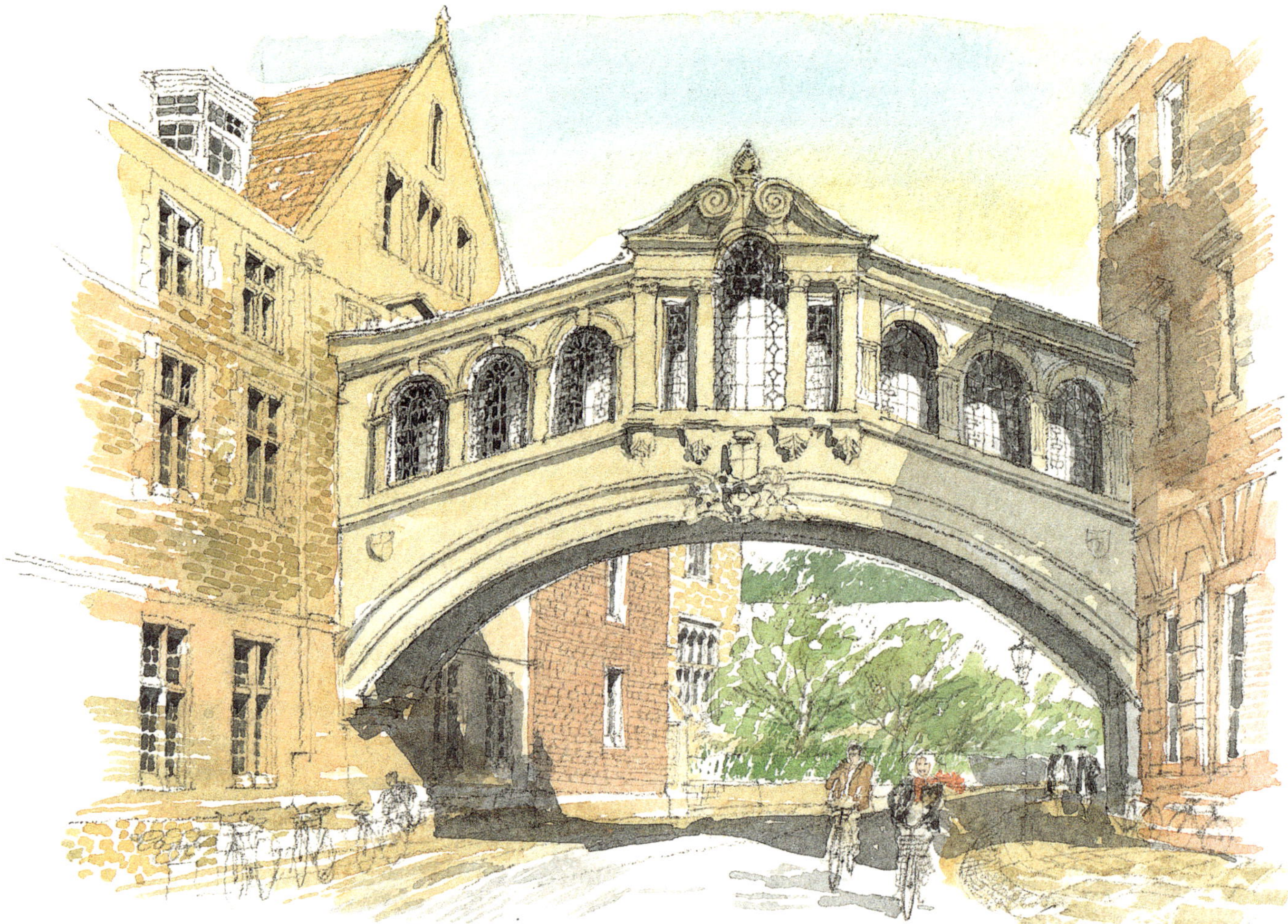

Hertford College owes much of its present appearance to the Victorian architect Sir Thomas Jackson, who designed the striking staircase (in the painting on the right) and also the so-called Bridge of Sighs, which connects two parts of the college across New College Lane. One of Hertford's most famous alumni was the novelist Evelyn Waugh.

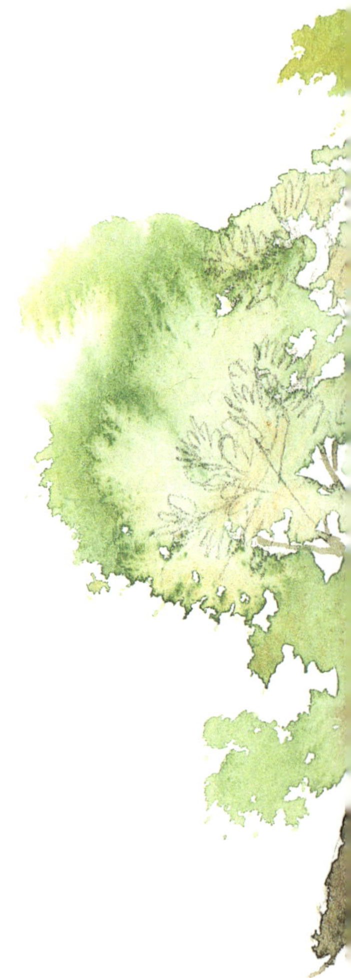

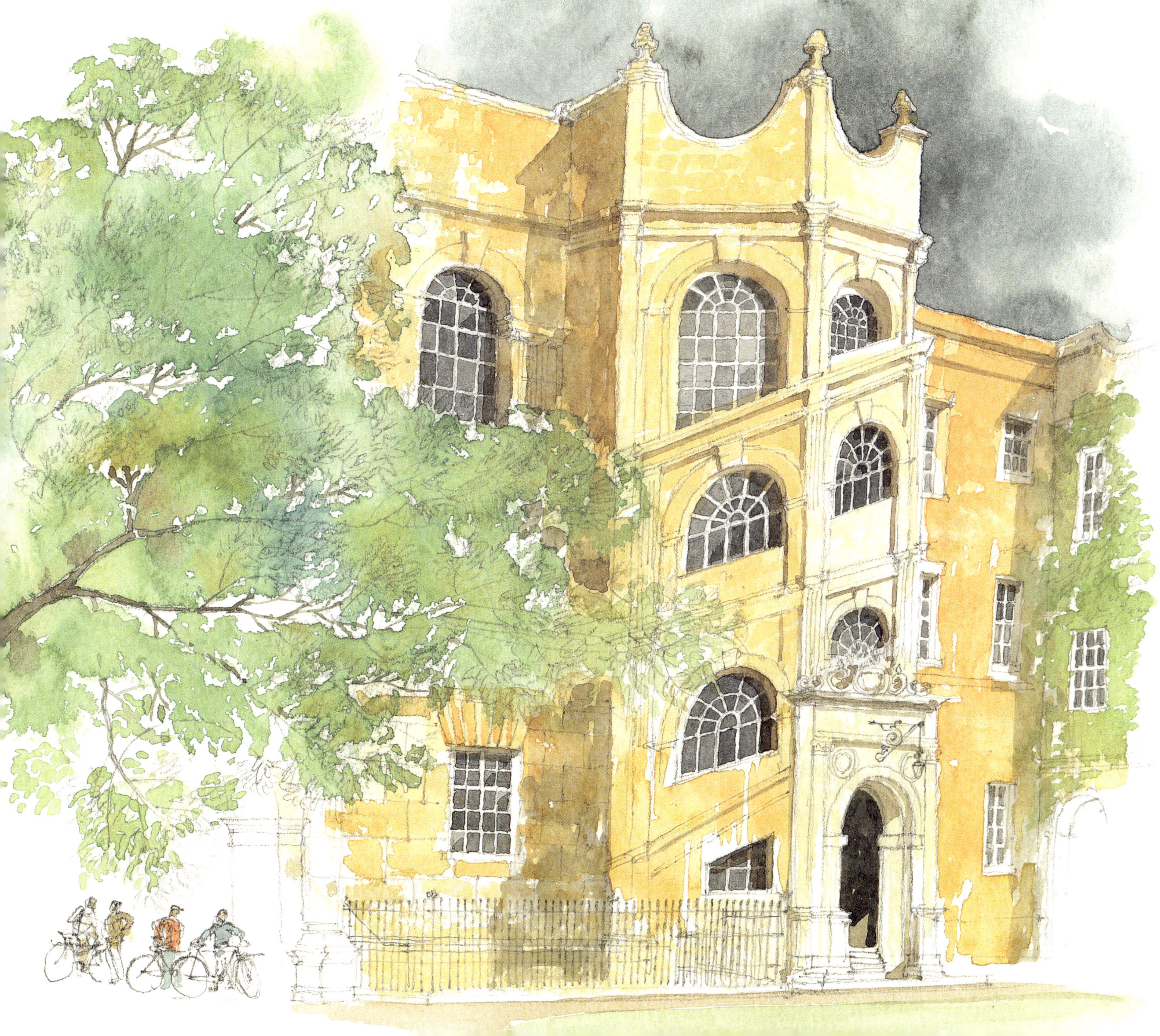

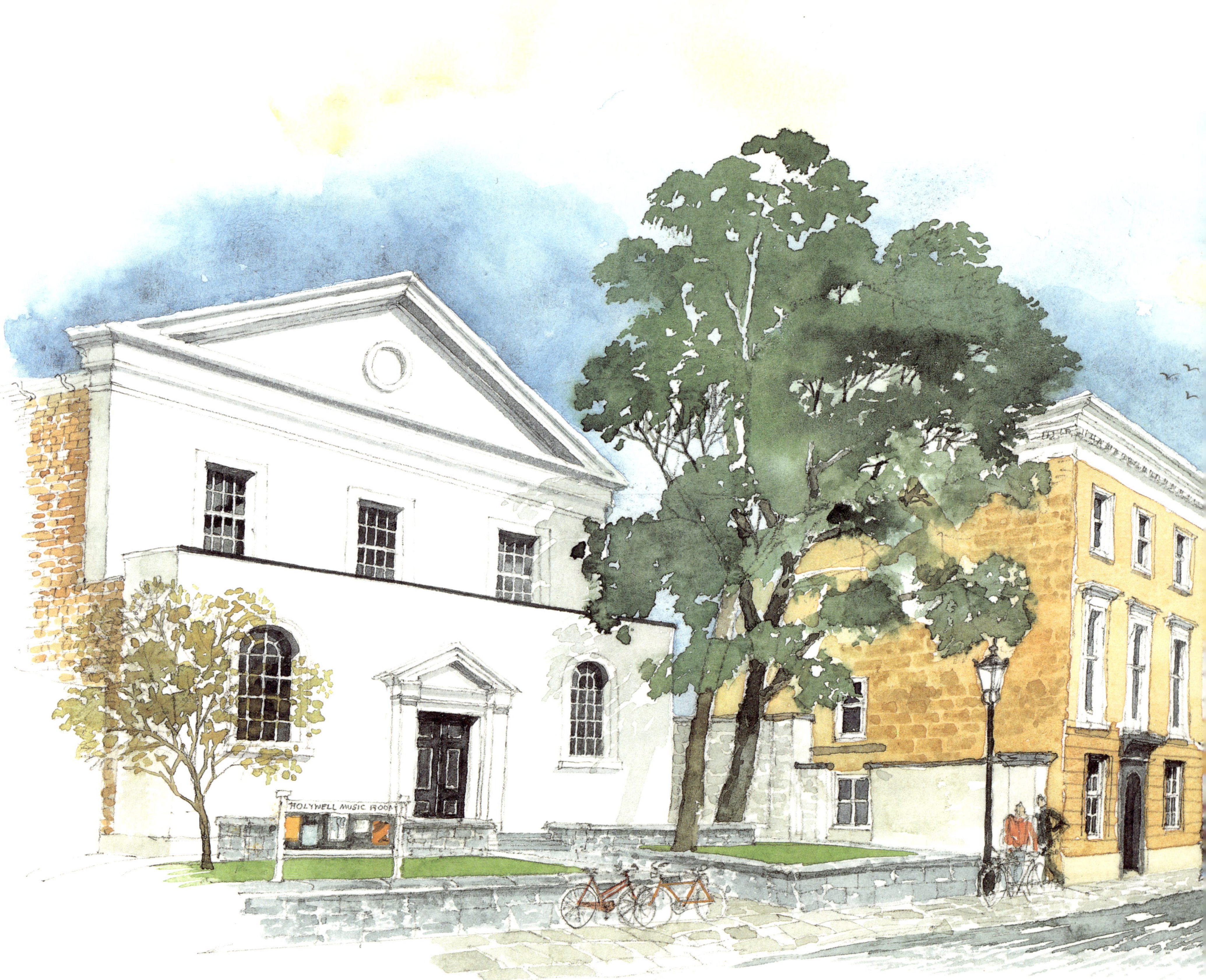
HOLYWELL MUSIC ROOM

Holywell Street is one of the city's most picturesque; the Music Room of the 1740s was England's first purpose-built concert hall. Framing the west end of the street are the King's Arms pub, popular with students, and the former Indian Institute.

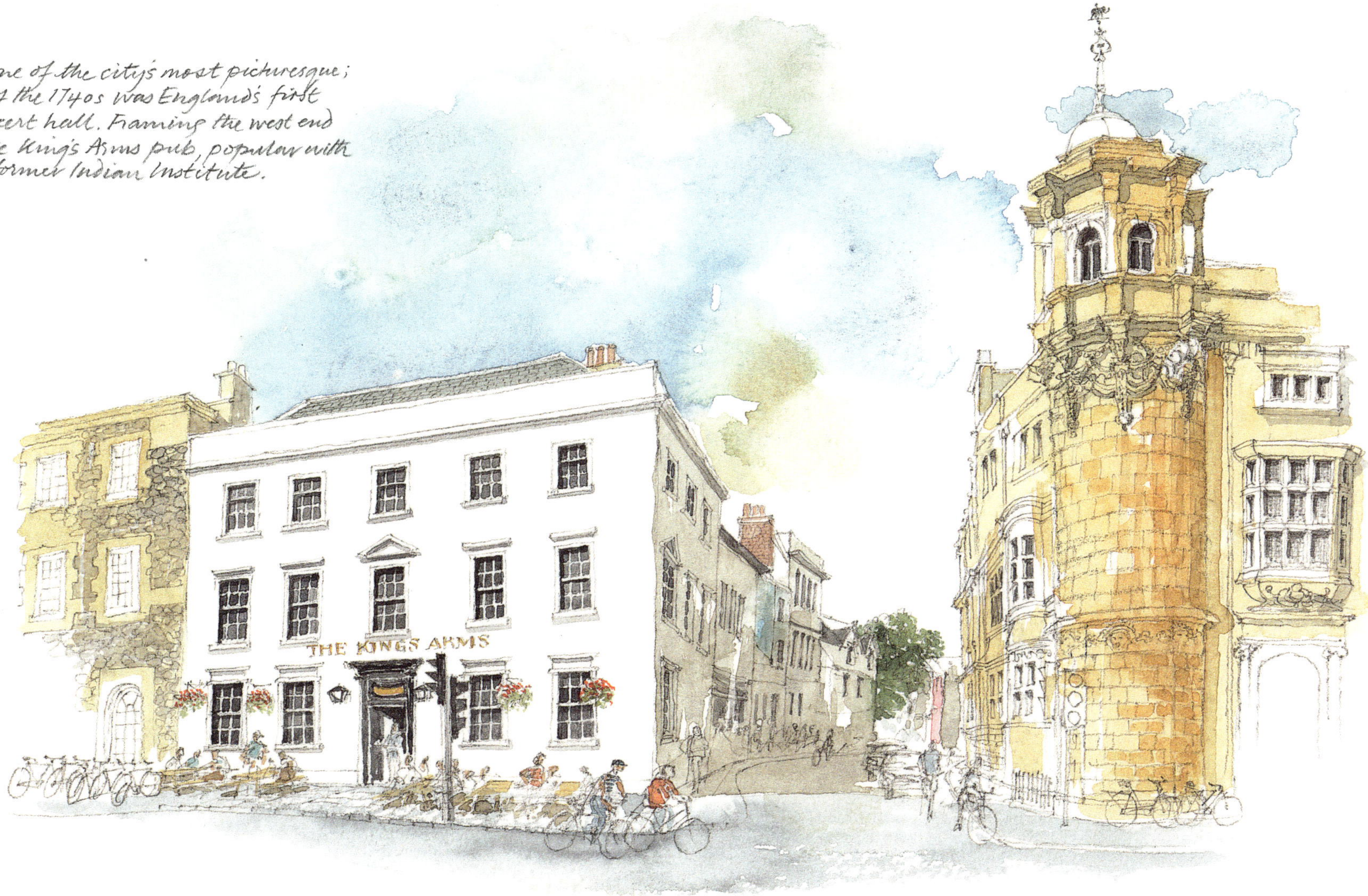

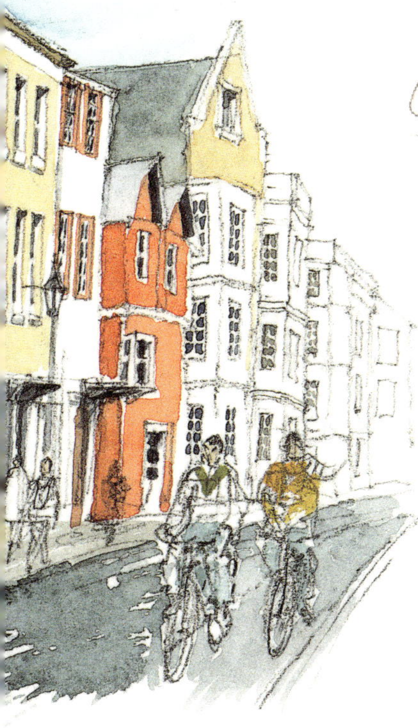

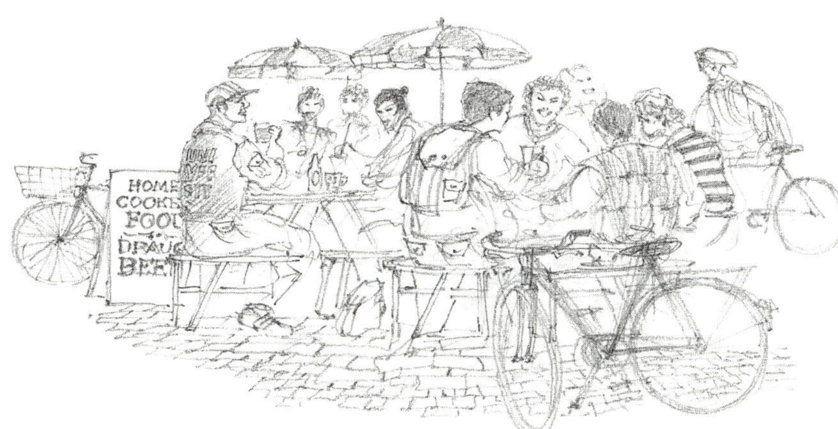

It's been a tradition for hundreds of years for students to drink at the many pubs in the city. Such famous names as Oscar Wilde and Kingsley Amis, C.S. Lewis and J.R.R. Tolkien were frequent vistors when they were students.

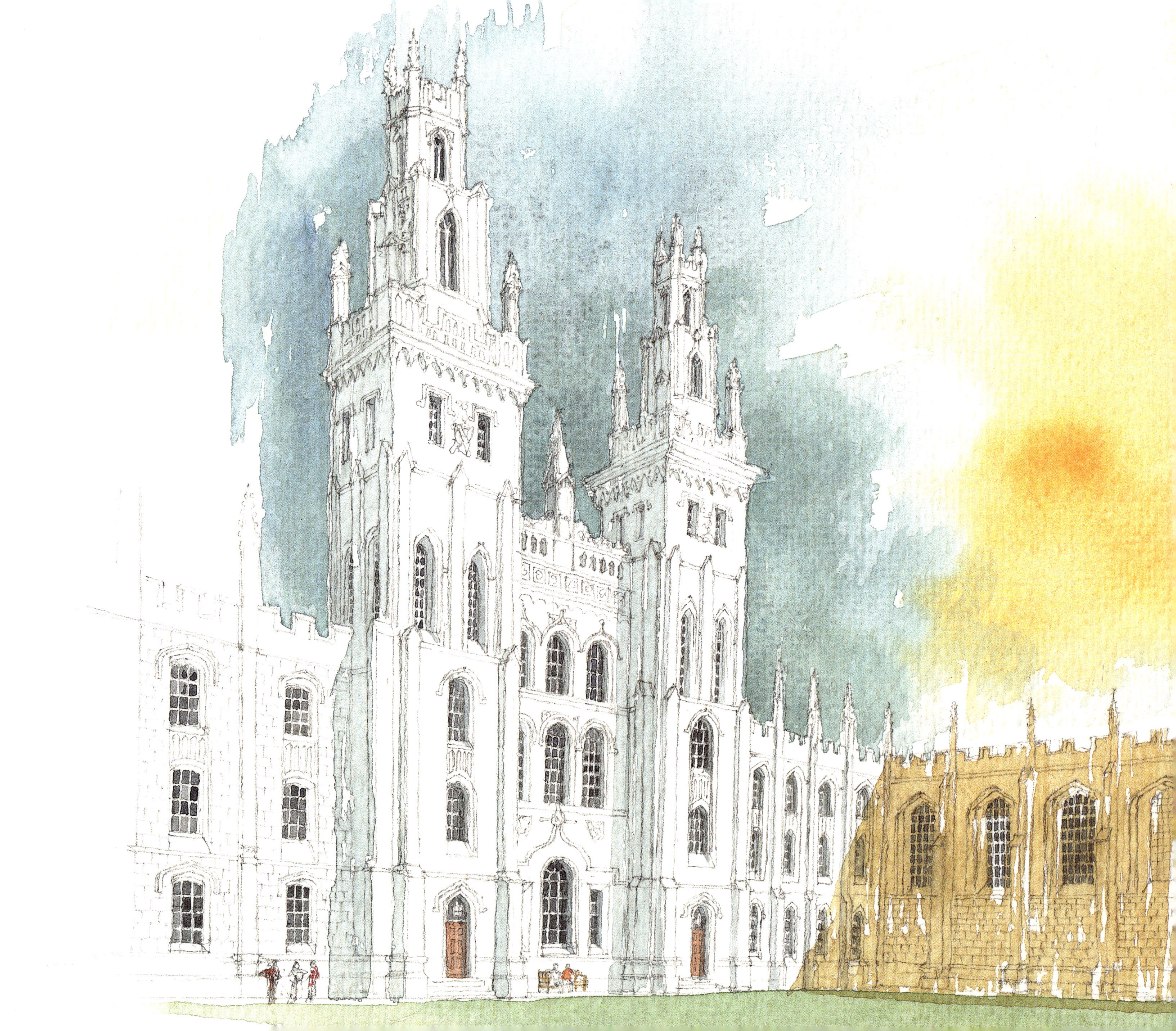

All souls is the only ancient college to have no undergraduates. Its splendid North Quad was designed in 1715 by Nicholas Hawksmoor, whose mentor Christopher Wren had probably designed the elaborate sundial during his year as Bursar of the college in 1658.

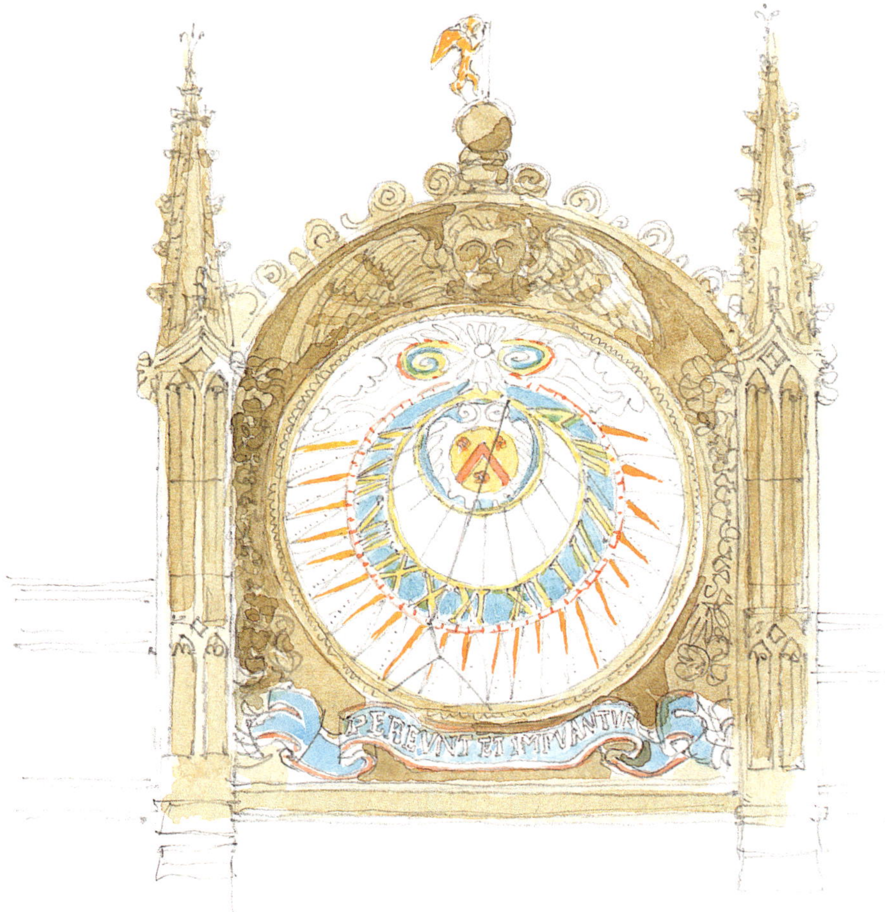

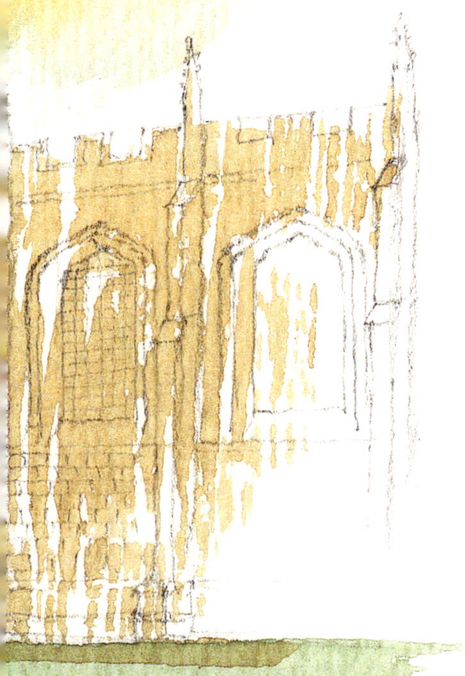

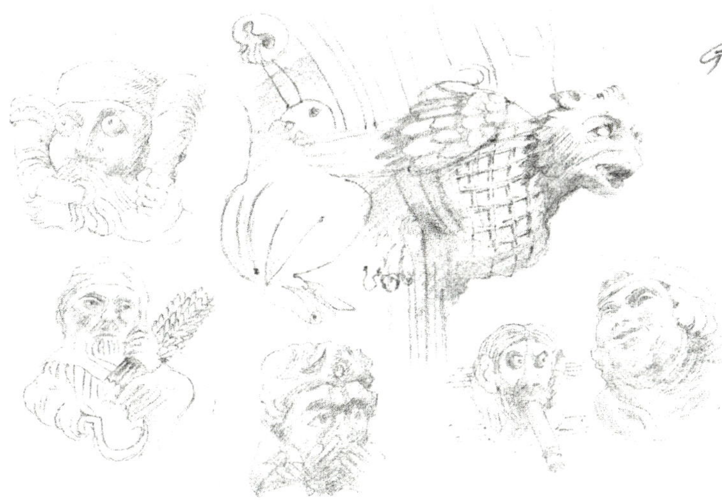

Grotesques and gargoyles can be seen attached to many of Oxford's buildings and date back to medieval times to ward off evil spirits and more practically to divert water.

Mansfield College began as a training college for Nonconformist ministers. Architect Basil Champneys was given the chance to design the college in a Tudor-Gothic style.

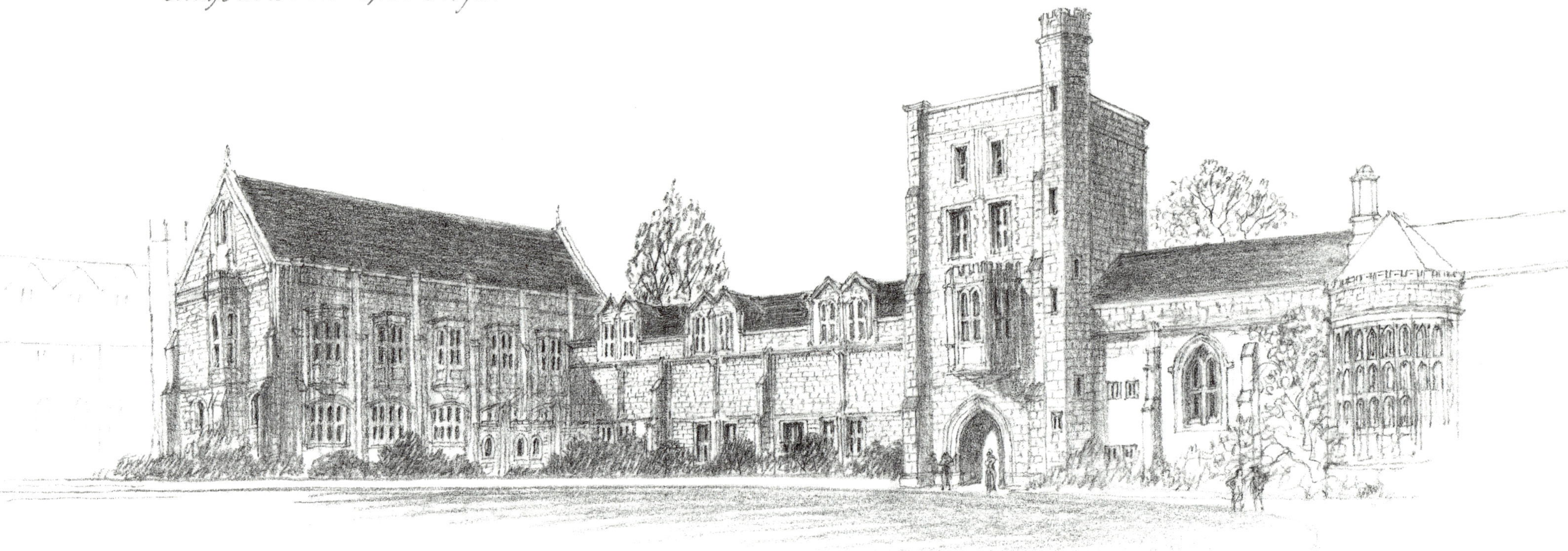

Rhodes House was built in the 1920s to commemorate the diamond magnate Cecil Rhodes. Rhodes Scholars who have gone on to achive fame and fortune count former President Bill Clinton among their number.

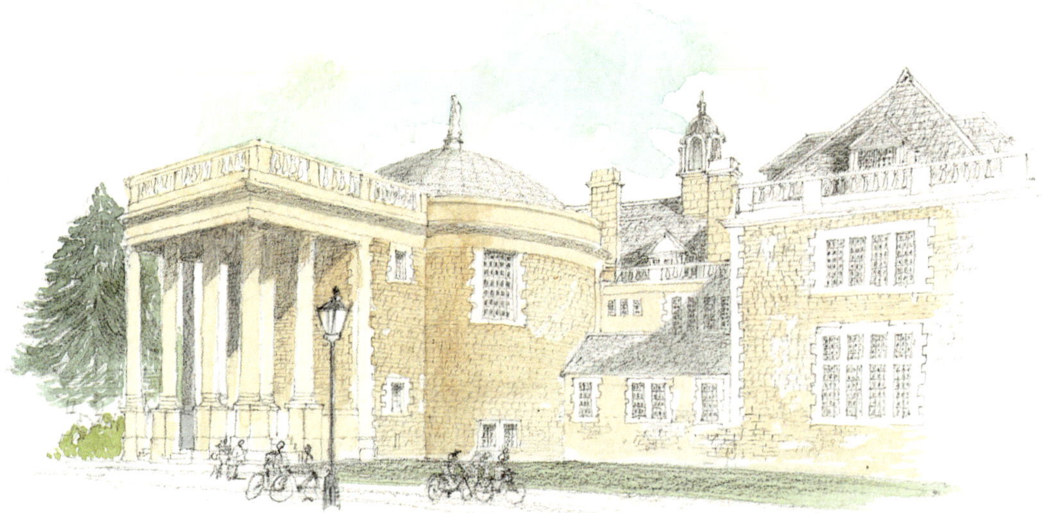

The imposing Front Quad at Wadham College remains exactly as it was first built in 1610-13. The porch to the hall is surmounted by statues of the founders, Nicholas and Dorothy Wadham, and above them is the then reigning monarch, James I. Within hangs the portrait of Christopher Wren, an undergraduate here in the early 1650s.

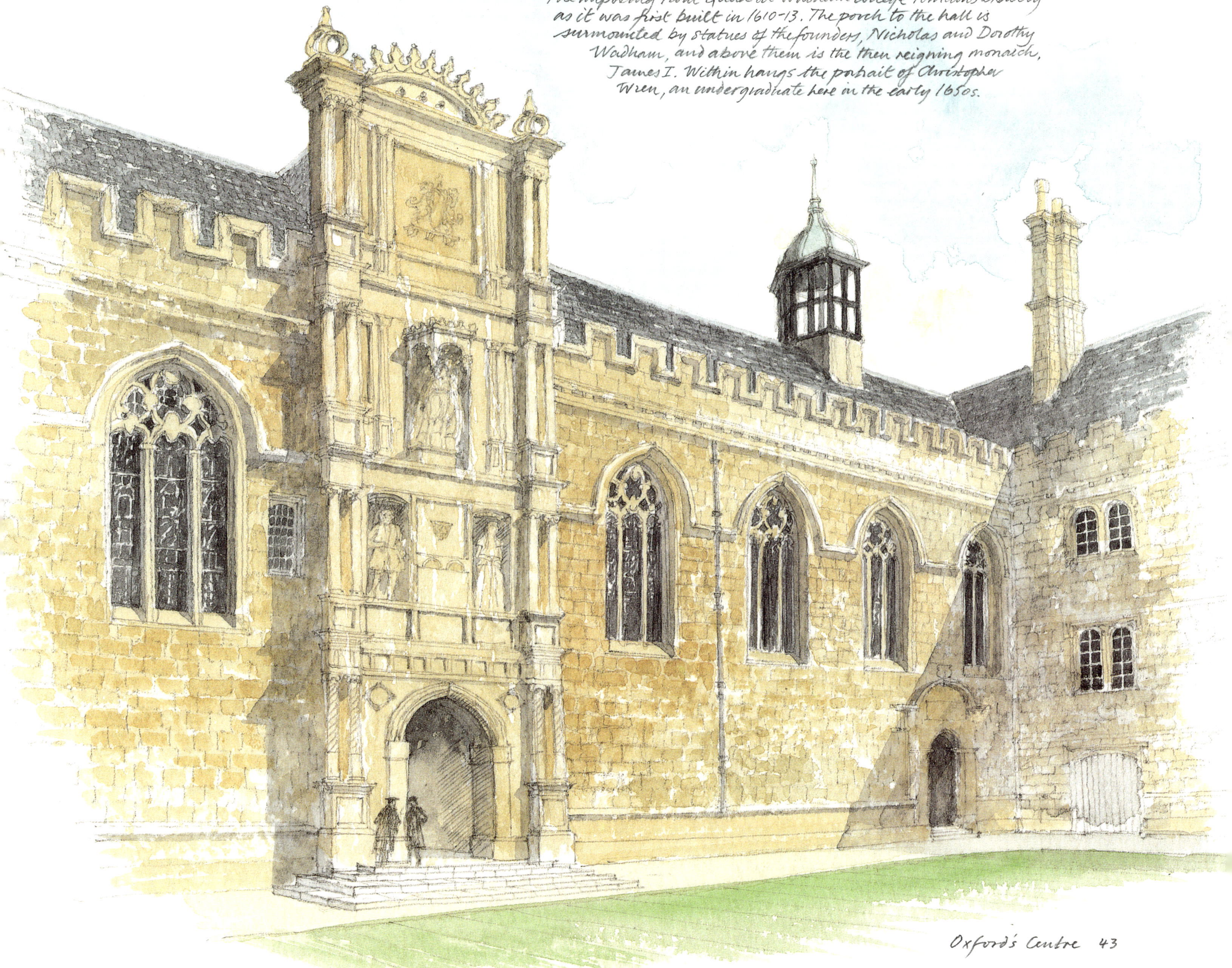

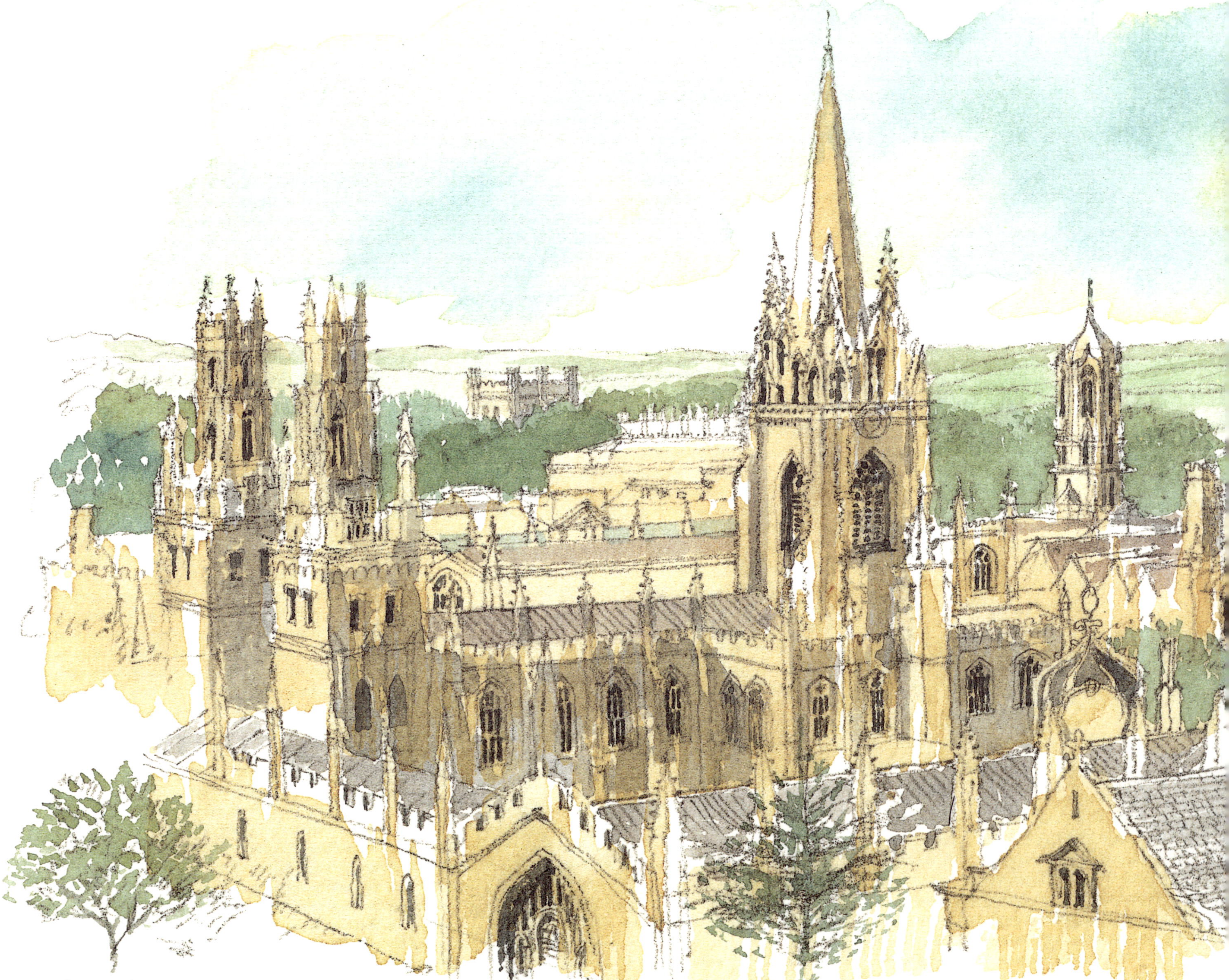

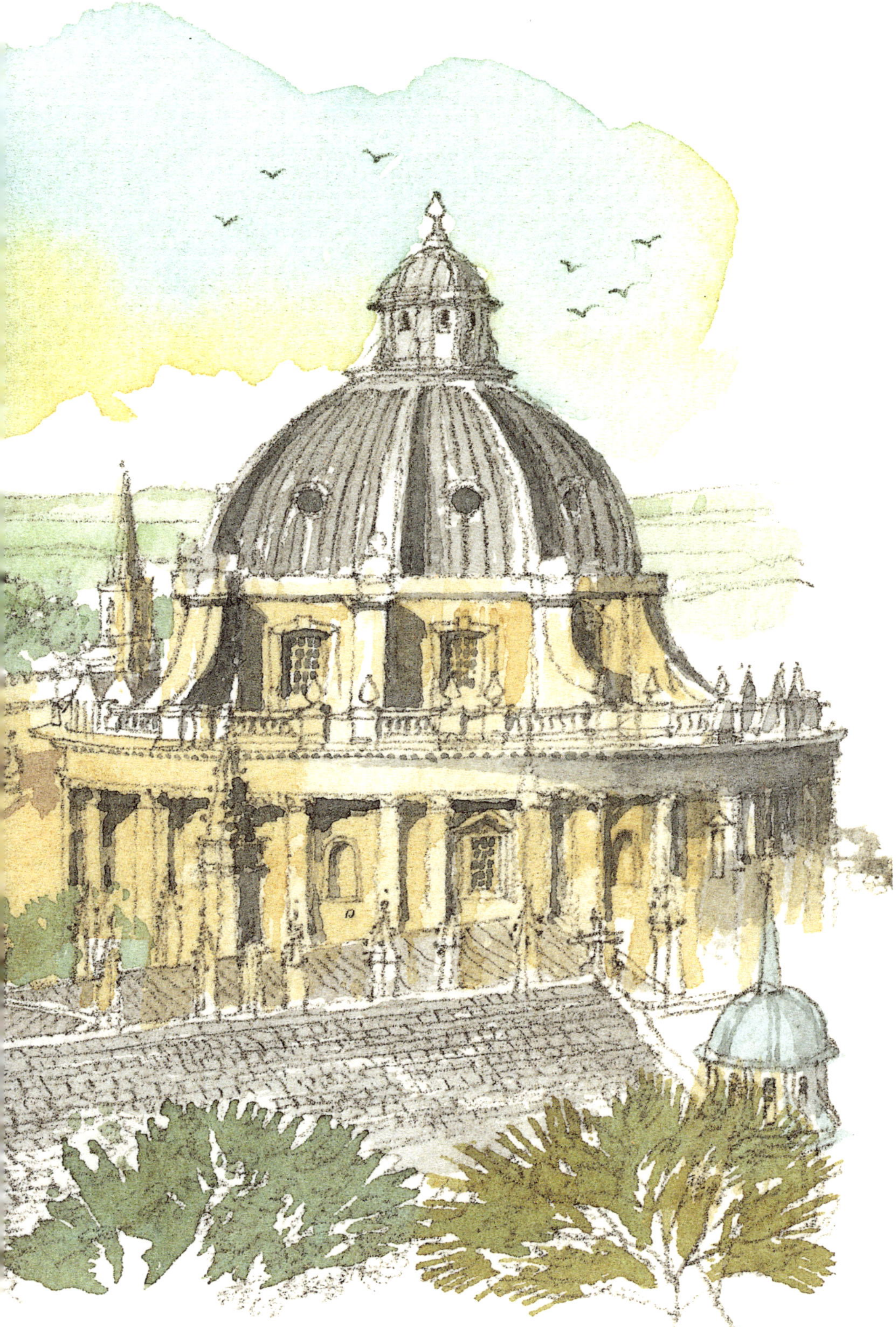

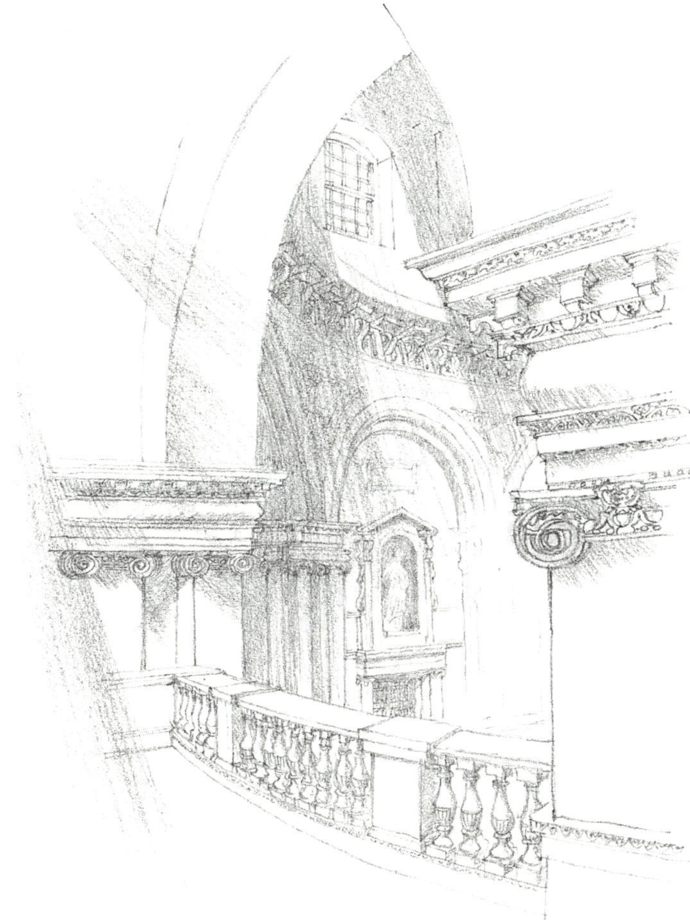

Among the most distinctive features of Oxford's skyline are (left to right) the twin towers of All Souls, the spire of St Mary the Virgin, Tom Tower (Christ Church), and the dome of the Radcliffe Camera. The Camera, now part of the Bodleian Library, is arguably the city's finest building.

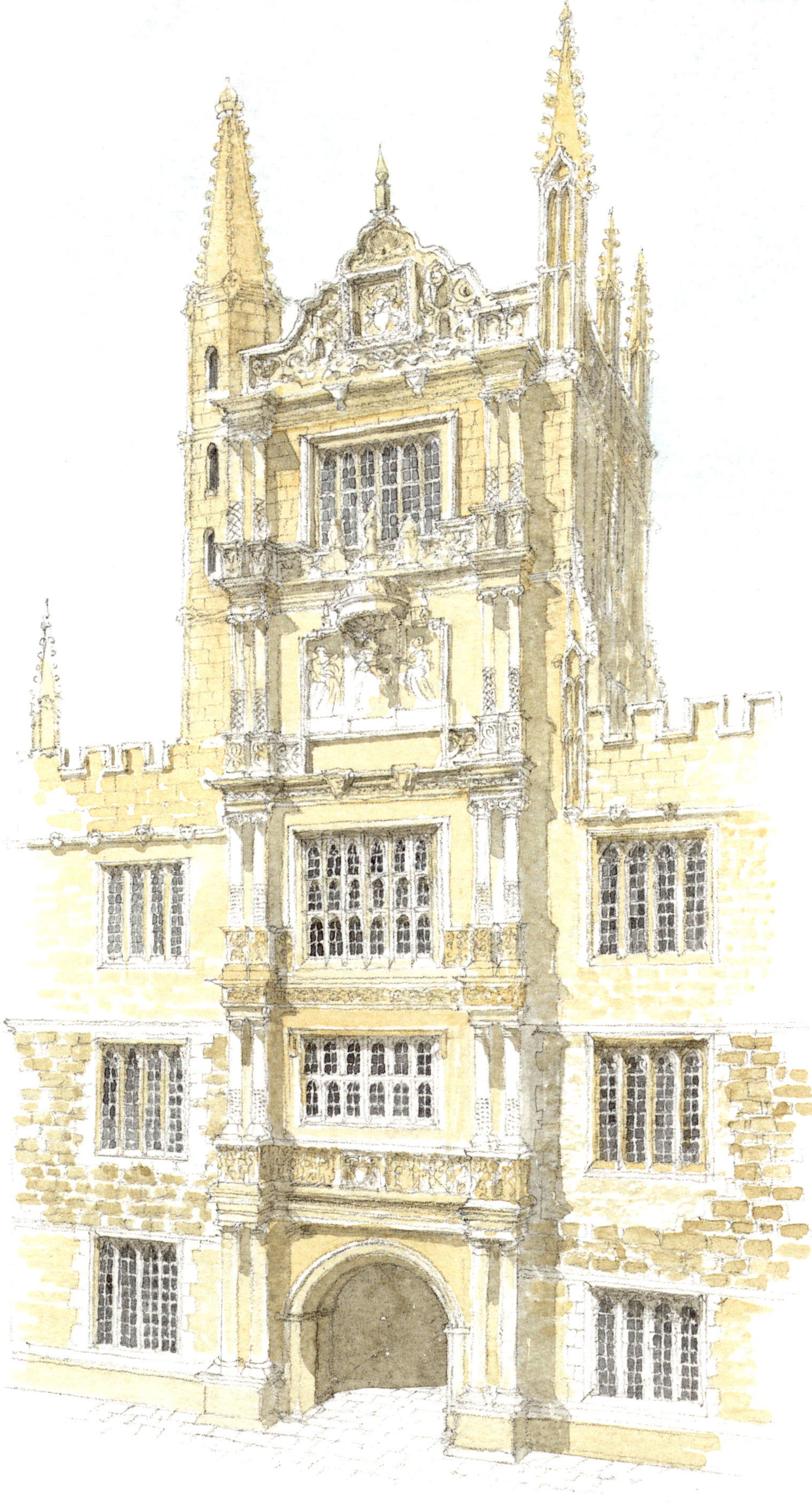

The Bodleian Library is one of six copyright libraries in the British Isles. It is named after Sir Thomas Bodley, who reorganised and enlarged it in the early 17th century and had the elaborate tower built.

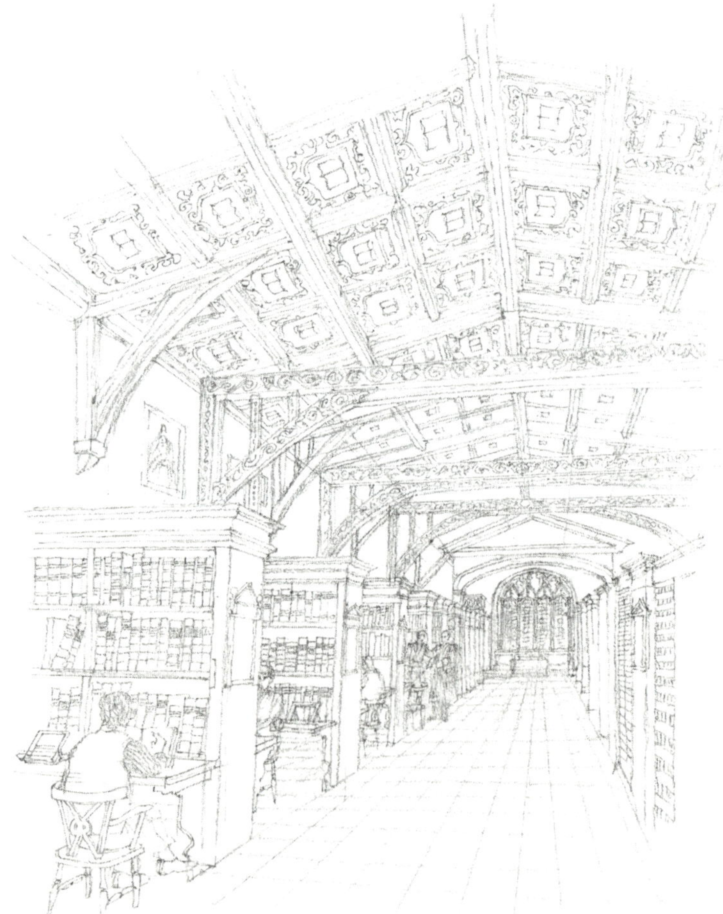

The historic core of the Bodleian is the 15th-century Duke Humphrey's Library. It takes its name from Duke Humphrey of Gloucester, who donated his books in 1444

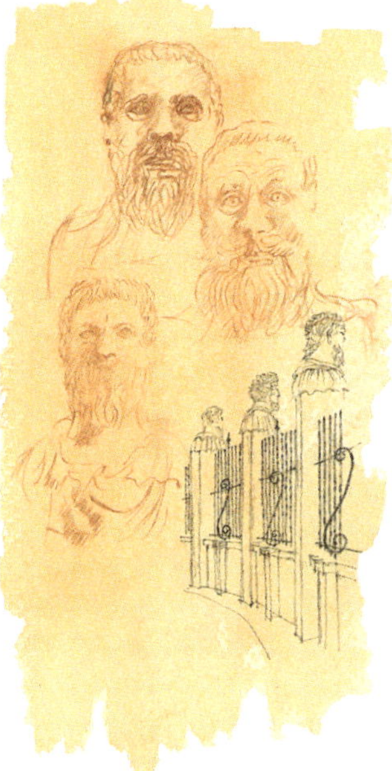

Twelve sculpted heads stand proudly on high plinths outside the Sheldonian Theatre facing Broad Street.

The Sheldonian Theatre was built in 1664-7 to Christopher Wren's design, as a suitably impressive setting for the university's ceremonies.

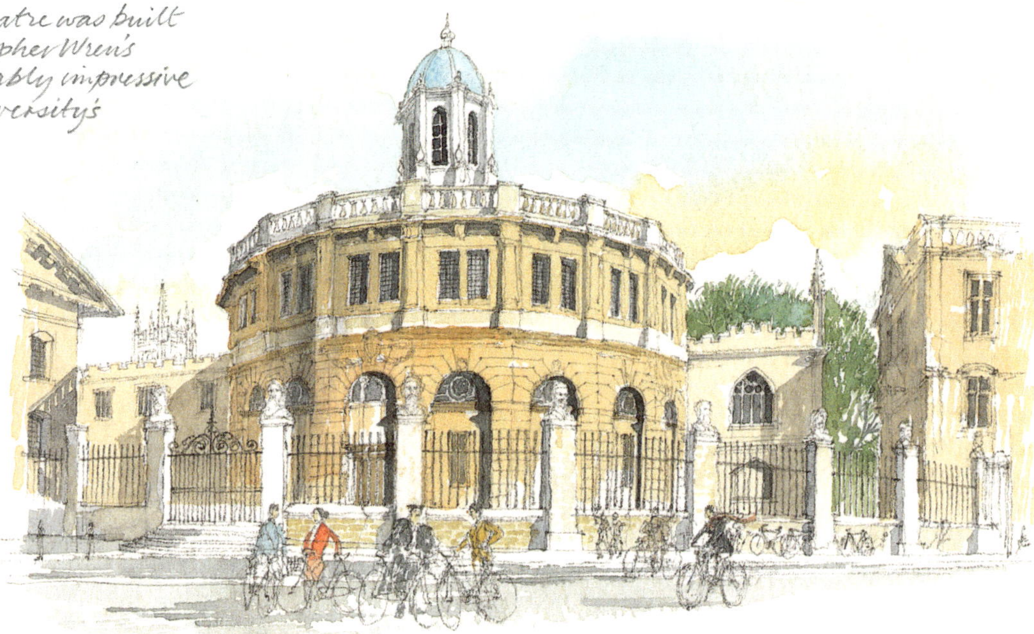

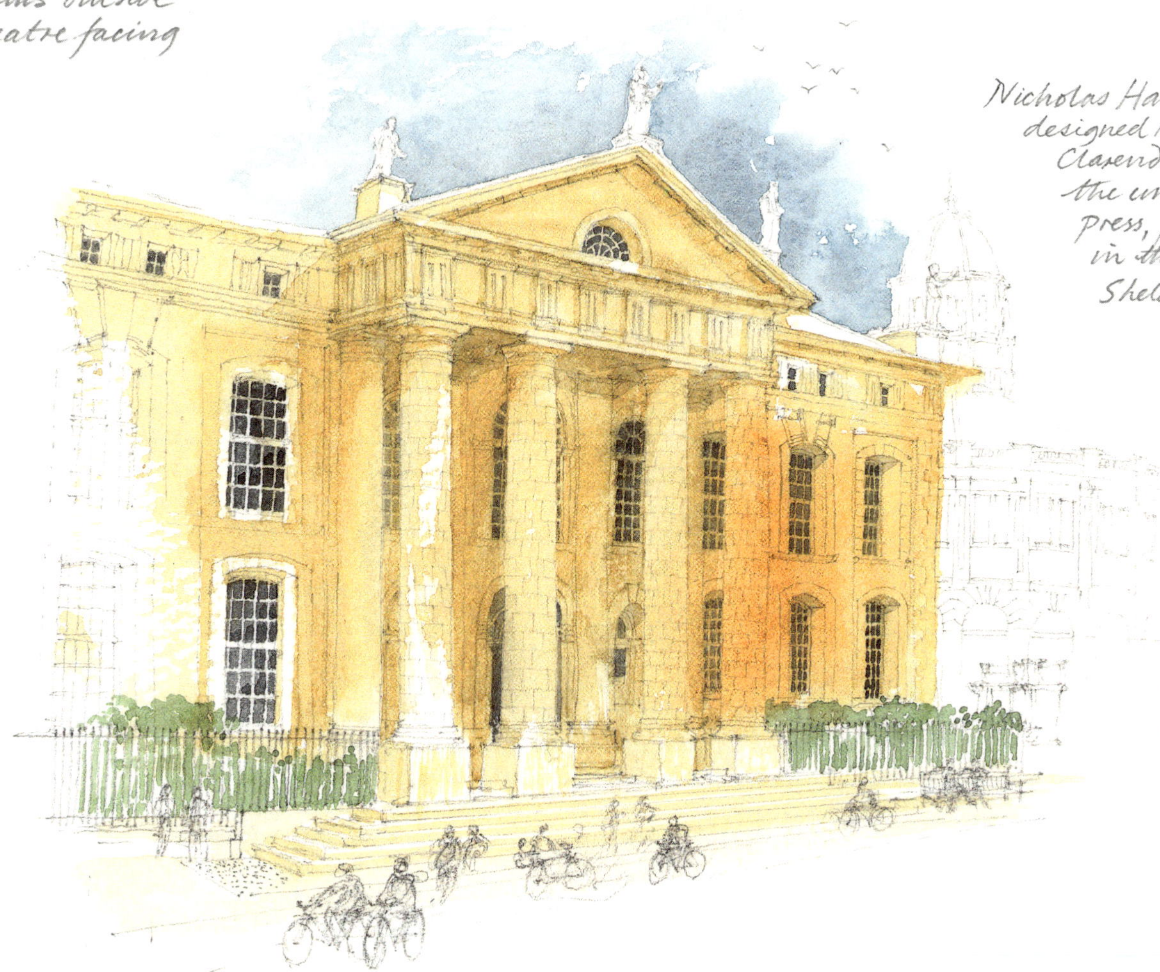

Nicholas Hawksmoor designed the adjoining Clarendon Building to house the university's printing press, previously located in the roof of the Sheldonian.

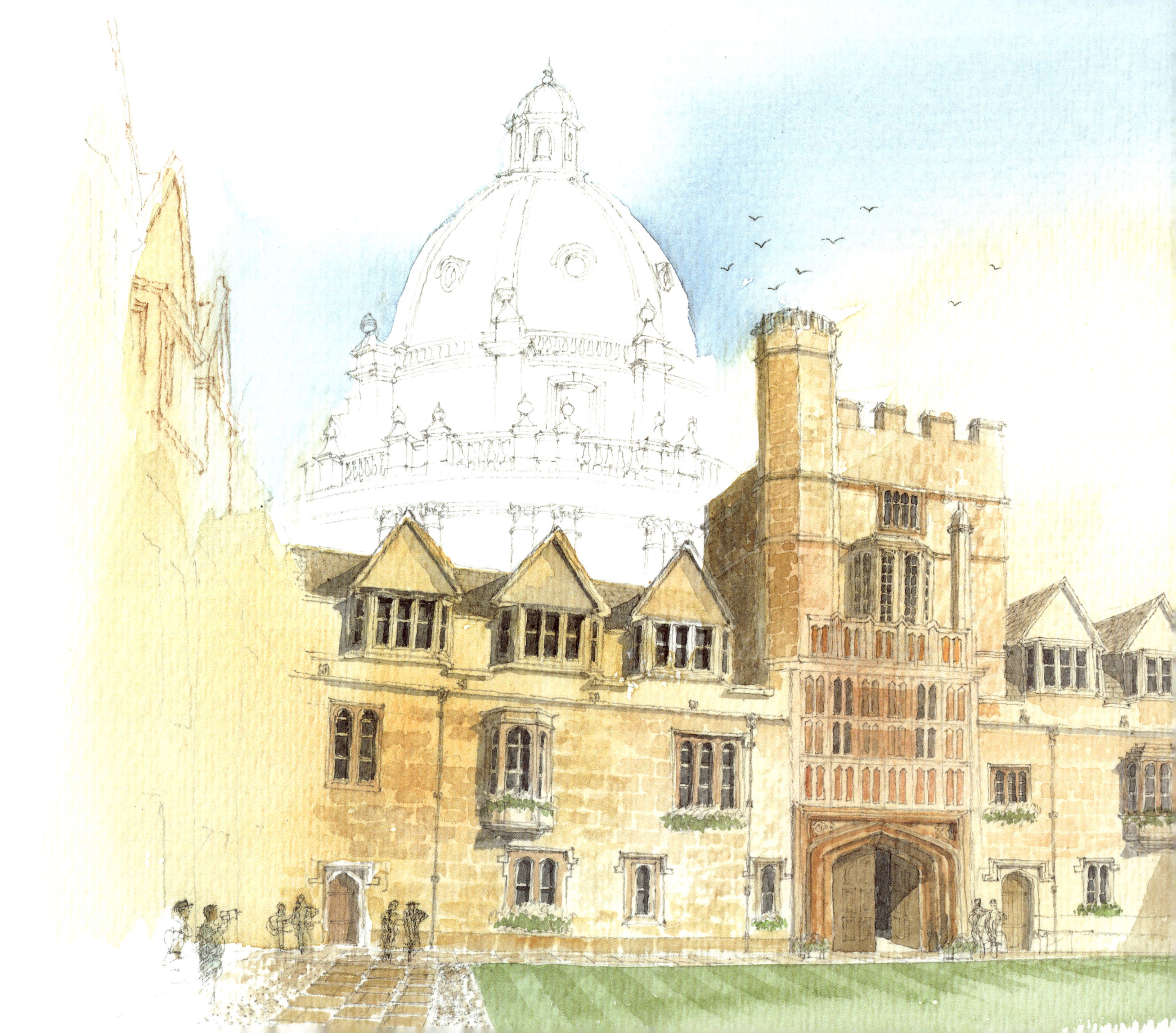

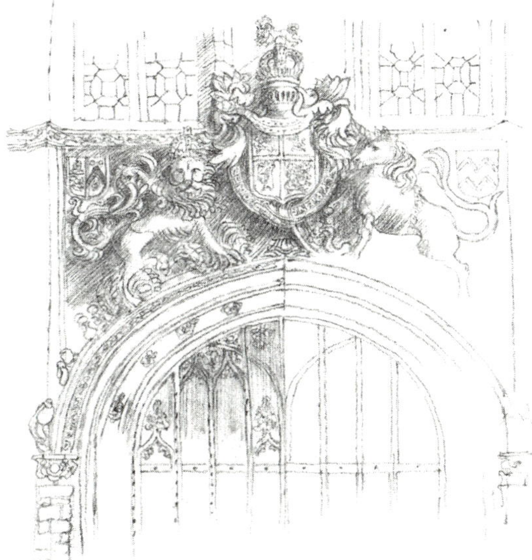

The Royal Arms above the High Street gate at Brasenose.

The chapel at Brasenose is in a strange mixture of Gothic and Classical, characteristic of mid-17th century Oxford.

Brasenose College founded in 1509, takes its curious name from a medieval brass door knocker in the shape of a nose. The dome of the Radcliffe Camera rises majestically above the Tudor quadrangle.

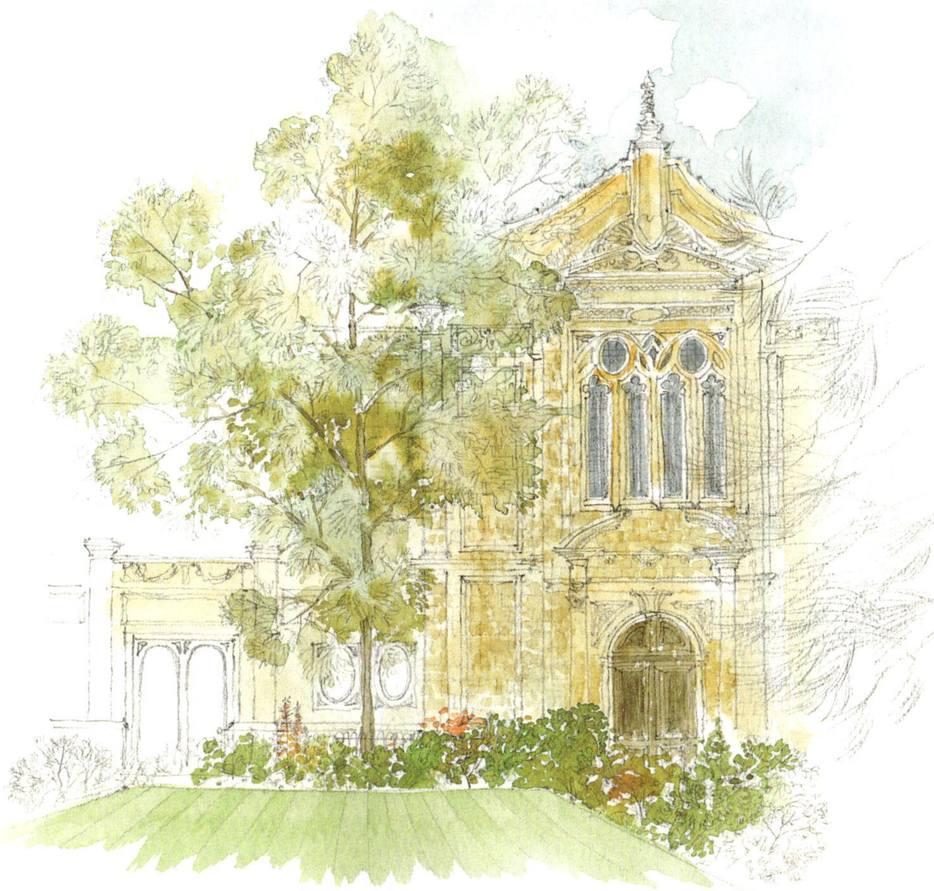

A creeper-clad wall of one of Lincoln College's quadrangles, transformed by glorious autumn colour.

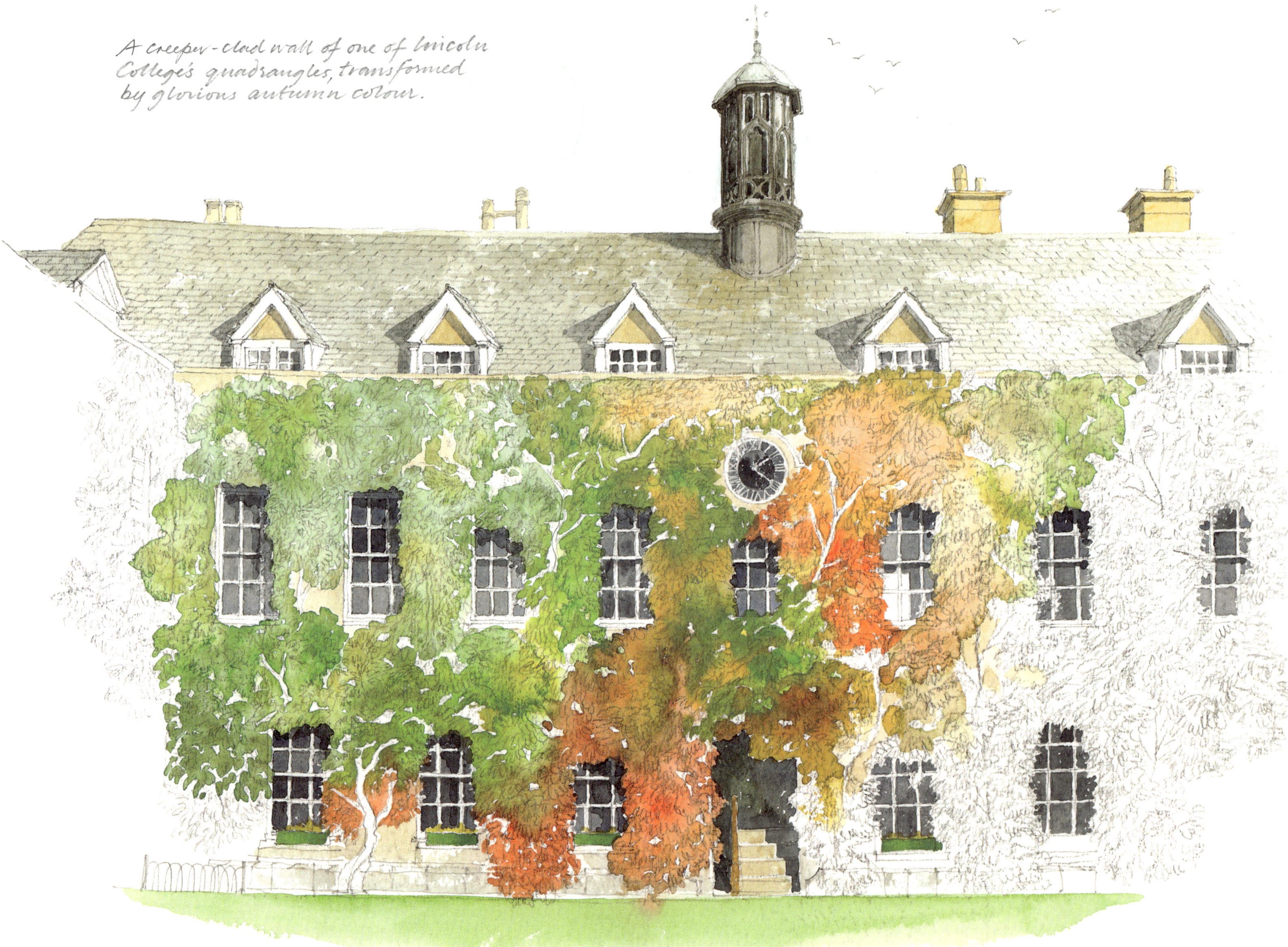

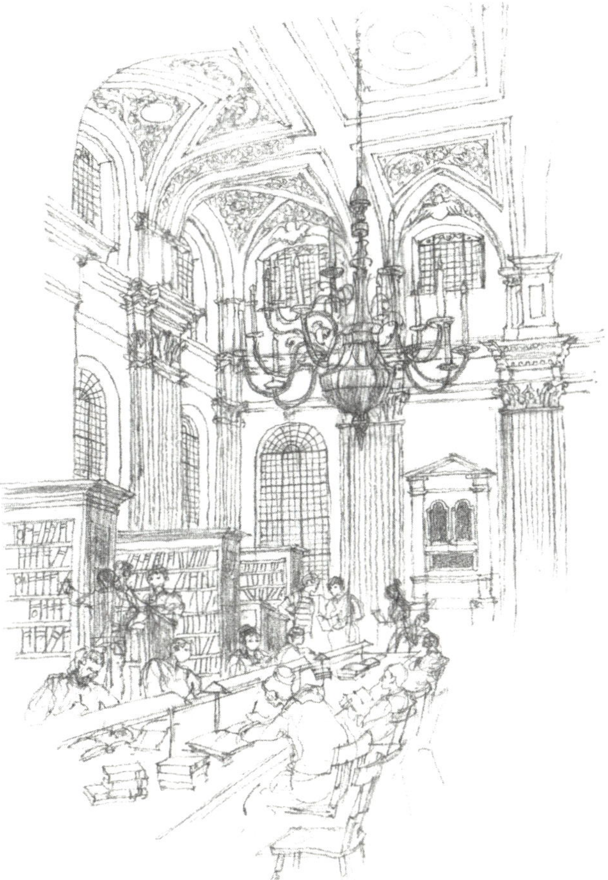

The view south down Turl Street ('The Turl') is closed by the spire of All Saints. This fine Baroque church has now been converted into a library for the adjacent Lincoln College (above).

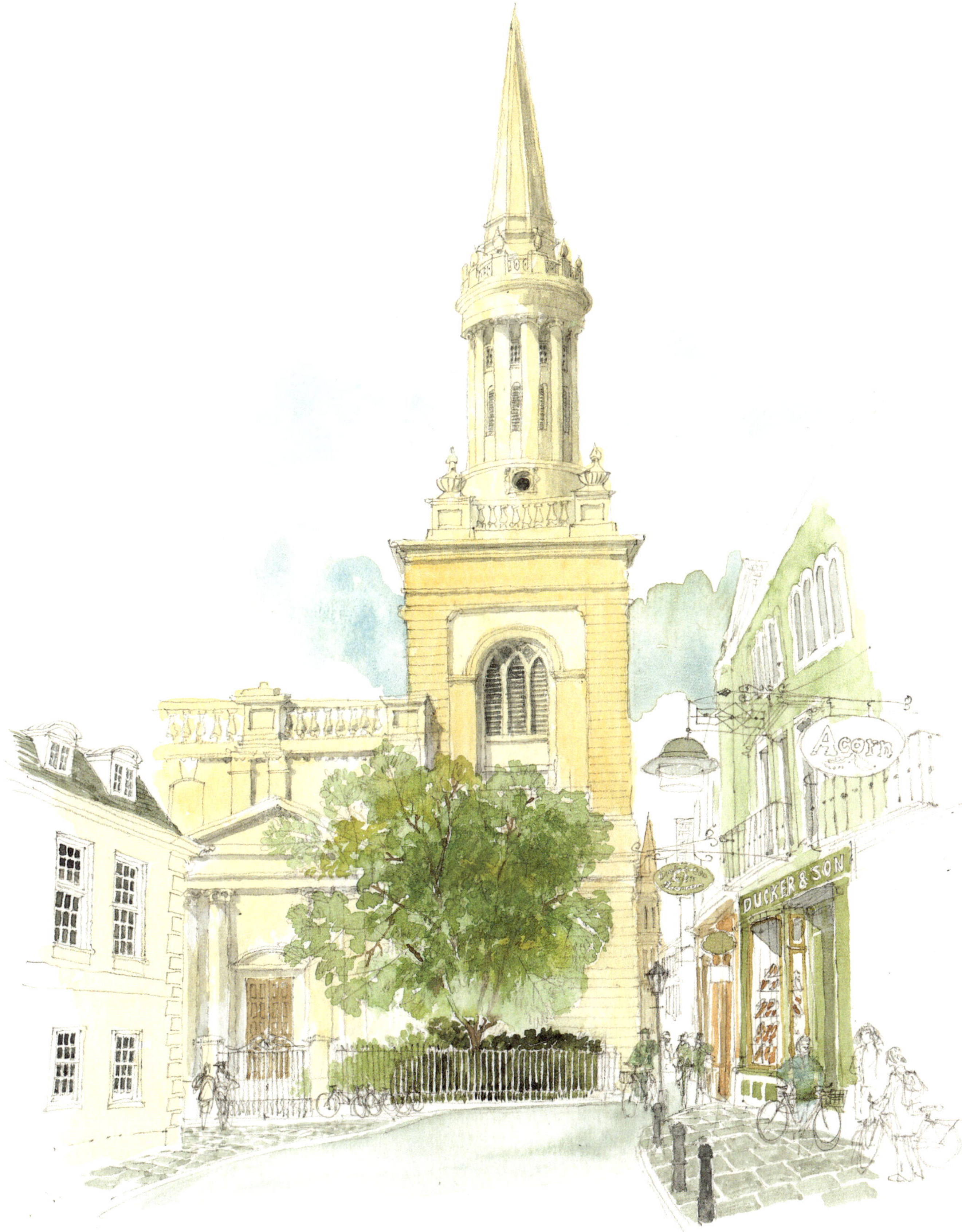

Exeter College is architecturally one of the most mixed; it was founded as early as 1314, but most of the buildings now date from the 17th century onwards. The High Victorian chapel by Sir George Gilbert Scott, though fine of its kind, was inspired by Sainte Chapelle in Paris and, to some, may appear alien to Oxford.

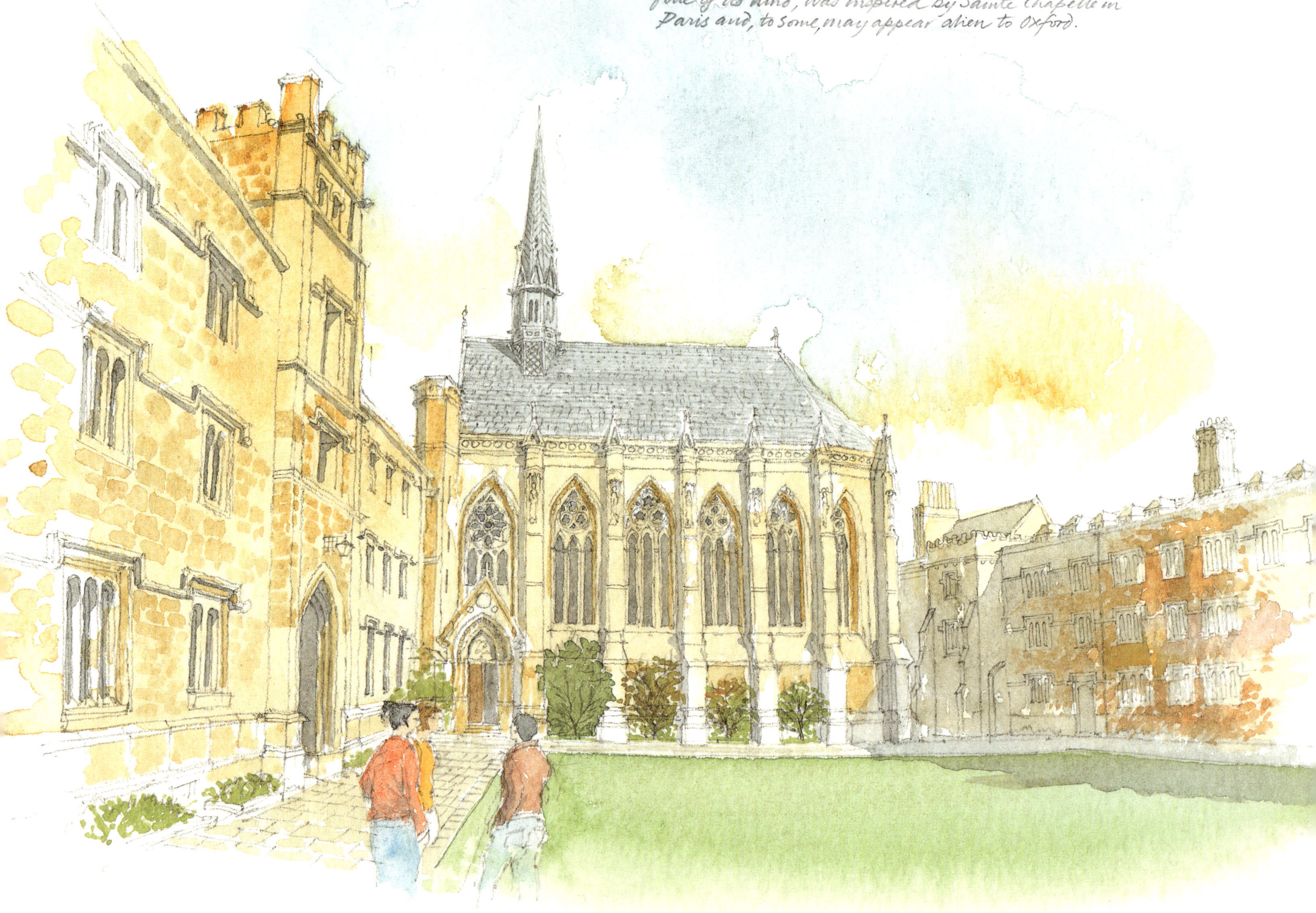

There can be few better places to relax with fellow students and friends than an Oxford quad.

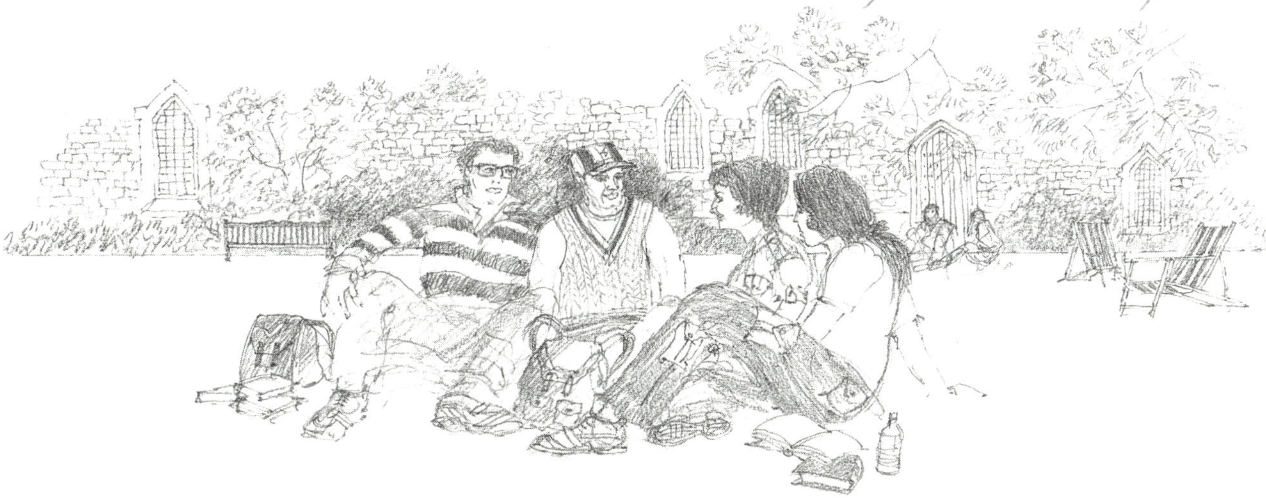

Exeter's garden is hidden away between the college buildings and those of the Bodleian Library.

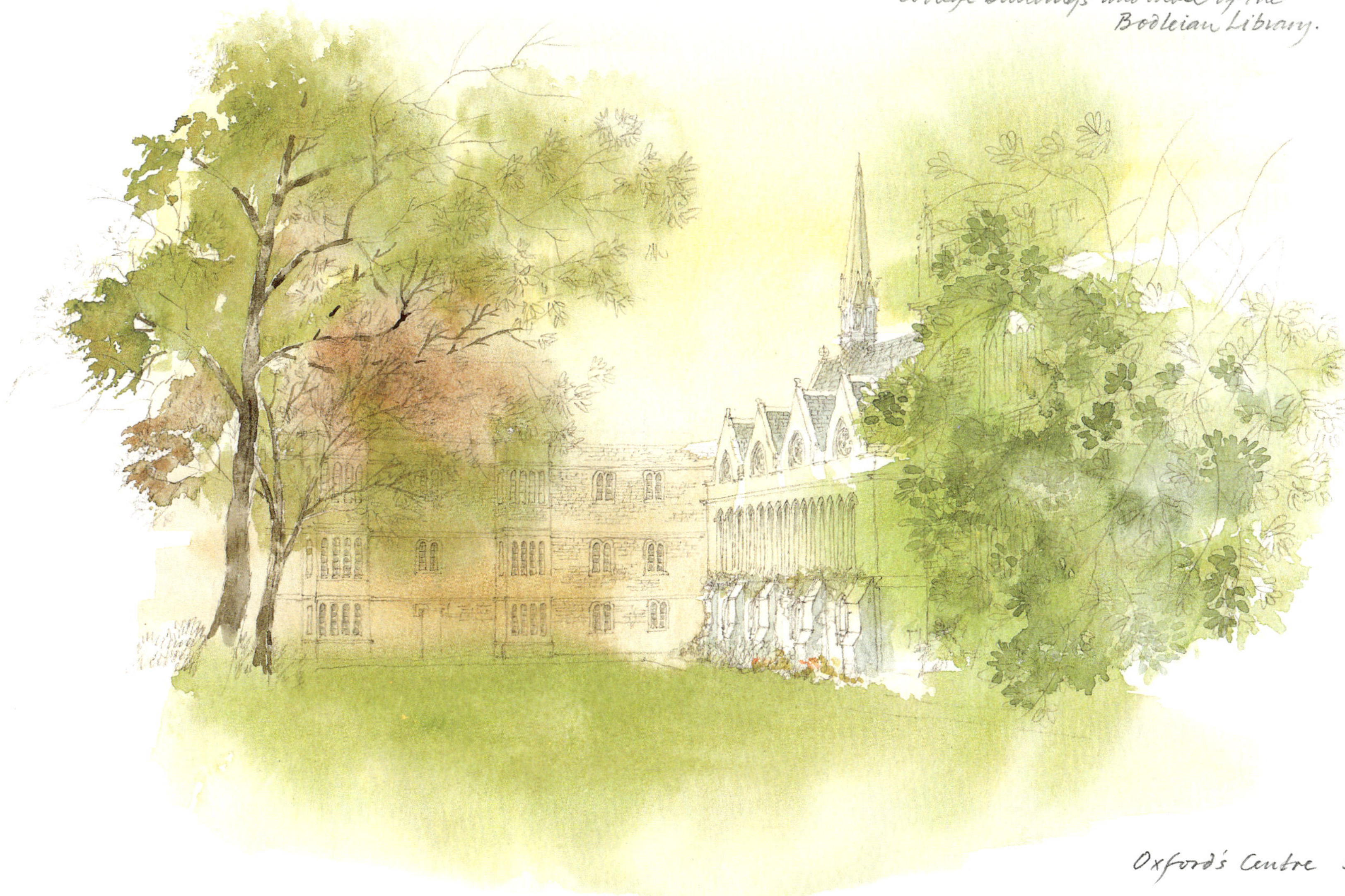

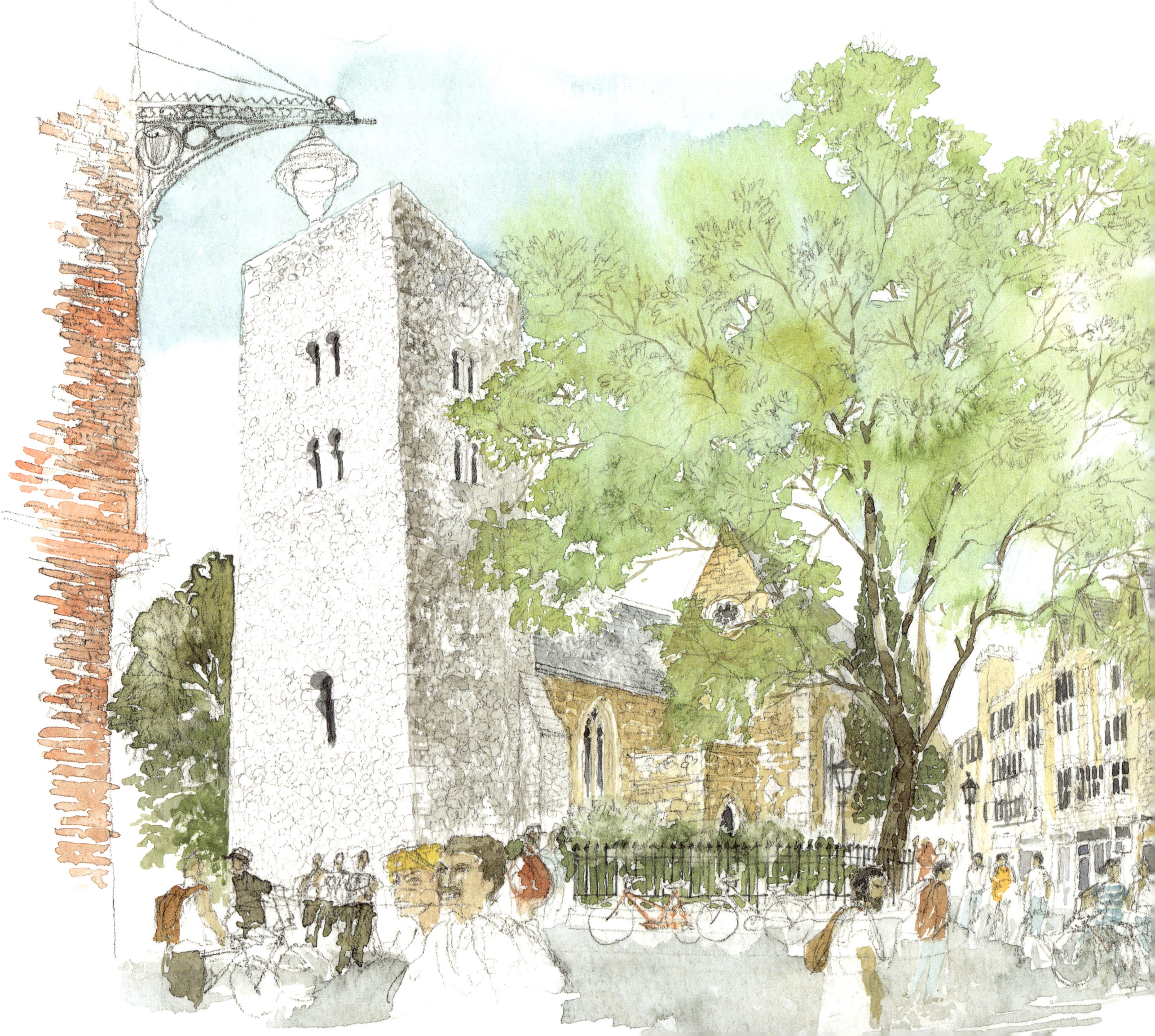

The former Golden Cross Inn on Cornmarket goes back at least to the 15th century, the date of the range on the left.

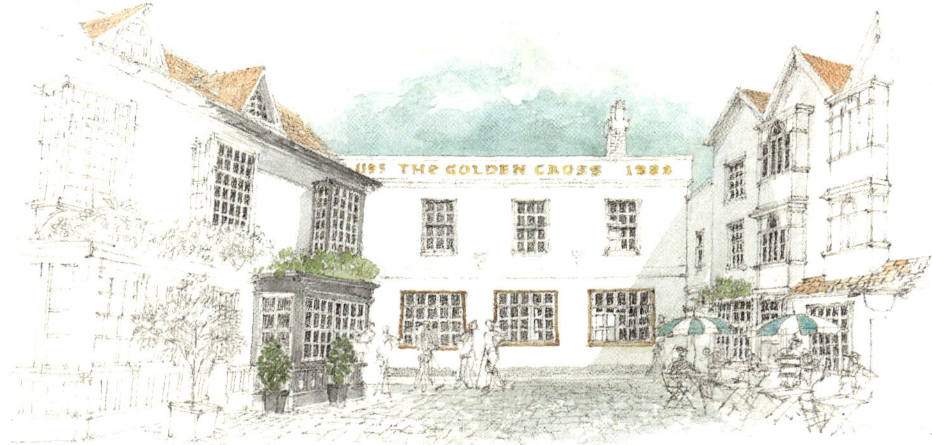

Cornmarket is Oxford's busiest shopping street. At its north end the mid-11th century tower of St Michael's church is the oldest surviving structure in the city. The half-timbered building to the right began life at the end of the 14th century as the New Inn.

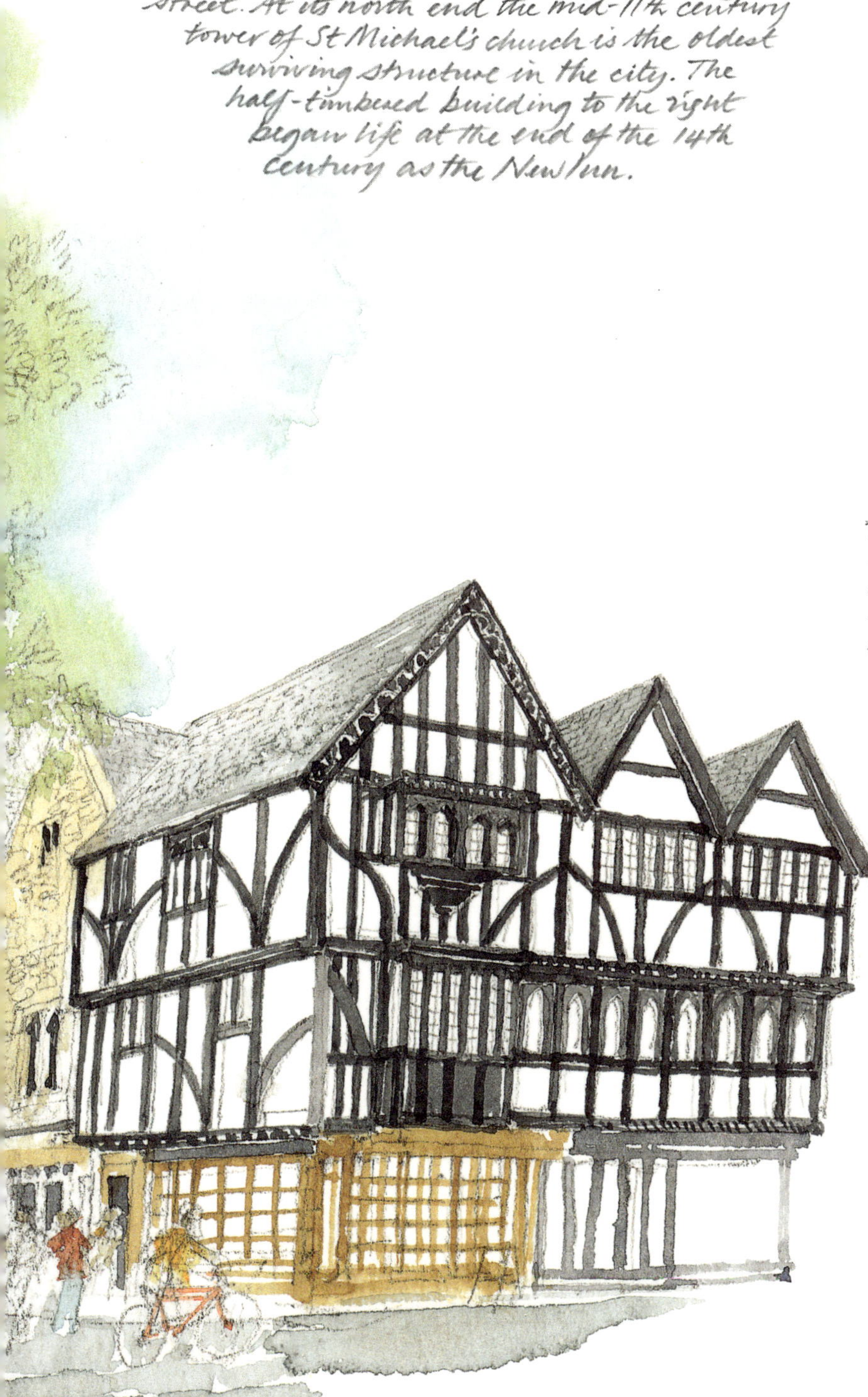

The 18th-century Covered Market was re-roofed at the end of the 19th. It is still a lively and attractive place to shop, although sadly many of the traditional traders have disappeared in recent years.

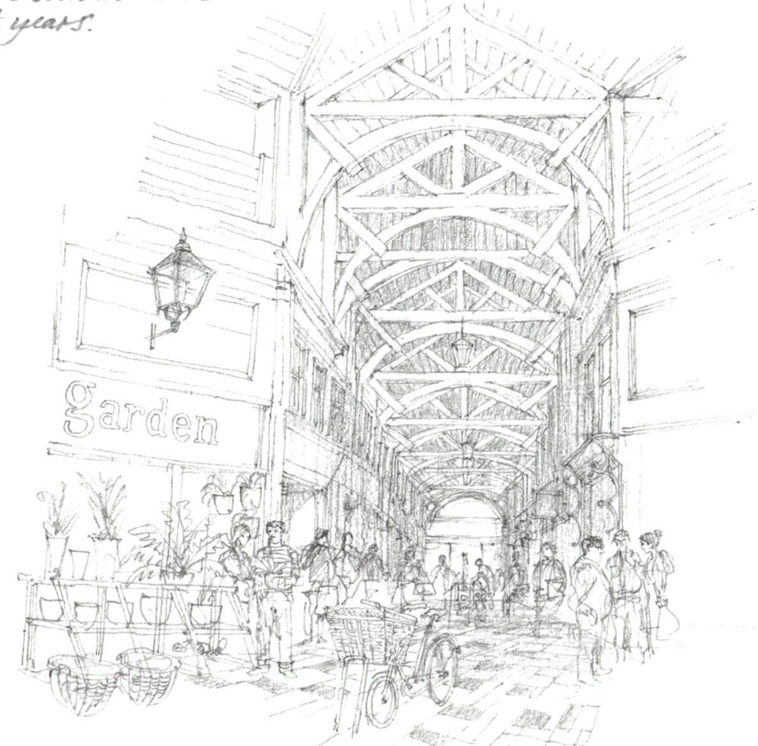

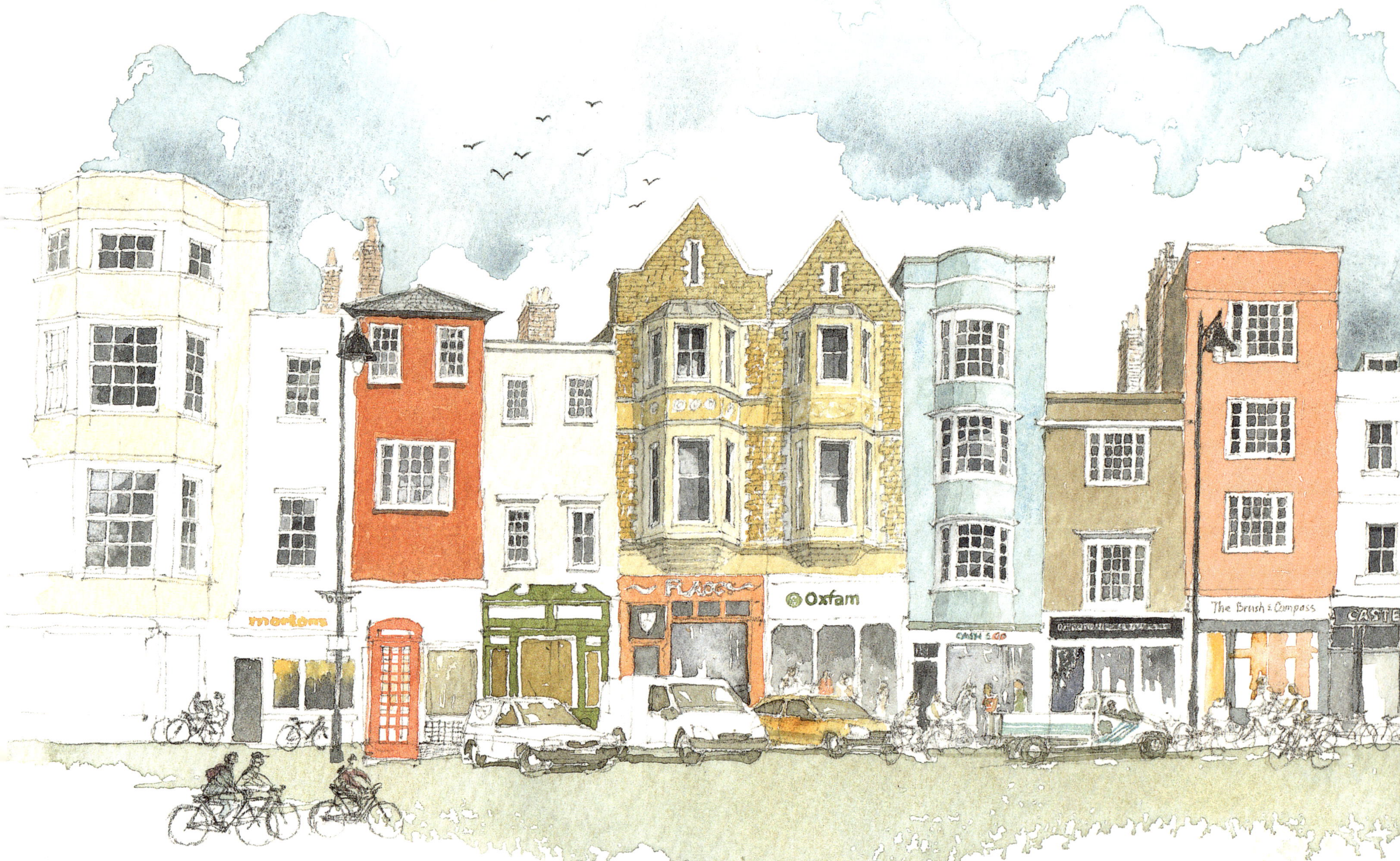

The aptly named Broad Street ('The Broad') developed to the north of the medieval city walls. It is now dominated by university and college buildings, but the south side retains a long range of narrow domestic frontages. A granite cross in the road marks the spot where, in 1556 Archbishop Cranmer and Bishops Latimer and Ridley were burned at the stake for their Protestant faith.

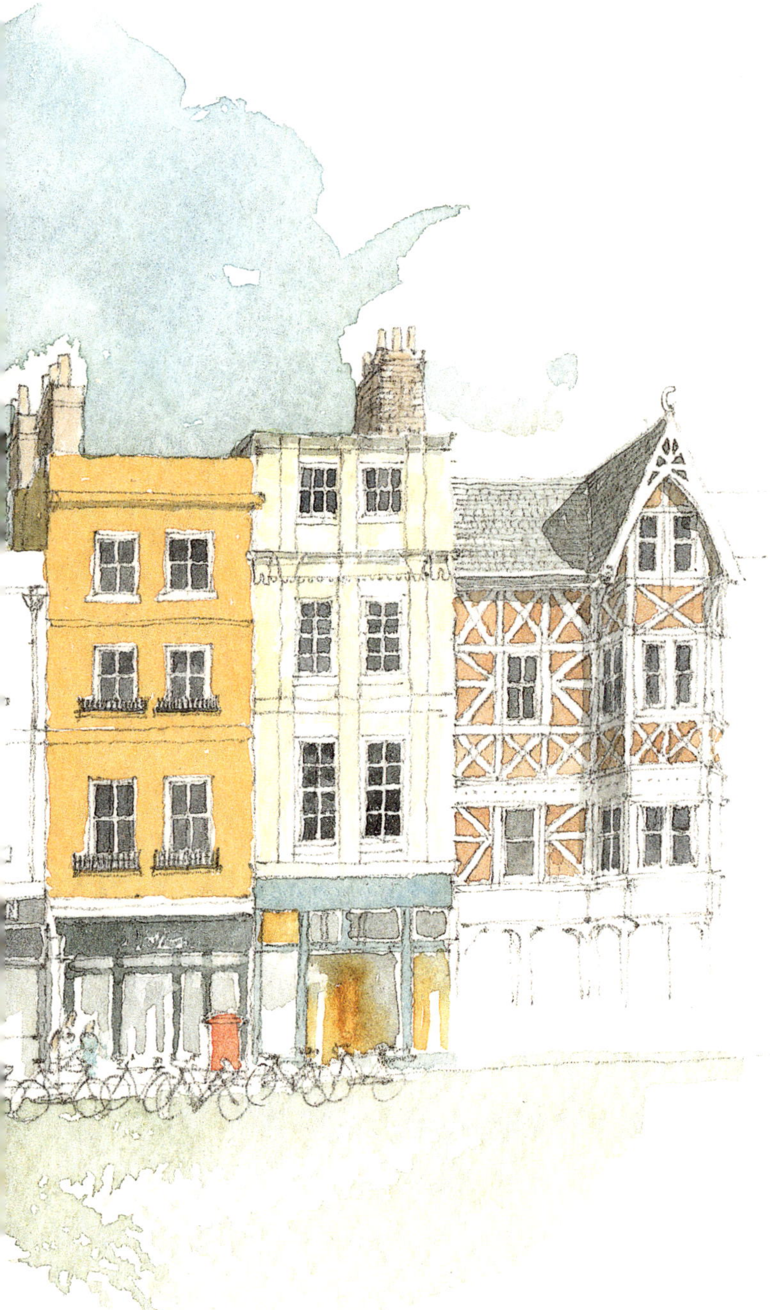

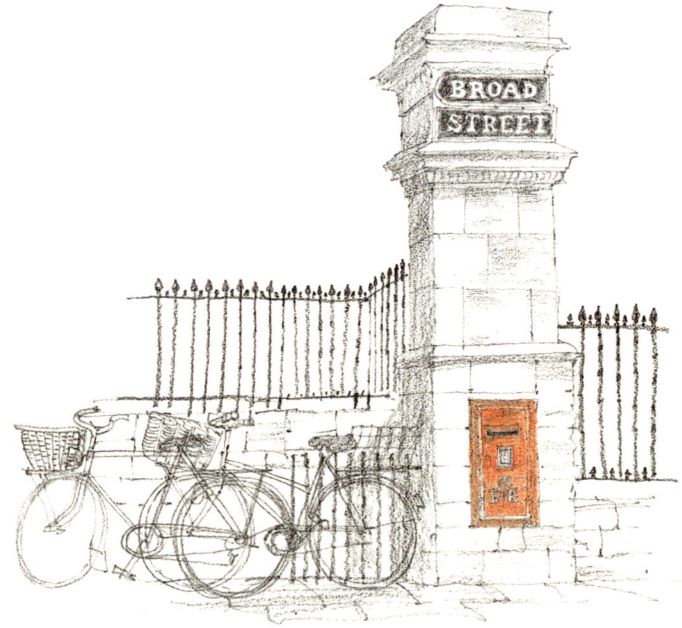

The north side of The Broad contains the buildings of Balliol and Trinity Colleges, and also Blackwell's bookshop used by thousands of students and tourists alike.

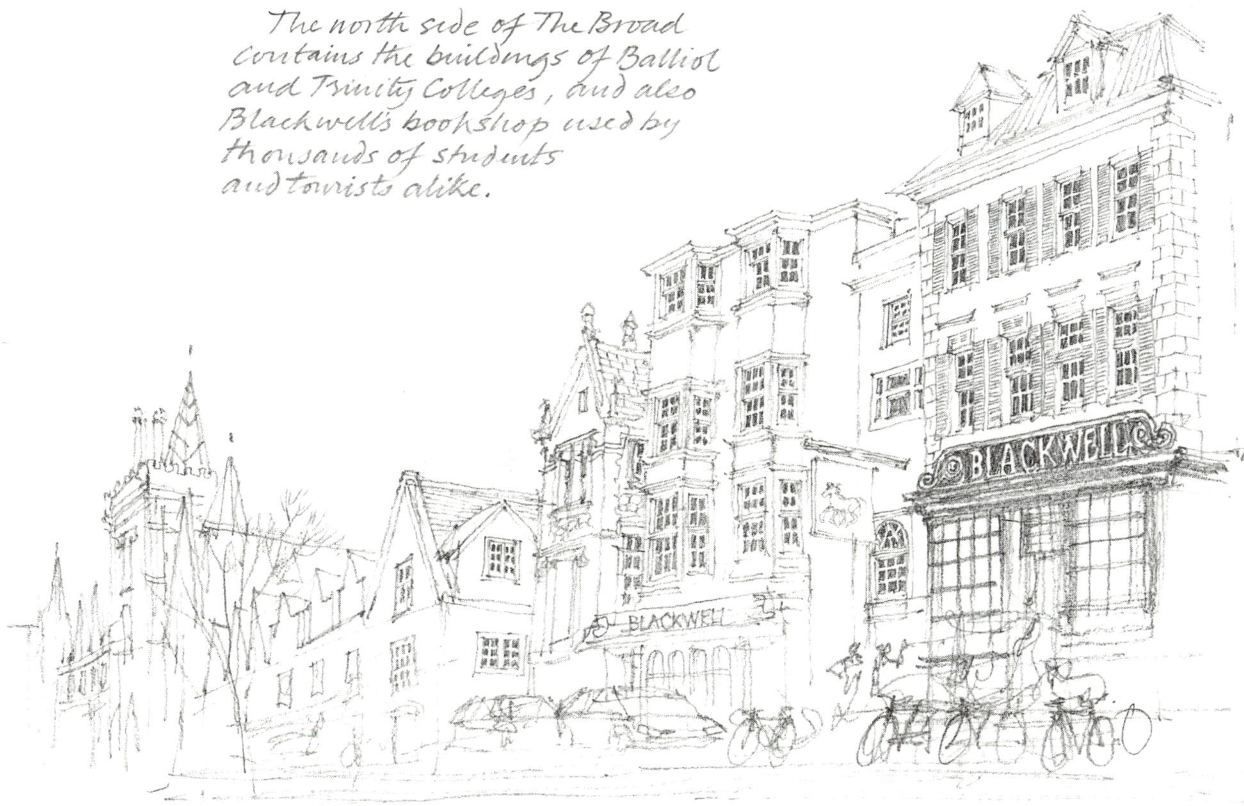

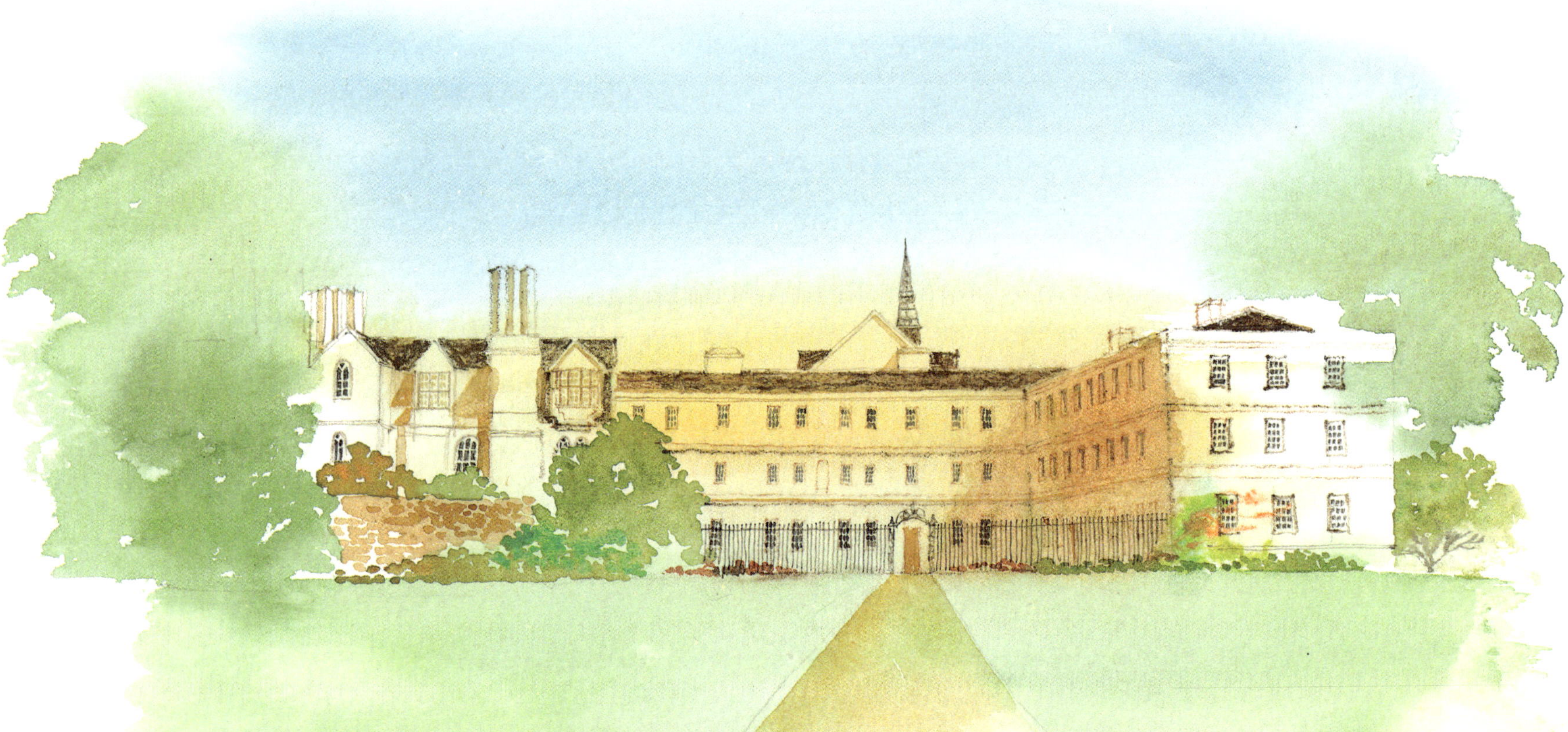

Trinity College has medieval origins, but was largely rebuilt from the late 17th century onwards. The spacious gardens can be glimpsed through the magnificent set of gates (built in 1713, below) opposite Wadham College.

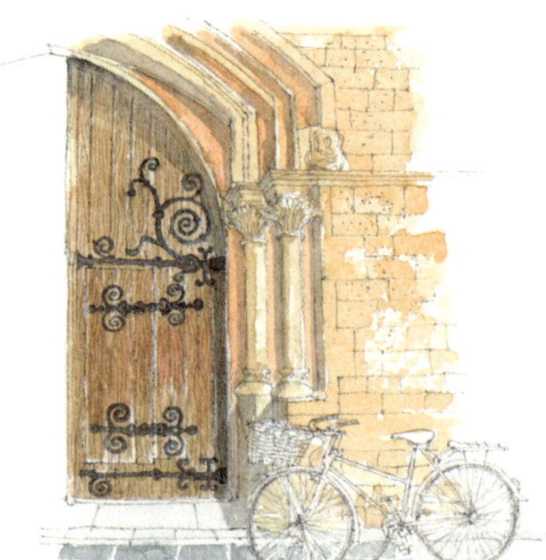

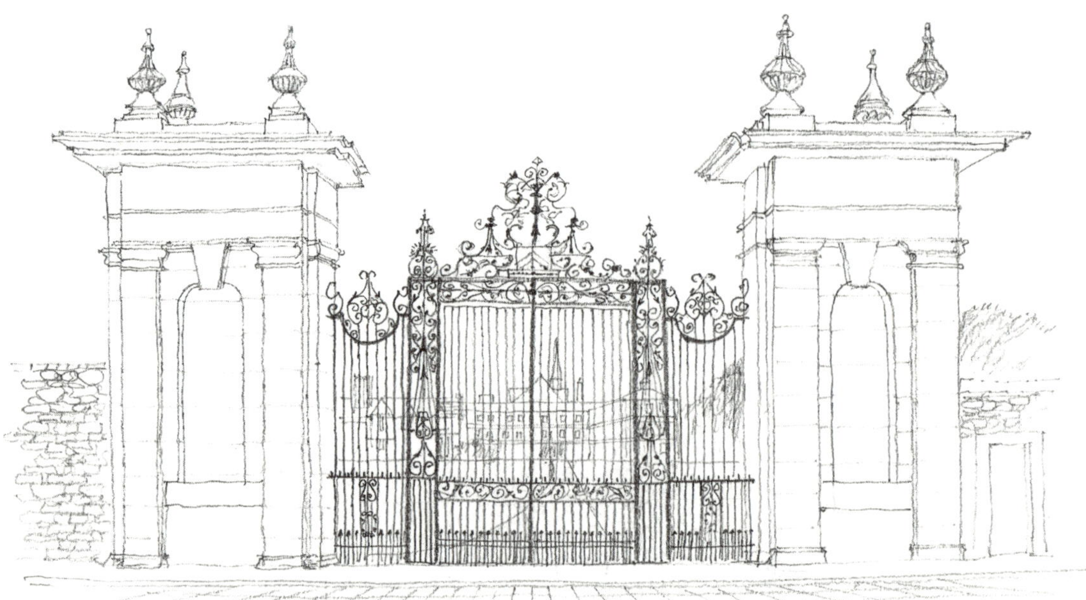

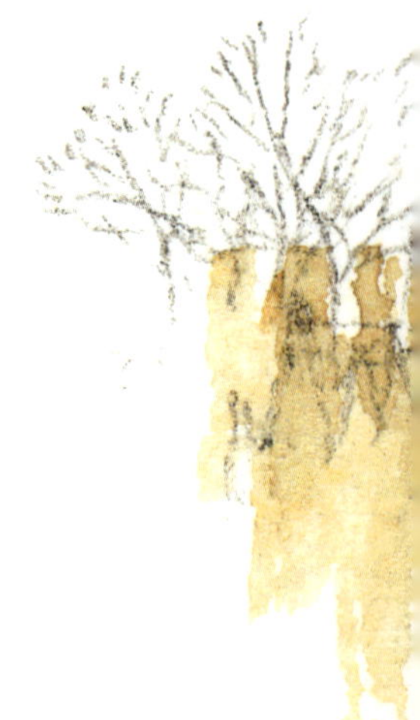

Despite its foundation in the 13th century, Balliol College is best known for its Victorian buildings with its somewhat dour frontage entered from The Broad by the doorway shown below left, usually surrounded by students' bikes. It is also known for its strong intellectual tradition and for the many leading politicians it has produced.

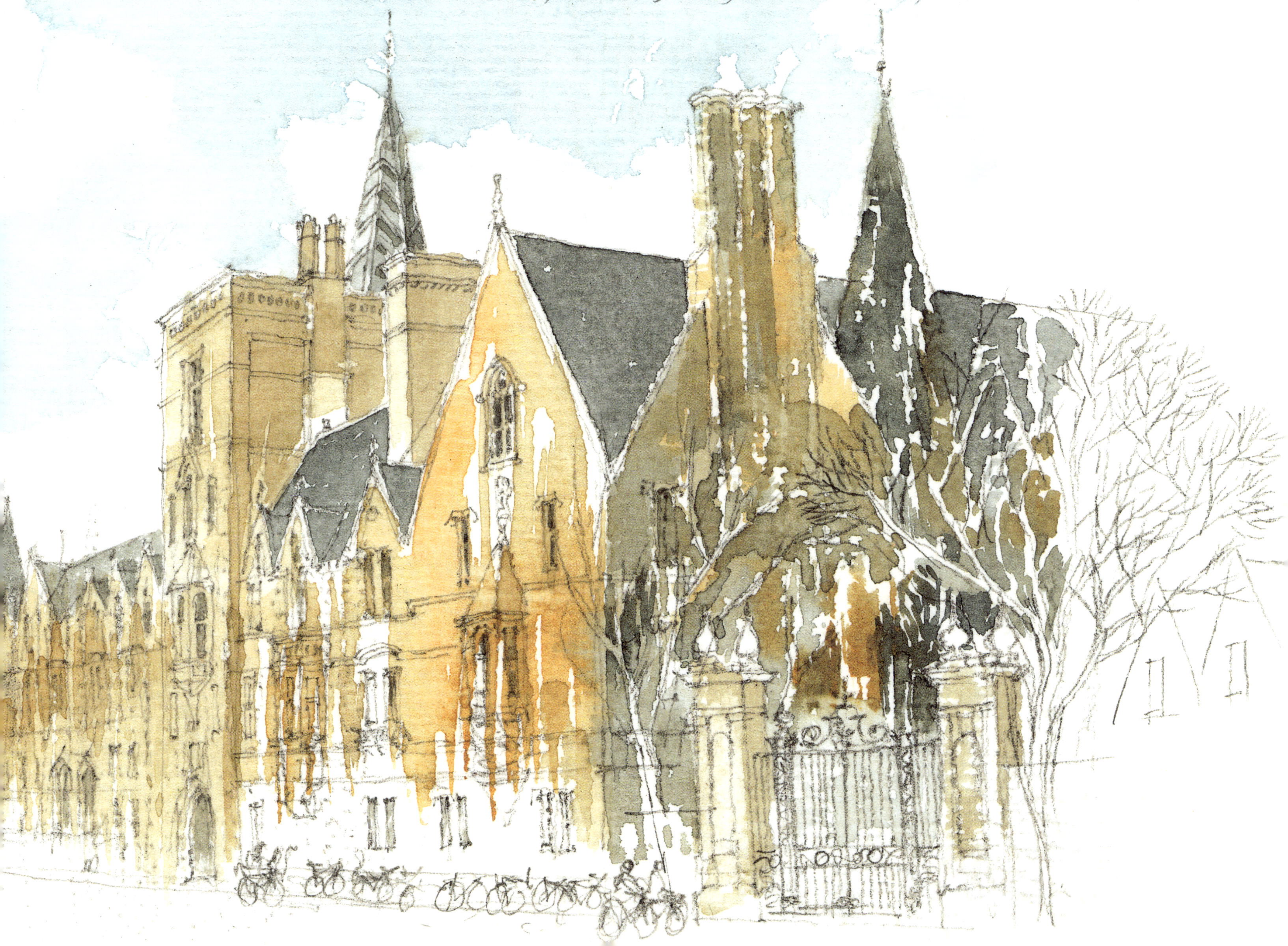

South of The High

Although it contains the sumptuous Victorian Town Hall, the area to the south of The High is given over even more completely to 'Gown' than that to the north. It is dominated by the buildings of two of the largest colleges, Christ Church (or 'The House', as it is alternatively known) and Merton. Three smaller colleges, Oriel, Corpus Christi and University, contribute strongly to its visual attractions. Thanks to Christ Church Meadow, which stretches south to the Thames (and was successfully defended by the university in the 1960s against a major road project proposed by the city council), the view of the historic centre from this direction still looks very much as it did before modern development engulfed the rest of Oxford. If the river itself (here sometimes known as the Isis) is now the preserve of college rowing teams and pleasure craft, the converted Georgian warehouse that is now the Head of the River pub offers a reminder that for most of Oxford's history the Thames was primarily a busy commercial artery. Keenly contested inter-collegiate rowing races take place here in May but punting, that other favourite summer-term leisure activity, is largely confined to the shallower River Cherwell that wraps around the eastern flank of the centre.

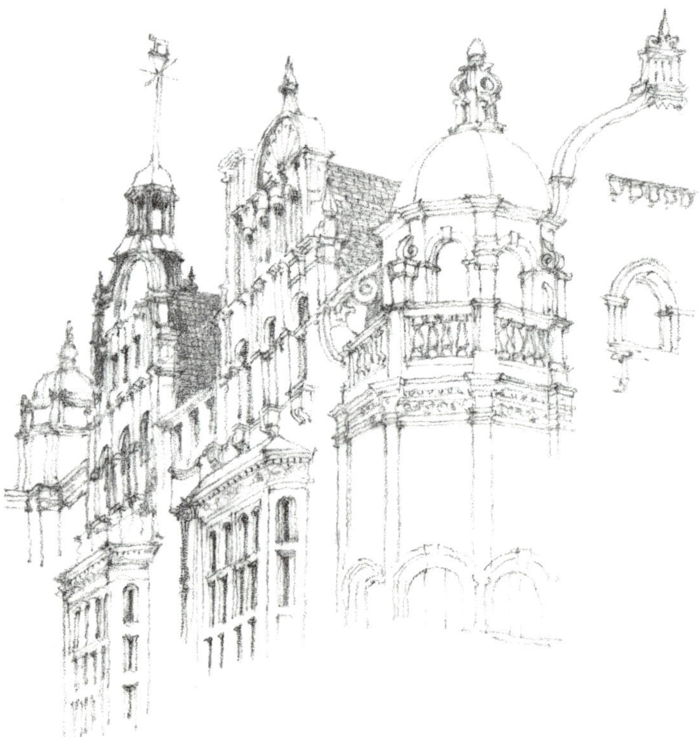

The elaborate neo-Jacobean gables of the Town Hall in St Aldate's.

Christ Church has produced many statesmen and other distinguished alumni; but it owes some of its worldwide renown to an otherwise obscure maths don, the Reverend Charles Dodgson, who spent his whole adult life in the college and produced his 'Alice' stories under the pseudonym Lewis Carroll. Alice was the daughter of the Dean, the head of the college, and the secret garden of Alice in Wonderland was the garden in which she played, tucked away within the sprawling complex of quadrangles and invisible to the outside world. In this last respect at least it could have been the garden of any one of Oxford's colleges.

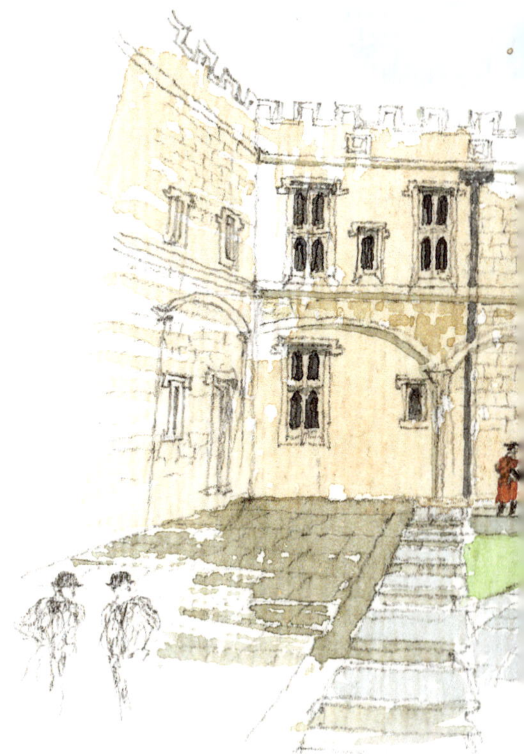

Tom Quad – the largest quadrangle in the university – and Tom Tower both take their names from Great Tom, the medieval bell moved here from Oseney Abbey at the Reformation, which still tolls a sonorous nightly curfew of 101 strokes. Cardinal Wolsey, the founder of Christ Church (or Cardinal College as it was originally known), intended the quad to be surrounded by a fan-vaulted cloister, but this was left unfinished at his fall from power in 1529.

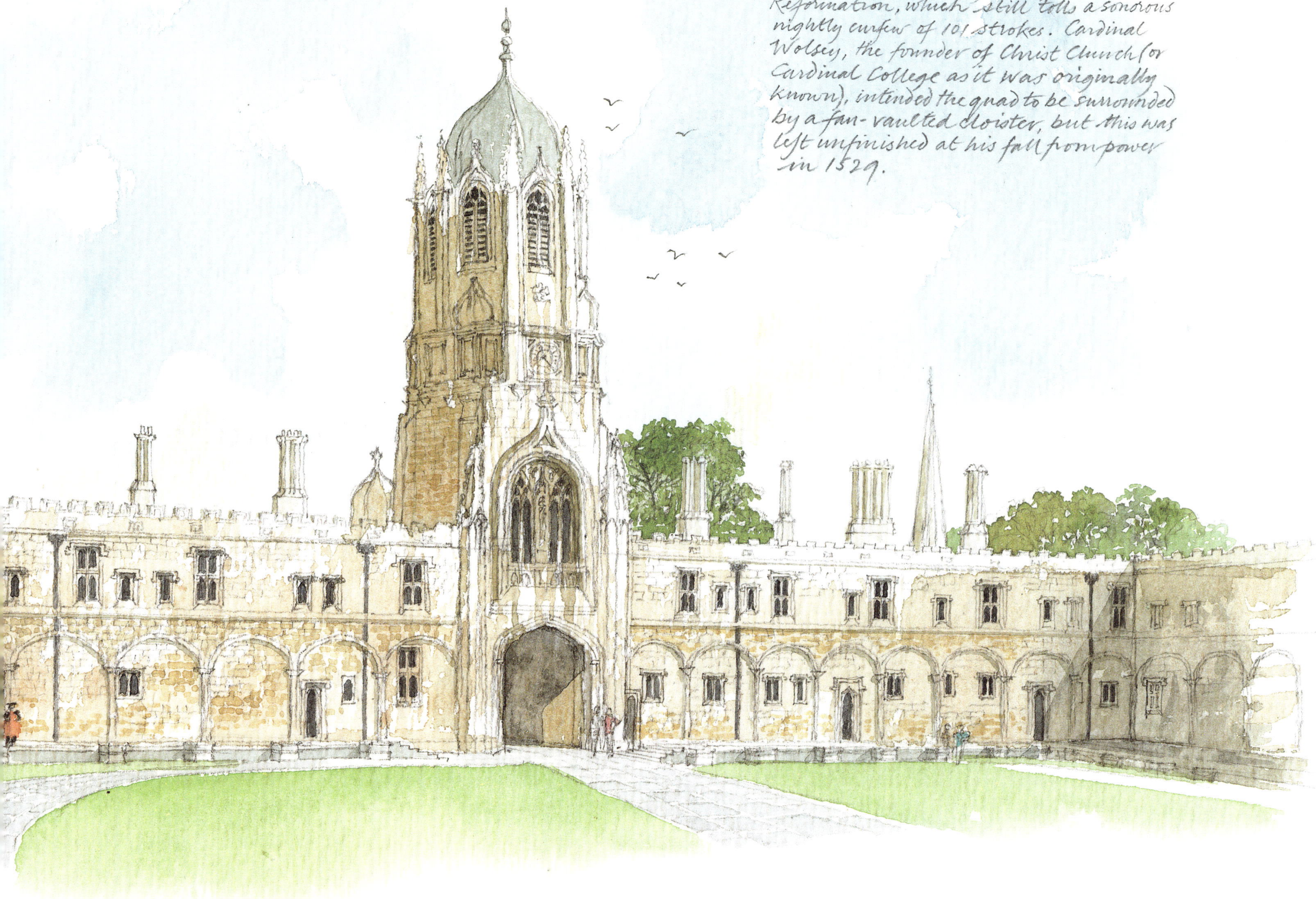

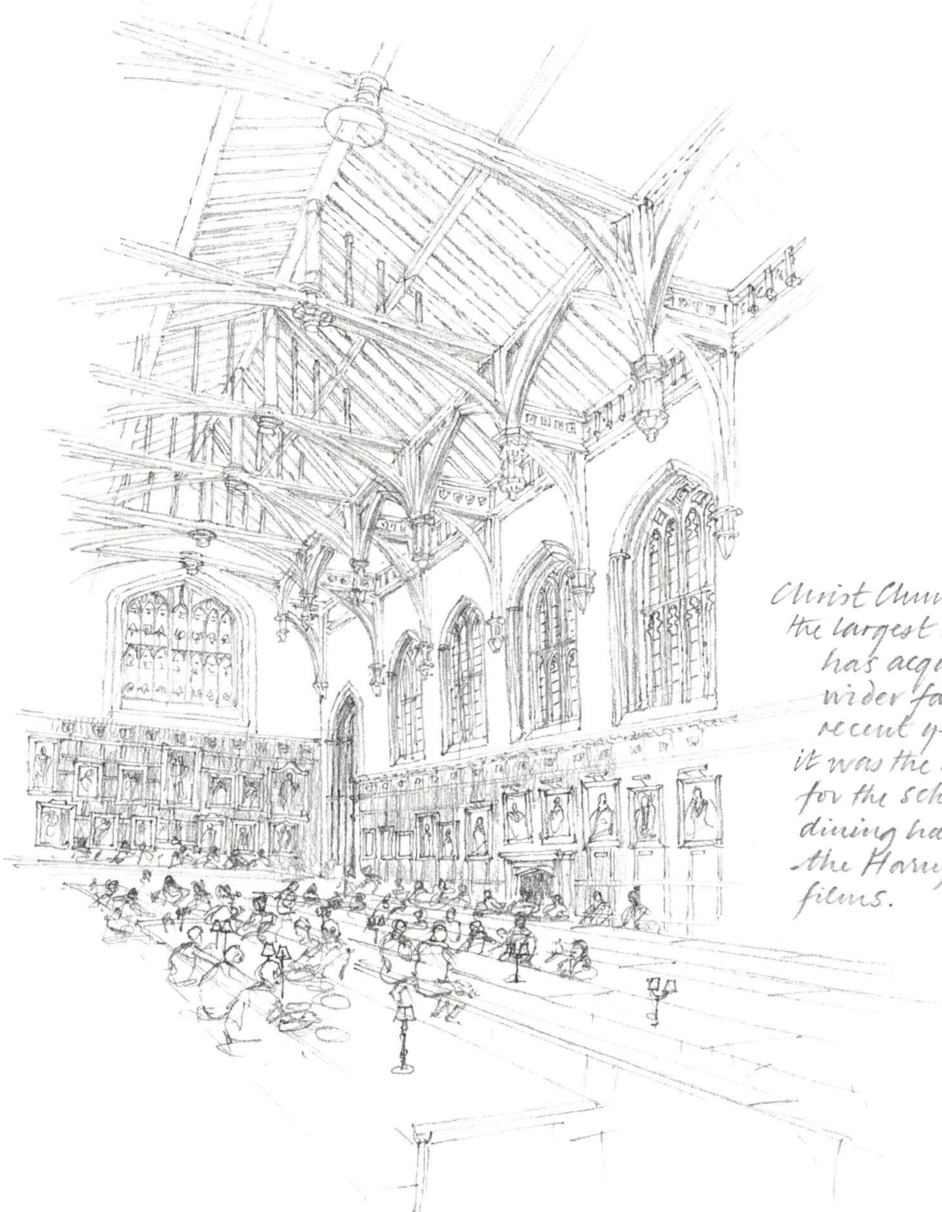

Christ Church's hall, the largest in Oxford, has acquired wider fame in recent years – it was the model for the school dining hall in the Harry Potter films.

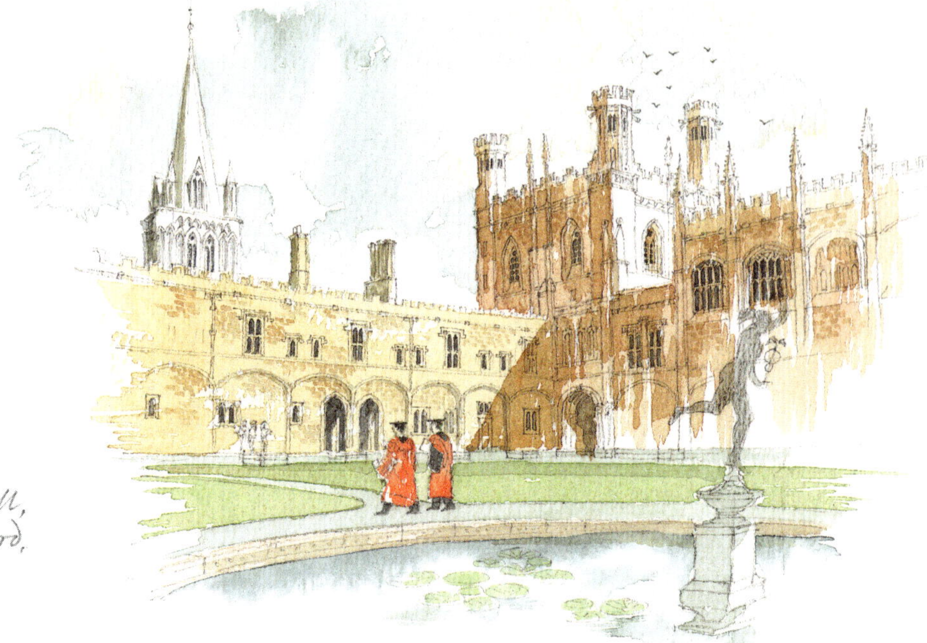

Oxford Cathedral, Christ Church's chapel is discreetly tucked behind Tom Quad.

The south flank of Christ Church seen from the entrance to the Broad Walk across Christ Church Meadow.

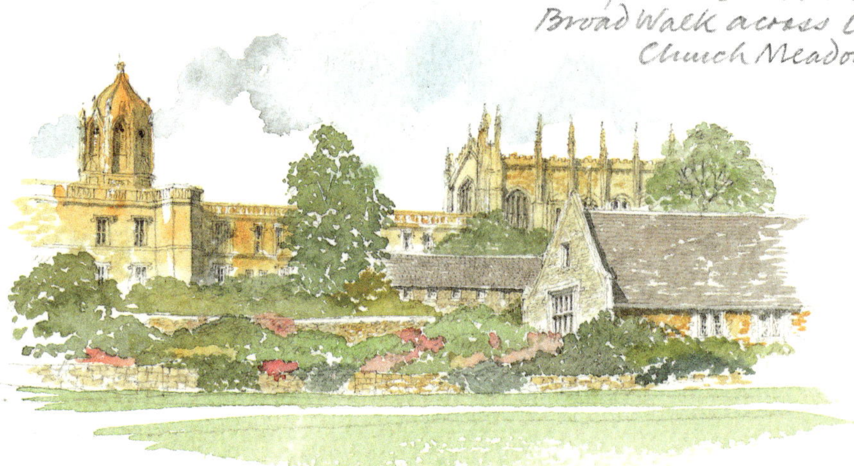

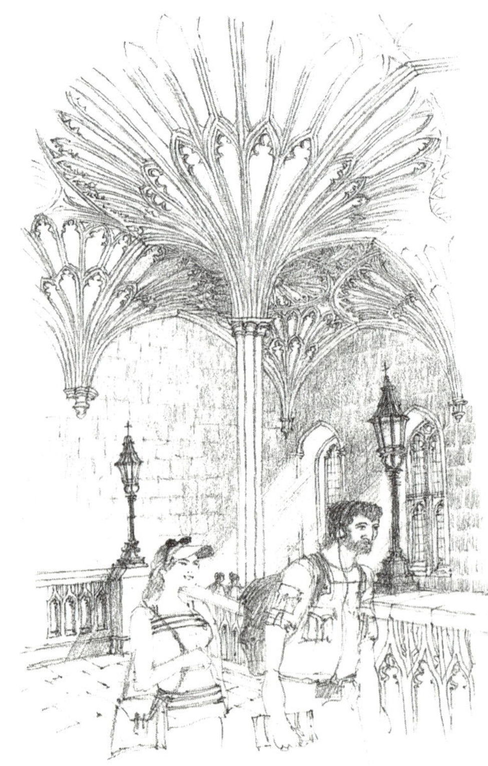

The grand staircase to the Christ Church Hall was inserted by James Wyatt in 1801, beneath a superb fan vault of 1638.

Maybe a little grim – the Meadow Building of the 1860s. In Evelyn Waugh's Brideshead Revisited, Anthony Blanche declaims T.S. Eliot from one of its balconies to suprised rowers on their way to the river.

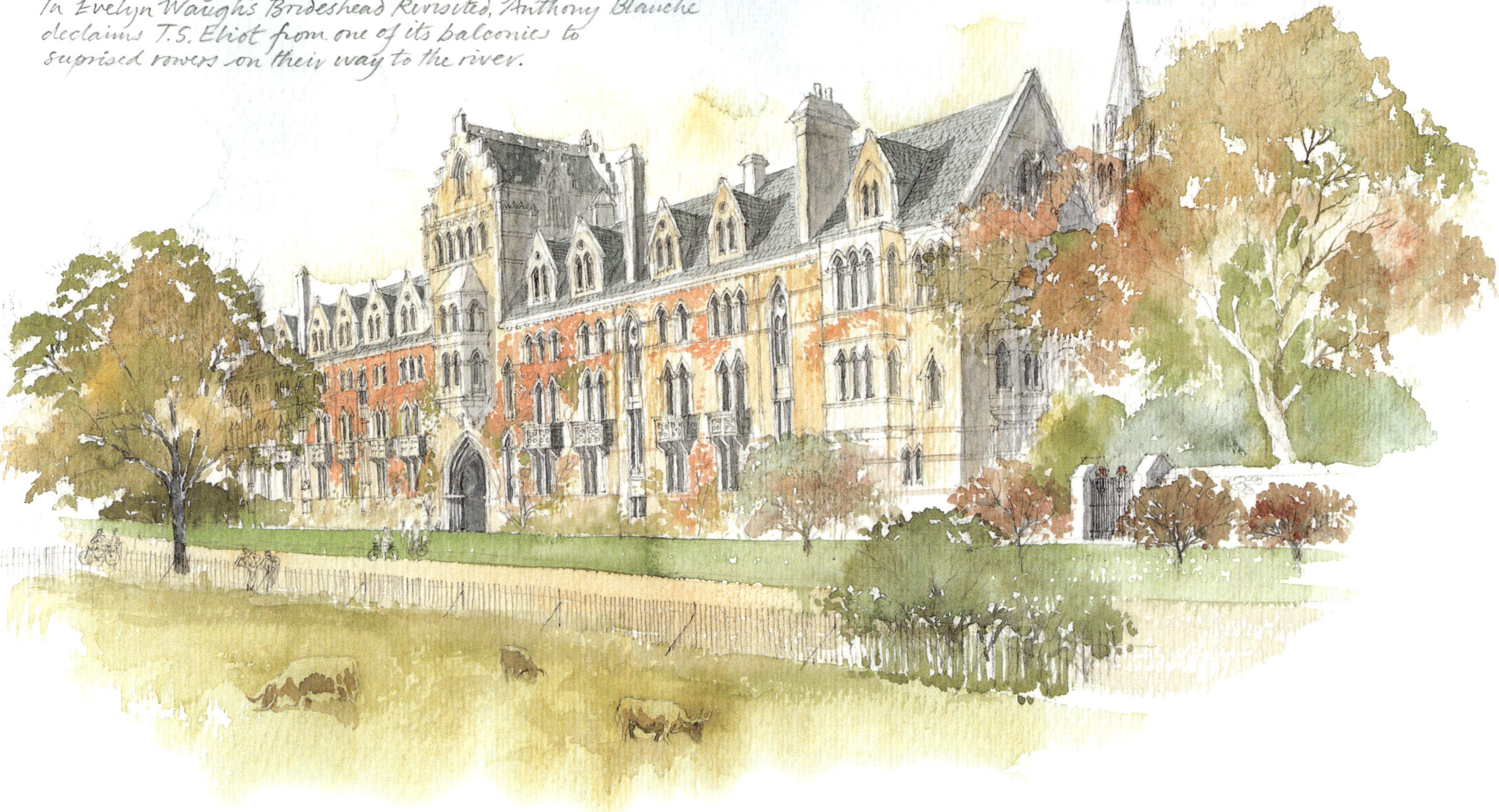

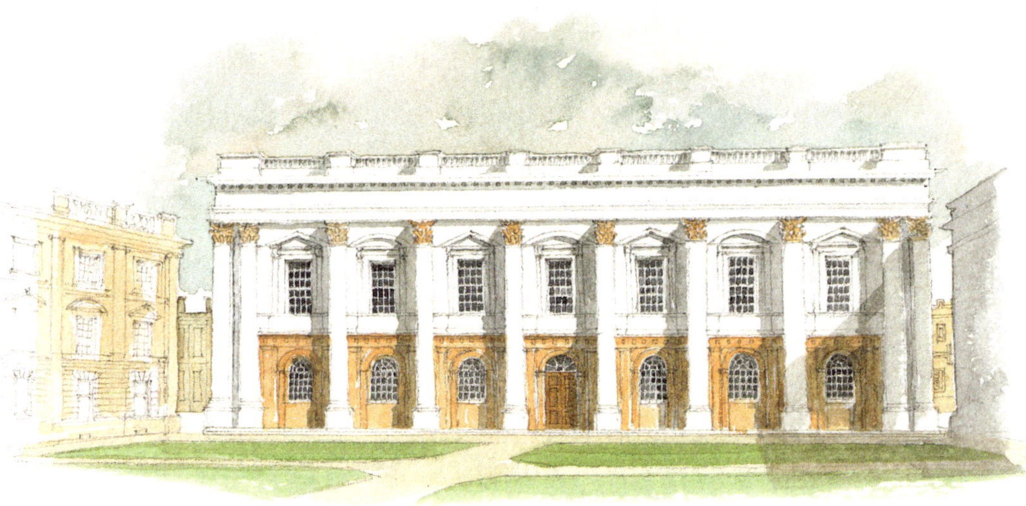

The magnificent library in Peckwater Quad contains what is said to be Cardinal Wolsey's red hat. The vast upper room is one of Oxford's finest 18th-century interiors.

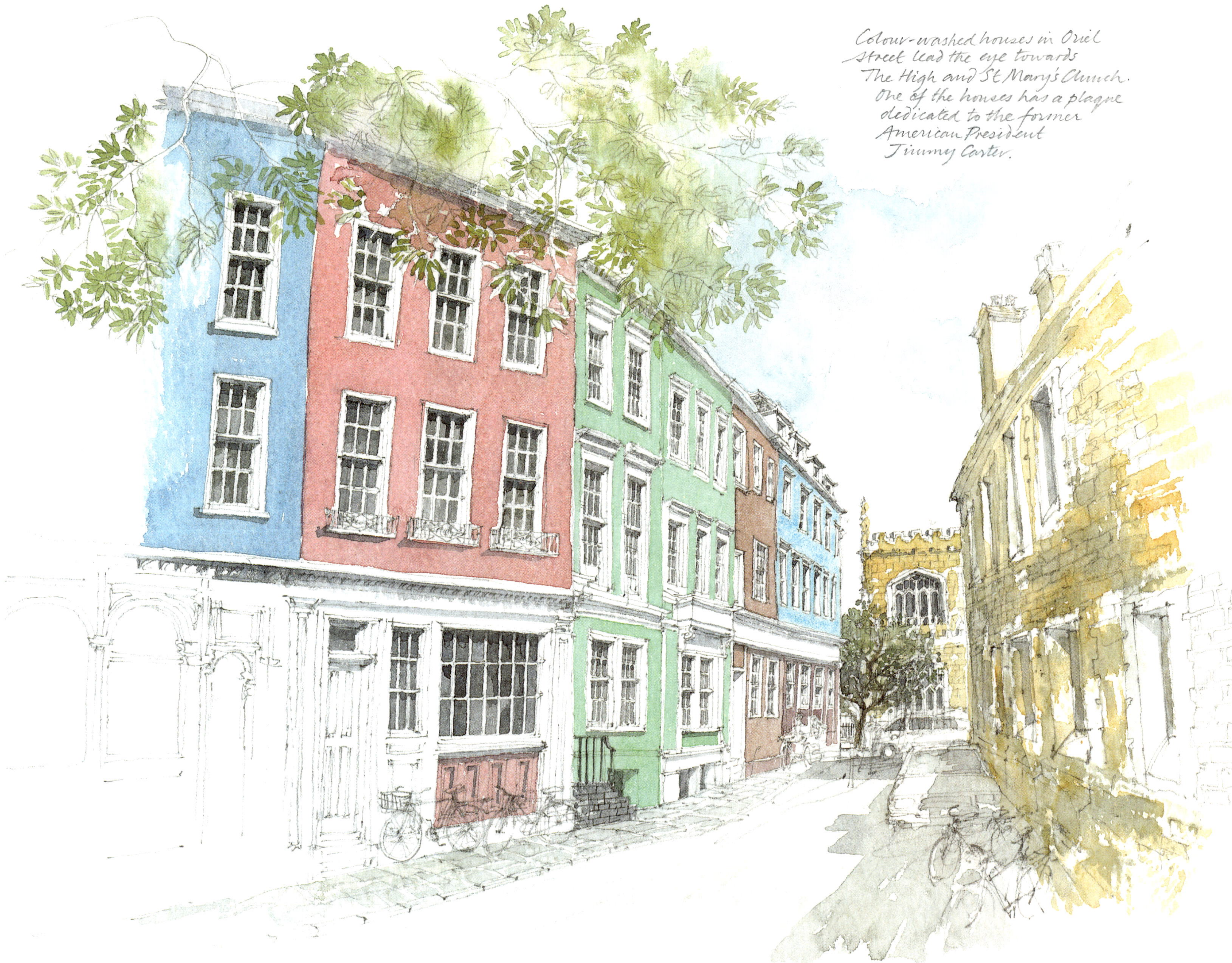

Colour-washed houses in Oriel Street lead the eye towards The High and St Mary's Church. One of the houses has a plaque dedicated to the former American President Jimmy Carter.

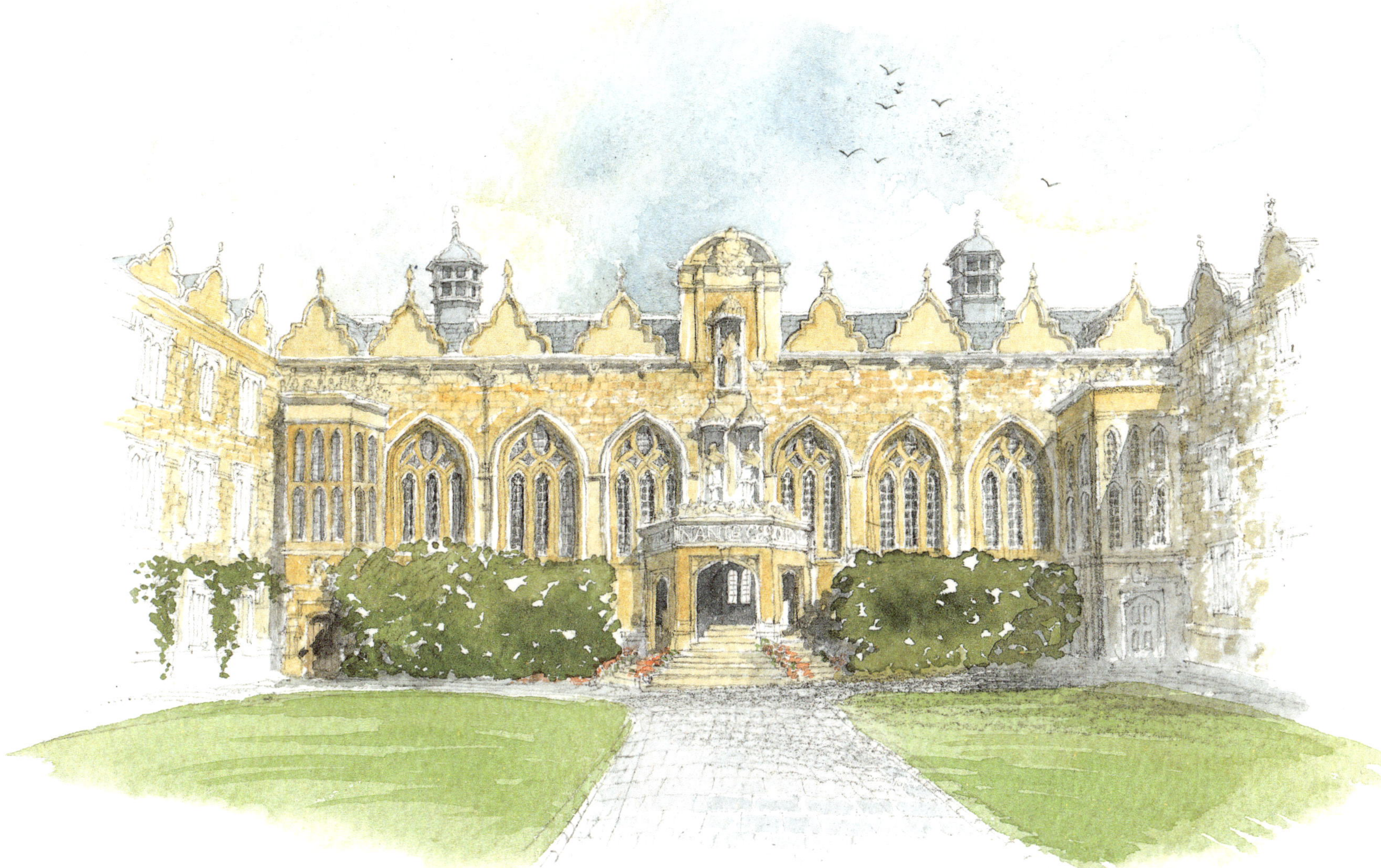

In the attractive early 17th-century Front Quad of Oriel College statues of two unidentified kings surmount the porch to the hall. A feature of the steps is the flower arrangements in the summer term.

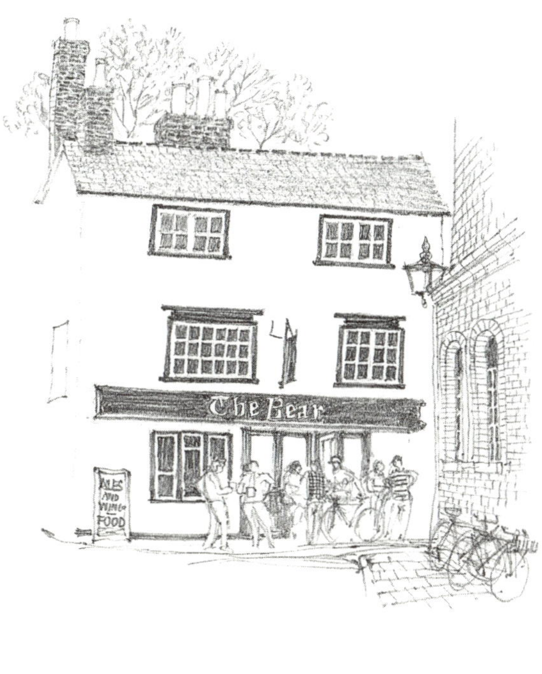

One of Oxford's oldest pubs is The Bear. Its intimate bar has thousands of ties mounted on its low ceilings. If you are having a drink do not wear an unusual tie!

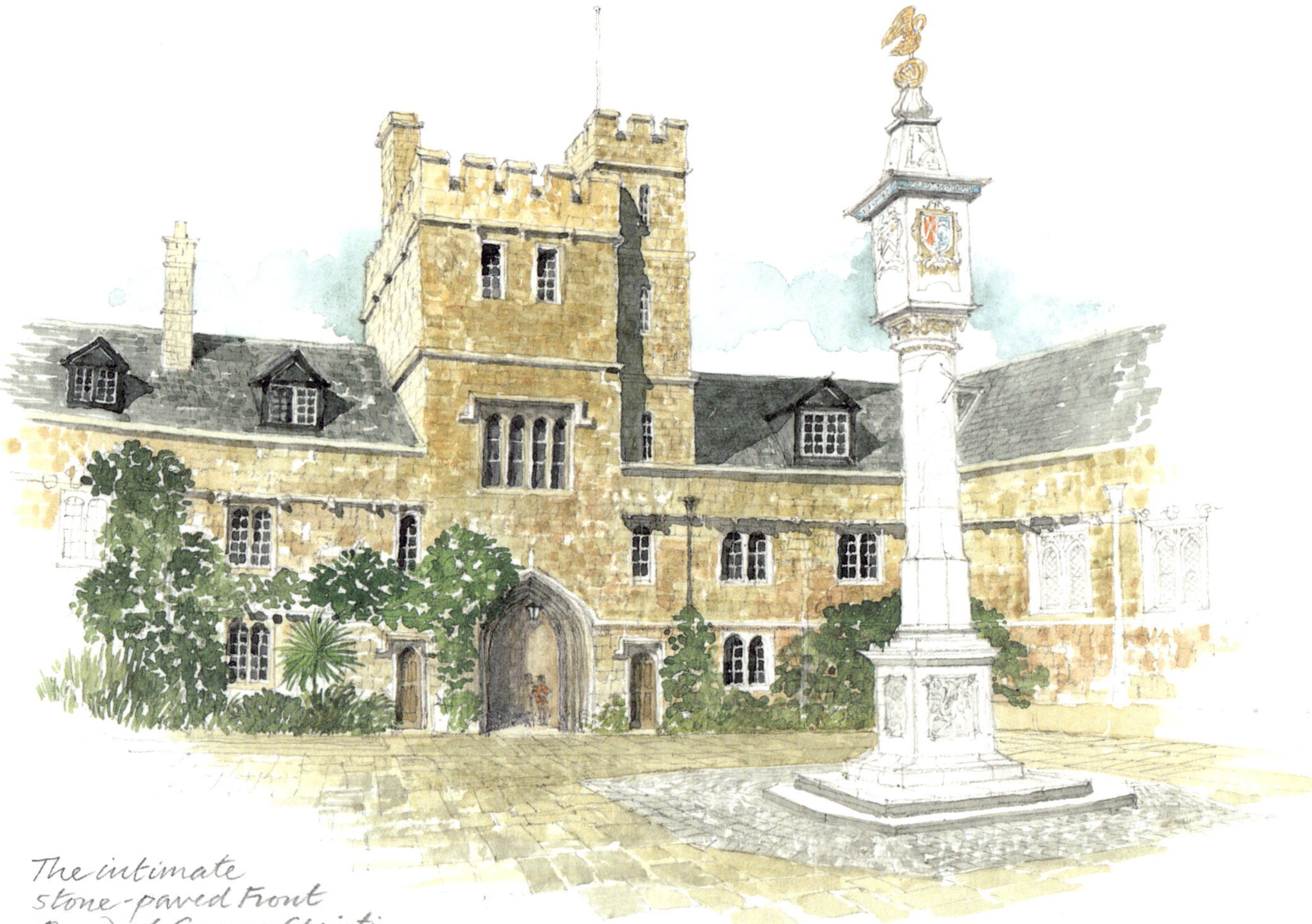

The intimate stone-paved Front Quad of Corpus Christi College, with its famous sundial topped by a pelican, contrasts with the scale of its grand neighbour Christ Church.

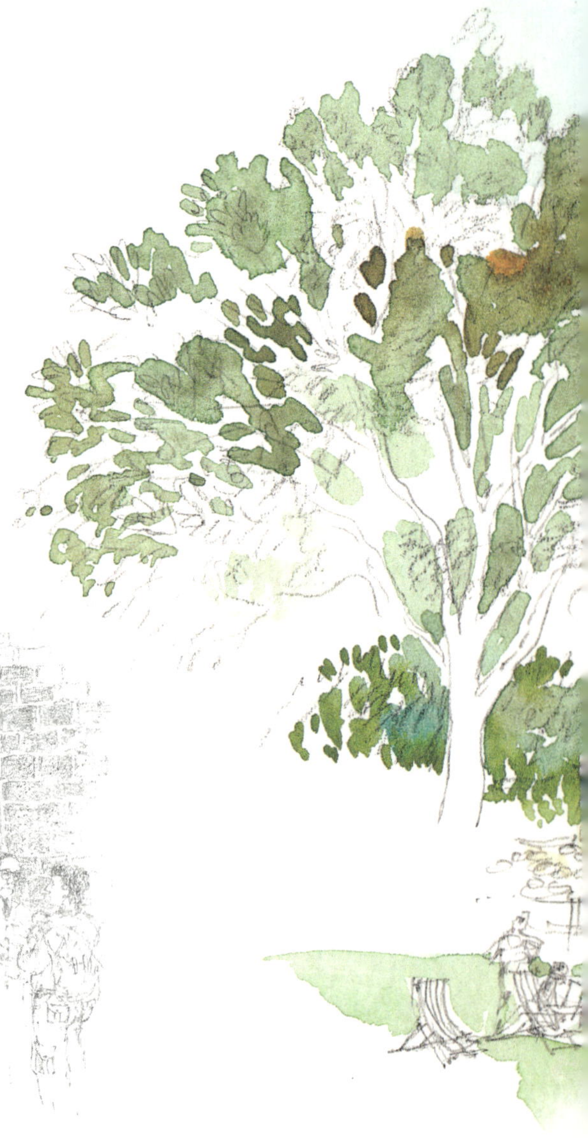

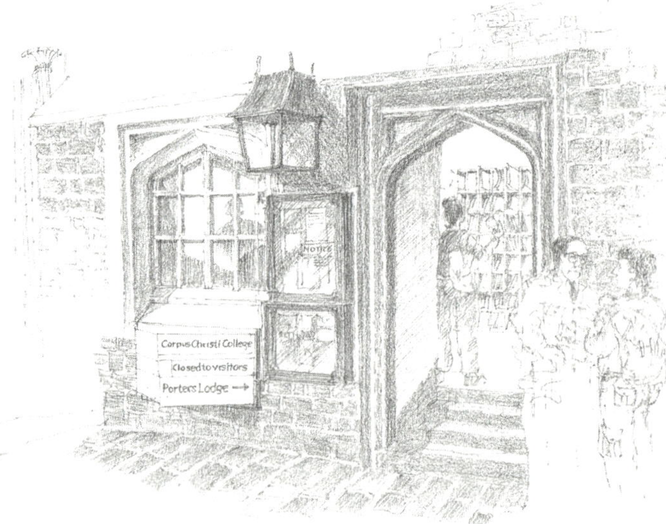

A traditional and important college figure is the porter who works in his lodge at the entrance of every college. His remit covers discipline, security, mail and reception. He commands respect from students and visitors alike.

Merton College, founded in 1264, is the oldest Oxford college. Seen from Christ Church Meadow, its buildings are dominated by the beautiful 15th-century tower of the chapel.

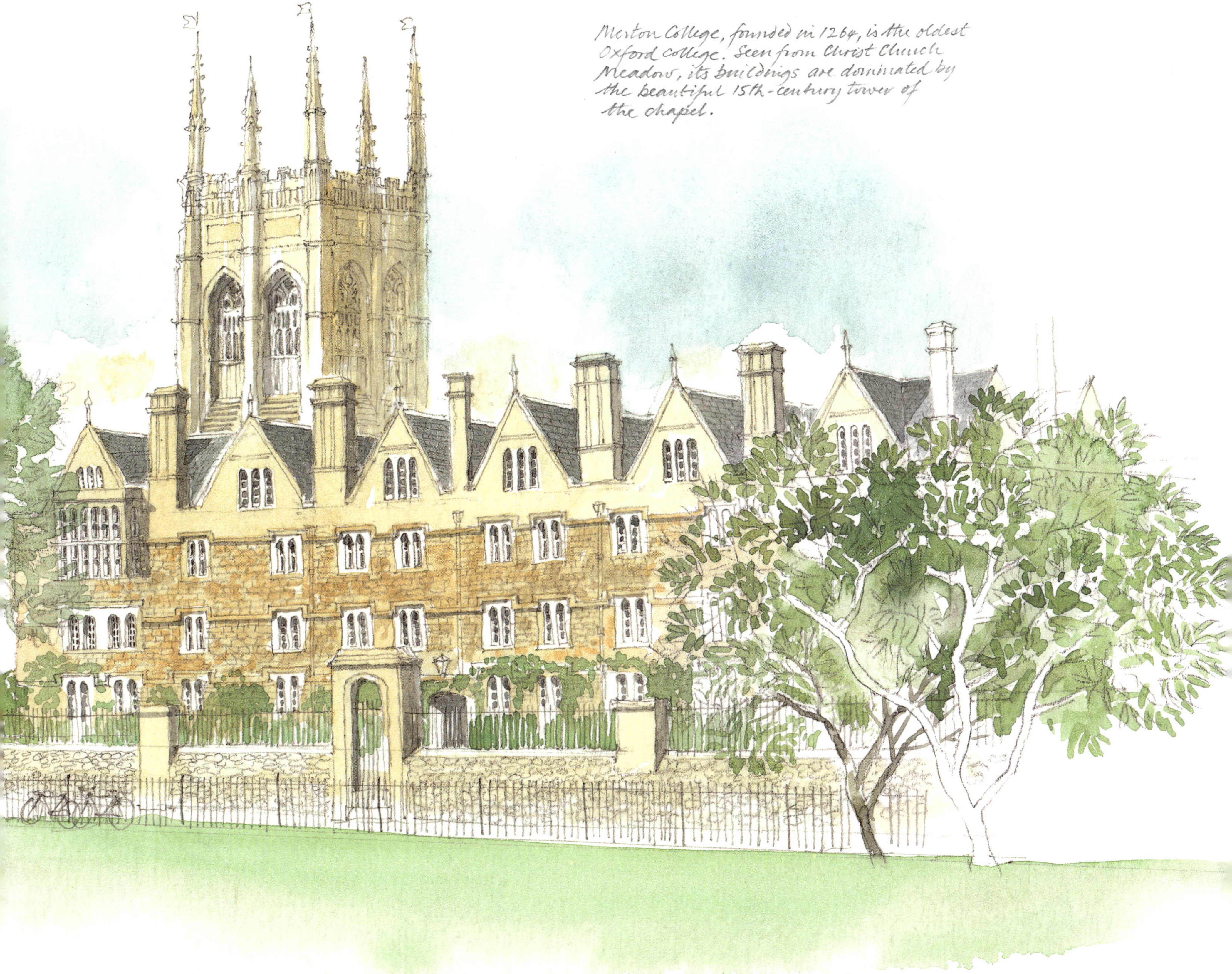

Radcliffe Quad at University College ('Univ') is entered from the High through a fan-vaulted gateway.

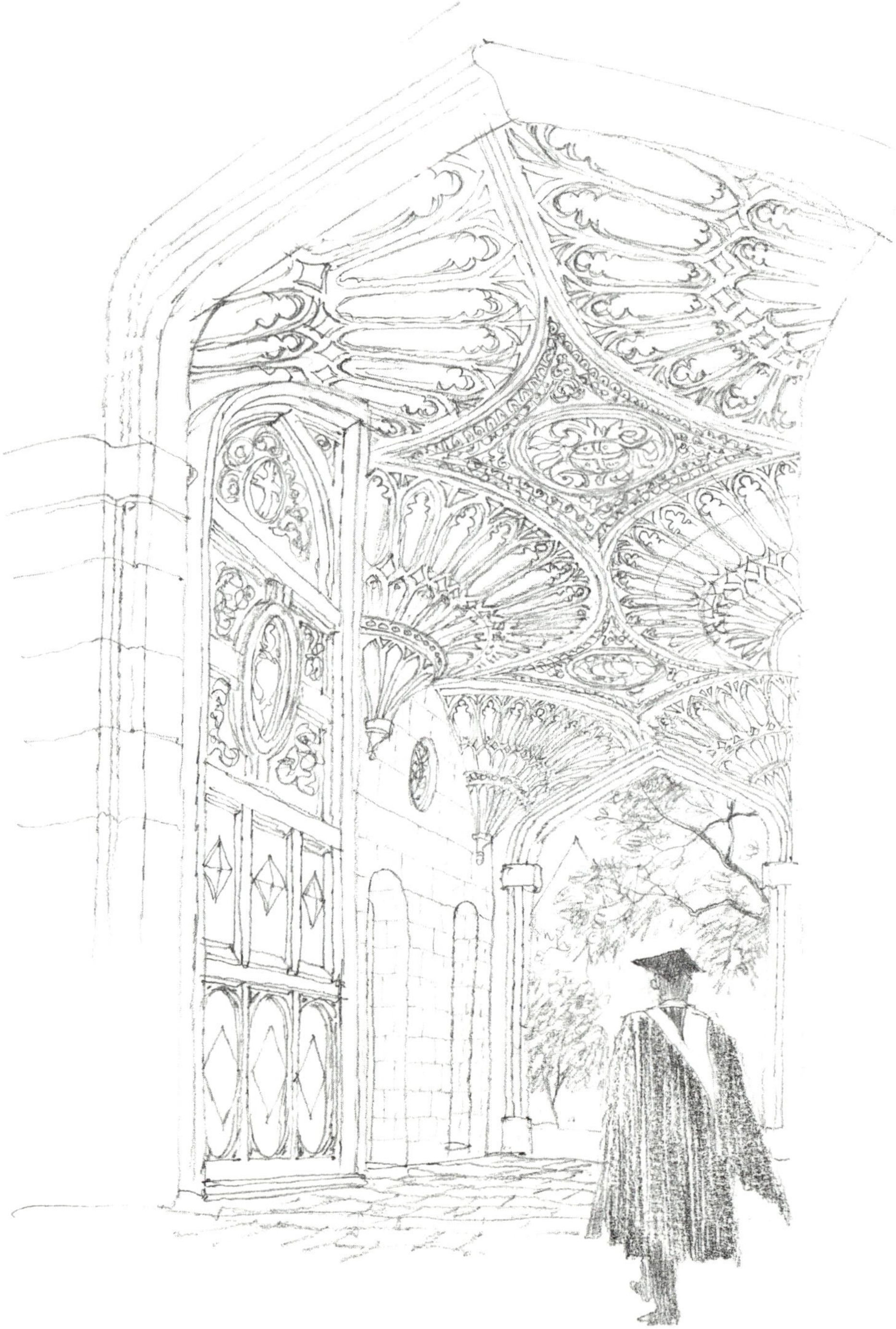

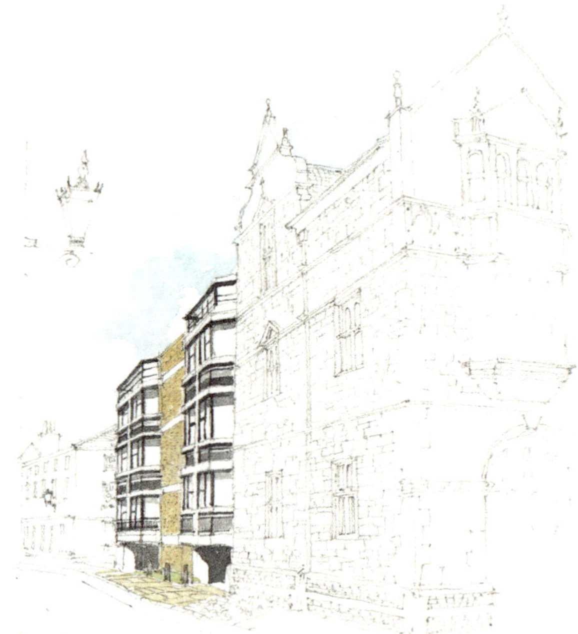

Corpus Christi College inserted a tactful new building into Magpie Lane in 1969.

Picturesque houses belonging to Corpus Christi on Merton Street.

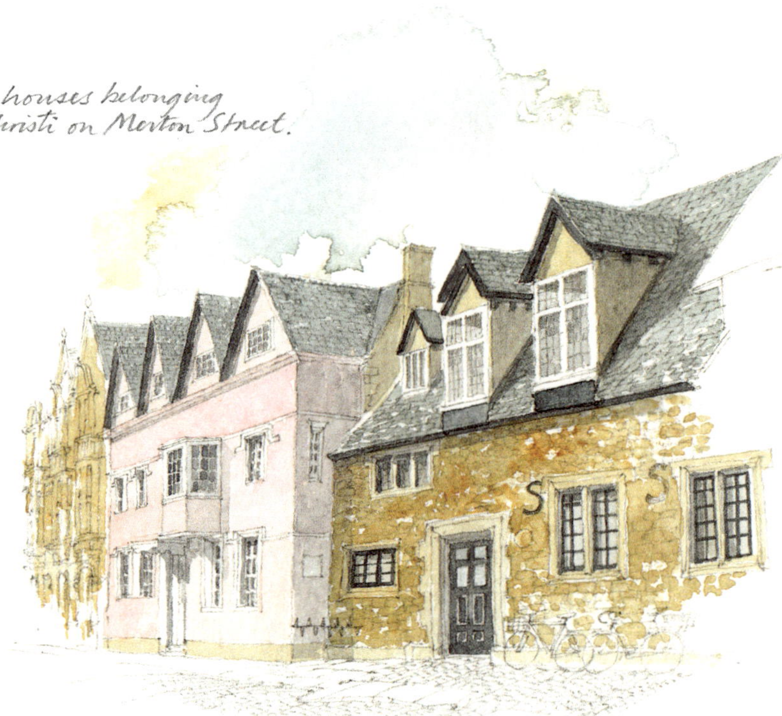

The Examination Schools, completed to Sir Thomas Jackson's designs in 1882, resemble a large Elizabethan country house. In May and June undergraduates can be observed sitting their exams here in the university dress code known as 'sub-fusc.'

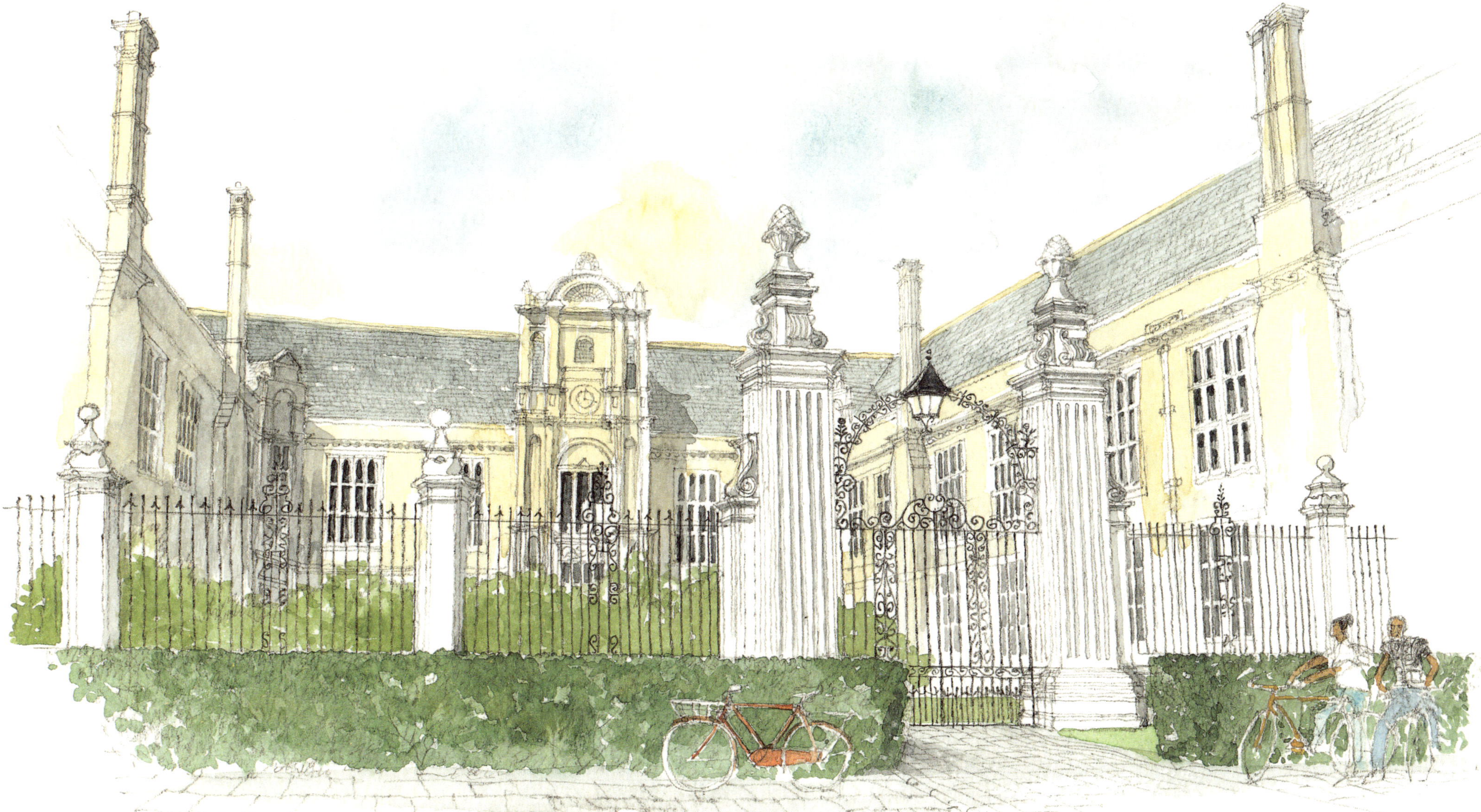

The Botanic Garden, founded in 1621 on the land that was formerly the medieval Jewish cemetery, was intended as a tool for scientific research rather than as a pleasure garden. Behind the gateway designed by Nicolas Stone rises the Magdalen bell tower.

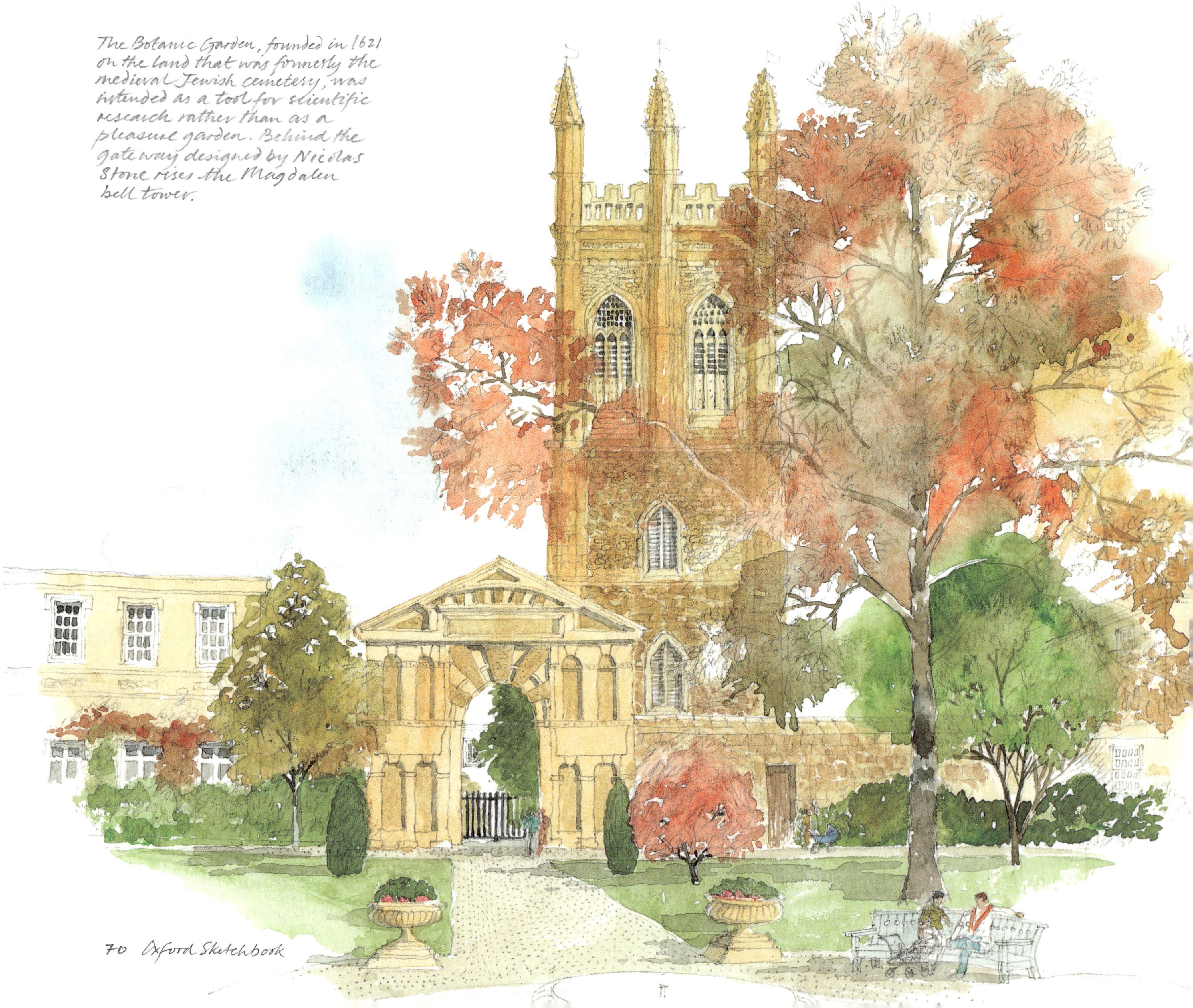

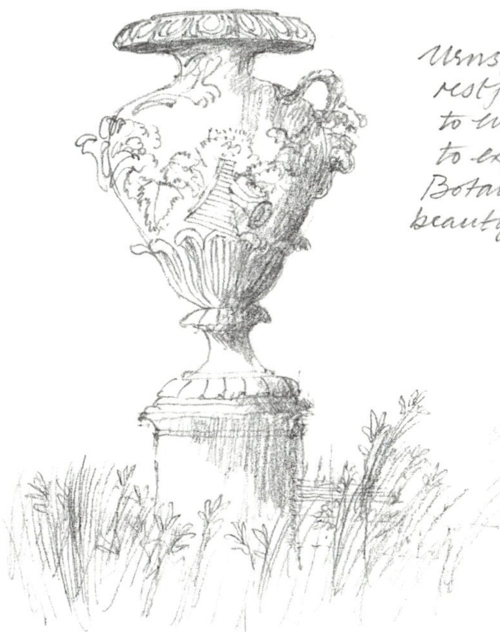

Urns, pots and restful benches serve to entice the visitor to explore the Botanic Garden's beautiful grounds.

On the grounds of Magdalen College School, the River Cherwell is spanned by this attractive bridge.

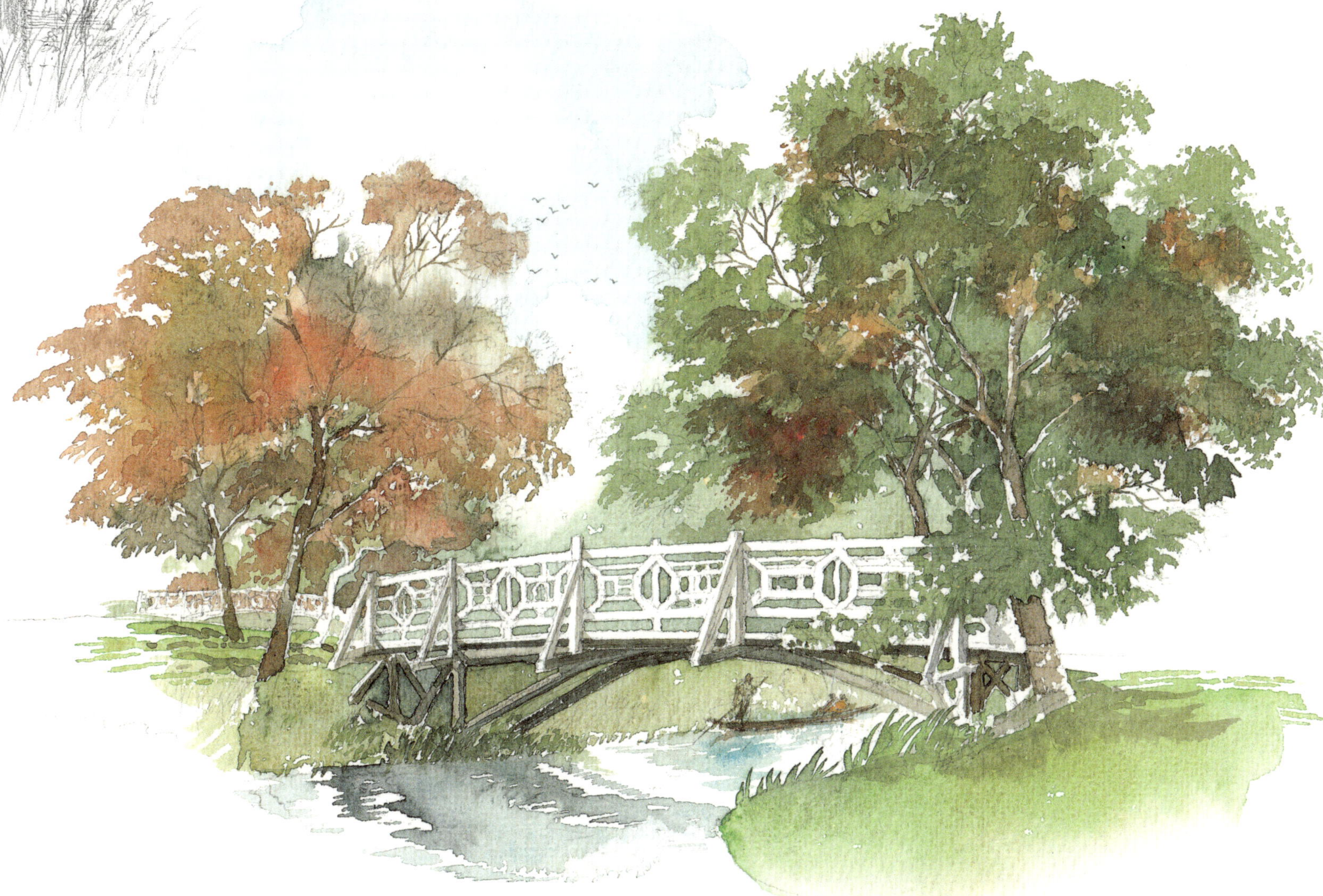

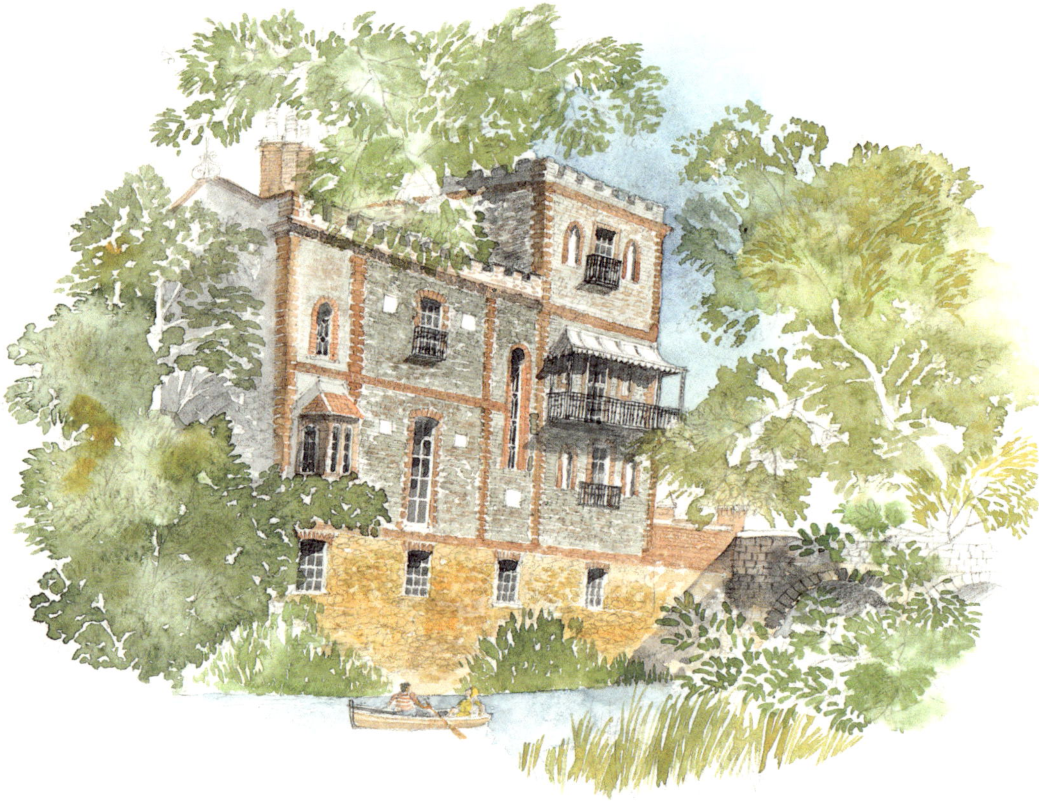

Isis House, adjoining Folly Bridge, was originally called Caudwell's Castle after the eccentric Joseph Caudwell, who built it in 1849.

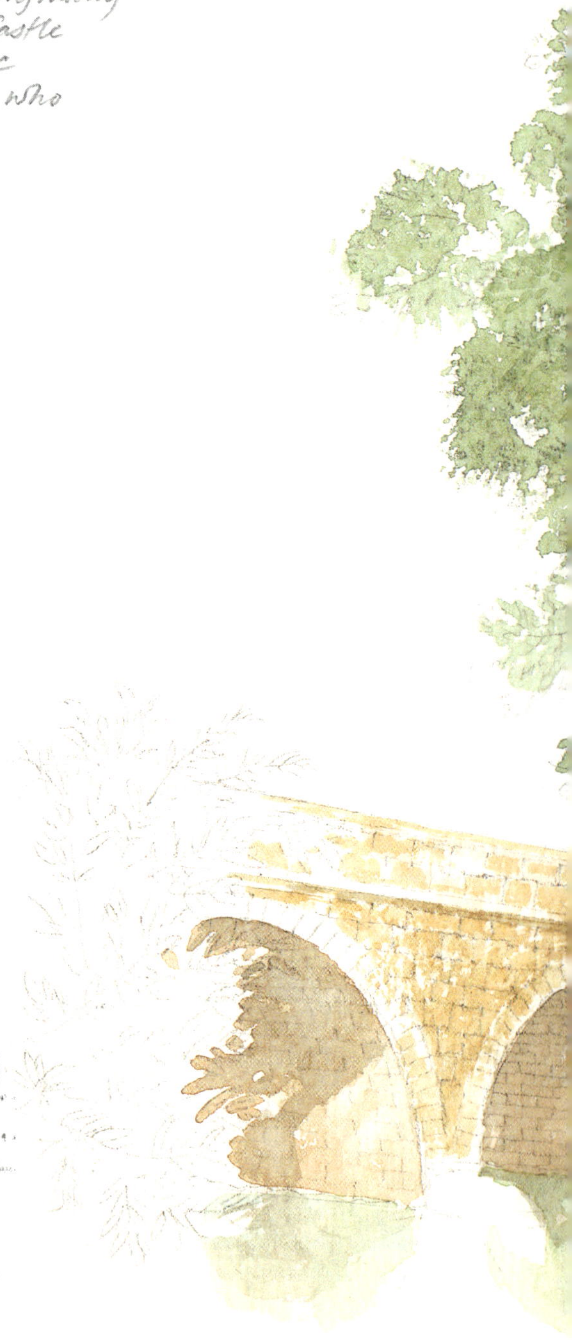

The College Boat Houses on the Thames is where The Eights Week races are held, when college 'eights' compete for the title of 'Head of the River'.

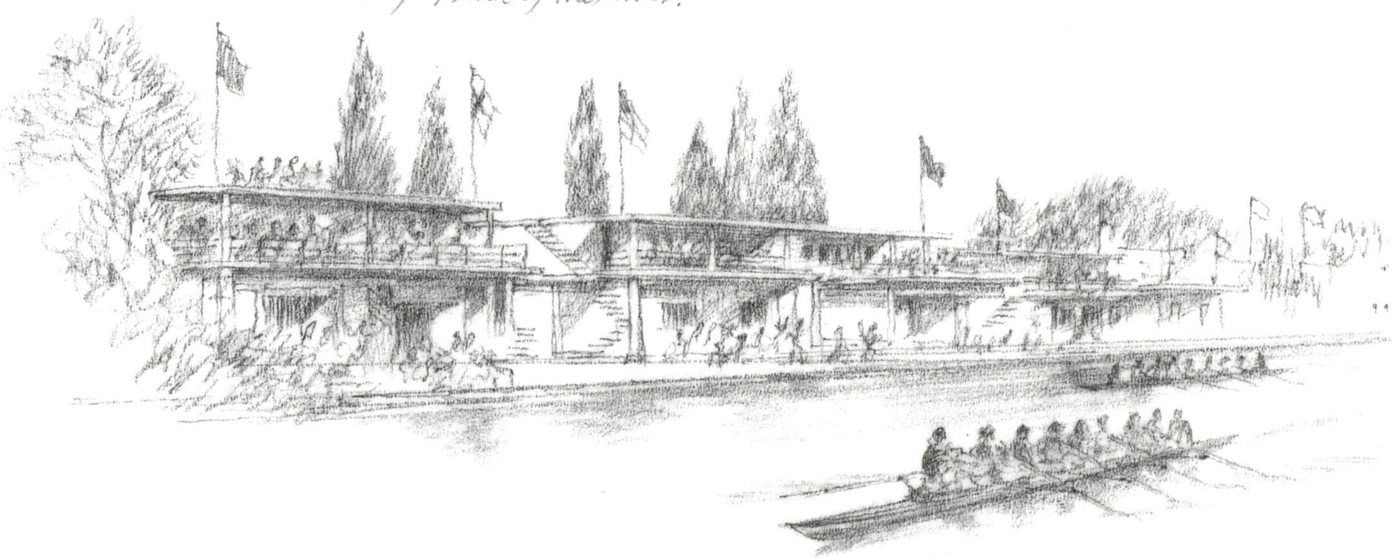

Folly Bridge replaced a picturesque medieval bridge in 1825-27. The adjoining warehouse, now Head of the River pub, was built shortly afterwards. For hundreds of years the Thames was a focus of commercial activity, but is now used almost exclusively by pleasure craft and rowing boats. It is said that the site of the original Folly Bridge was once the crossing for oxen, namely 'oxen-ford'.

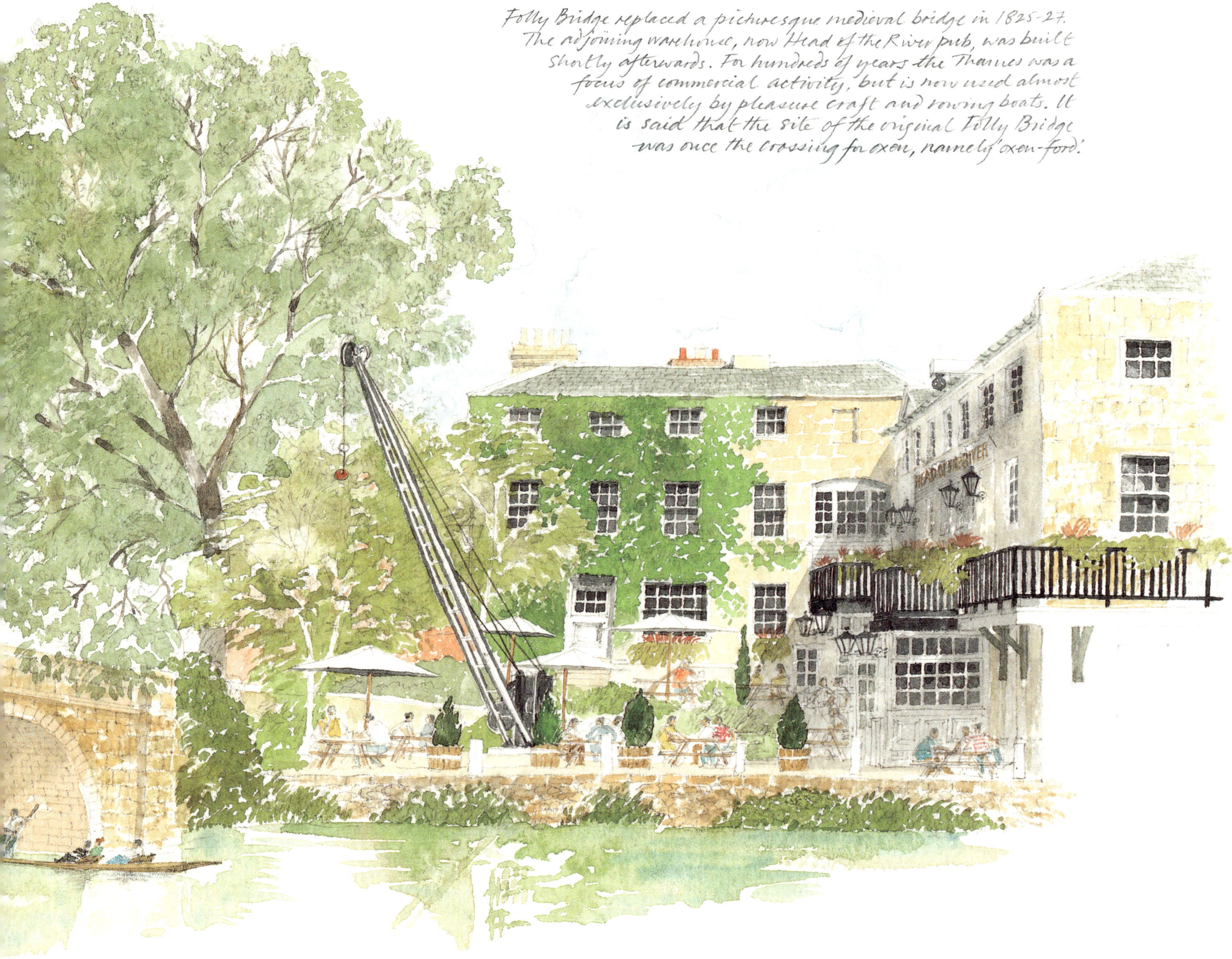

Looking West

An axis formed by Cornmarket and St Aldate's runs north-south through the centre of Oxford. The university and college buildings which dominate the area to the east are very much less in evidence to the west, which is emphatically 'Town'. Though at least as historic, containing as it does the sites of the Norman castle and the vanished royal palace of Beaumont, and those of several medieval monasteries, time and the tide of development have treated it far less gently. The western fringe suffered from the early industrialisation that attended the arrival of first the Oxford and Coventry Canal and then the railway. With Victorian commercial redevelopment the city's main shopping streets ceased to be charming, and they have since succumbed to the relentless advance of the standard multiples with their brash fascias. In the 1960s much of the picturesquely decayed south-west quarter known as St Ebbe's was cleared away by the council to make way for a ring road, multi-storey car parks and the dreadful Westgate shopping centre.

The approach to the centre from the railway station is correspondingly uninspiring, although the new Said Business School and the cupola'd Gloucester Green development have recently injected a welcome note of architectural consequence. Not surprisingly the relatively few college buildings have a rather beleaguered air - charming but cash-strapped Pembroke, and stripped-Cotswold-Gothic Nuffield. The exception is Worcester, whose handsome Georgian ranges and unexpectedly spacious grounds provide a wonderful oasis amid the dross. What really raises the tone, however, is the university's Ashmolean Museum, housed in a nobly Grecian building of the 1840s by C.R. Cockerell - one of the finest public buildings of its age - and containing a cornucopia of the fine arts.

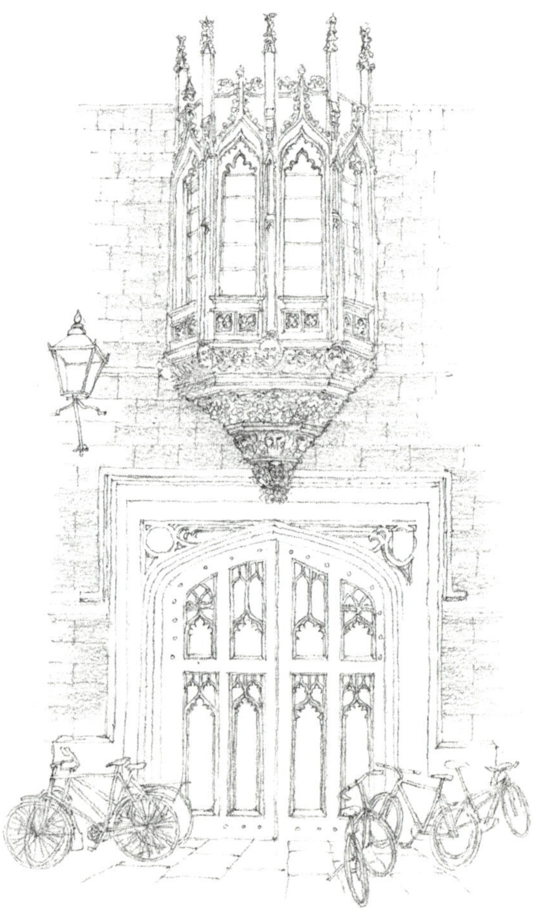

The entrance to Pembroke College is tucked inconspicuously into a corner behind St Aldate's church.

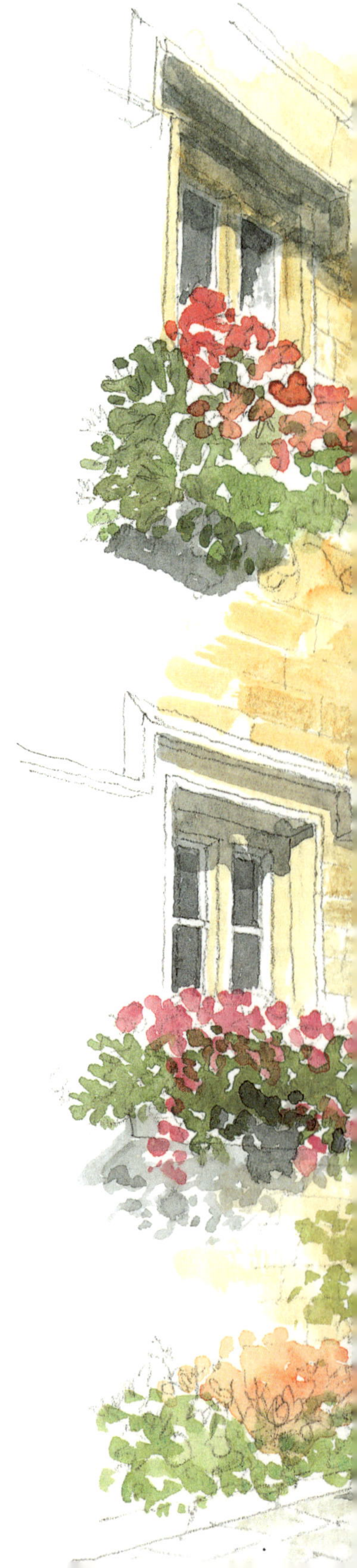

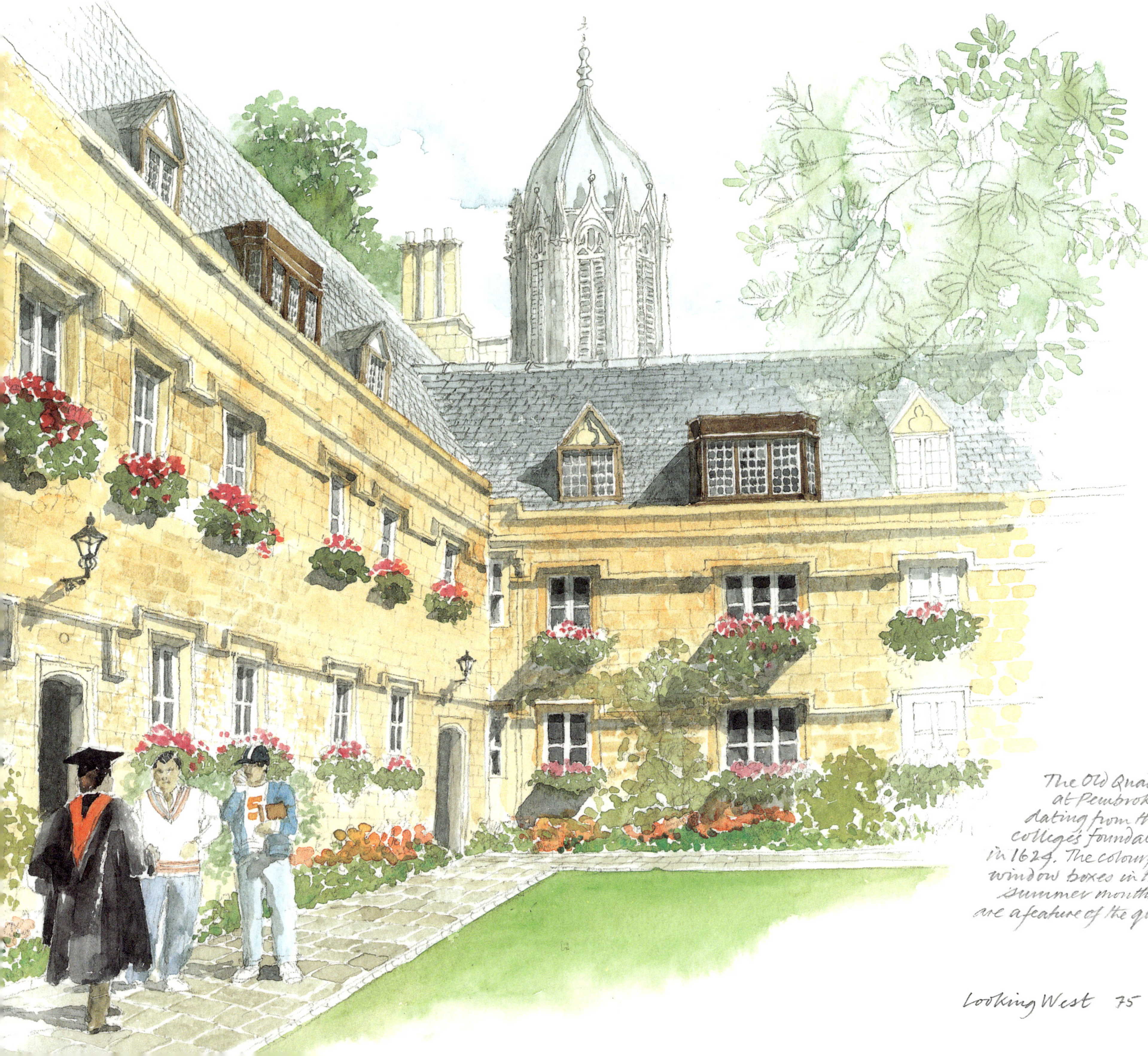

The Old Quad at Pembroke, dating from the college's foundation in 1624. The colourful window boxes in the summer months are a feature of the quad.

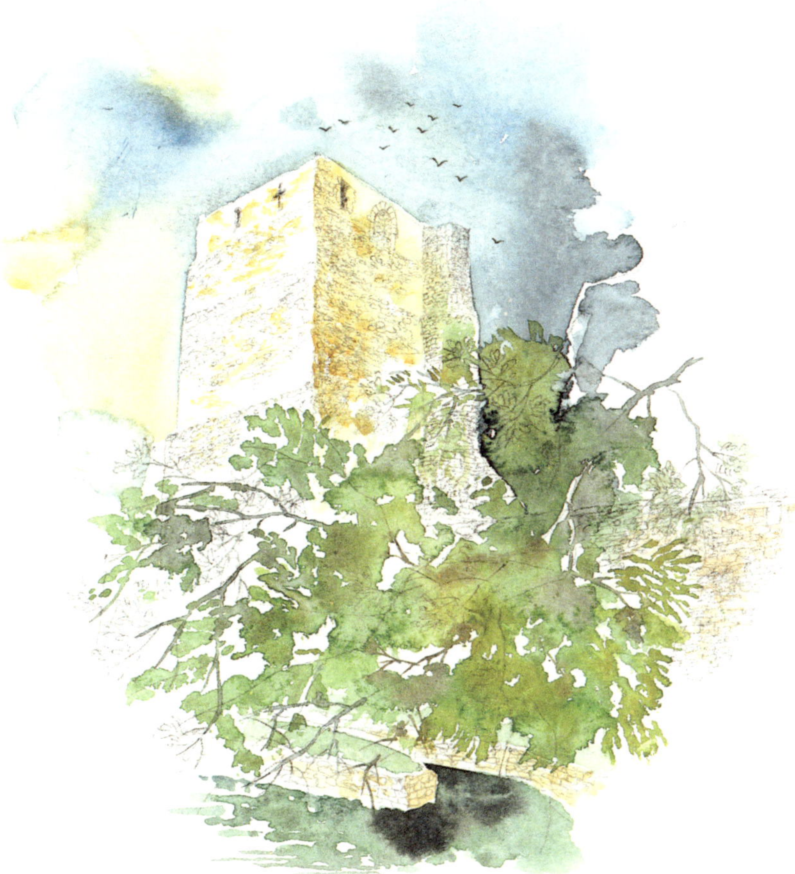

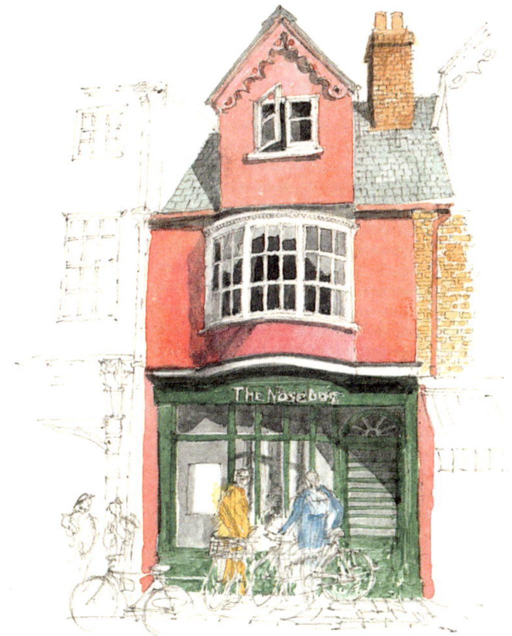

The Nosebag is an inexpensive and well frequented restaurant near the Oxford Union on St Michael's St.

St George's Tower is all that remains of the Norman castle begun in 1071.

Nuffield College was built between 1949 and 1960 at the expense of the car manufacturer Lord Nuffield. The tower functions as a library bookstack.

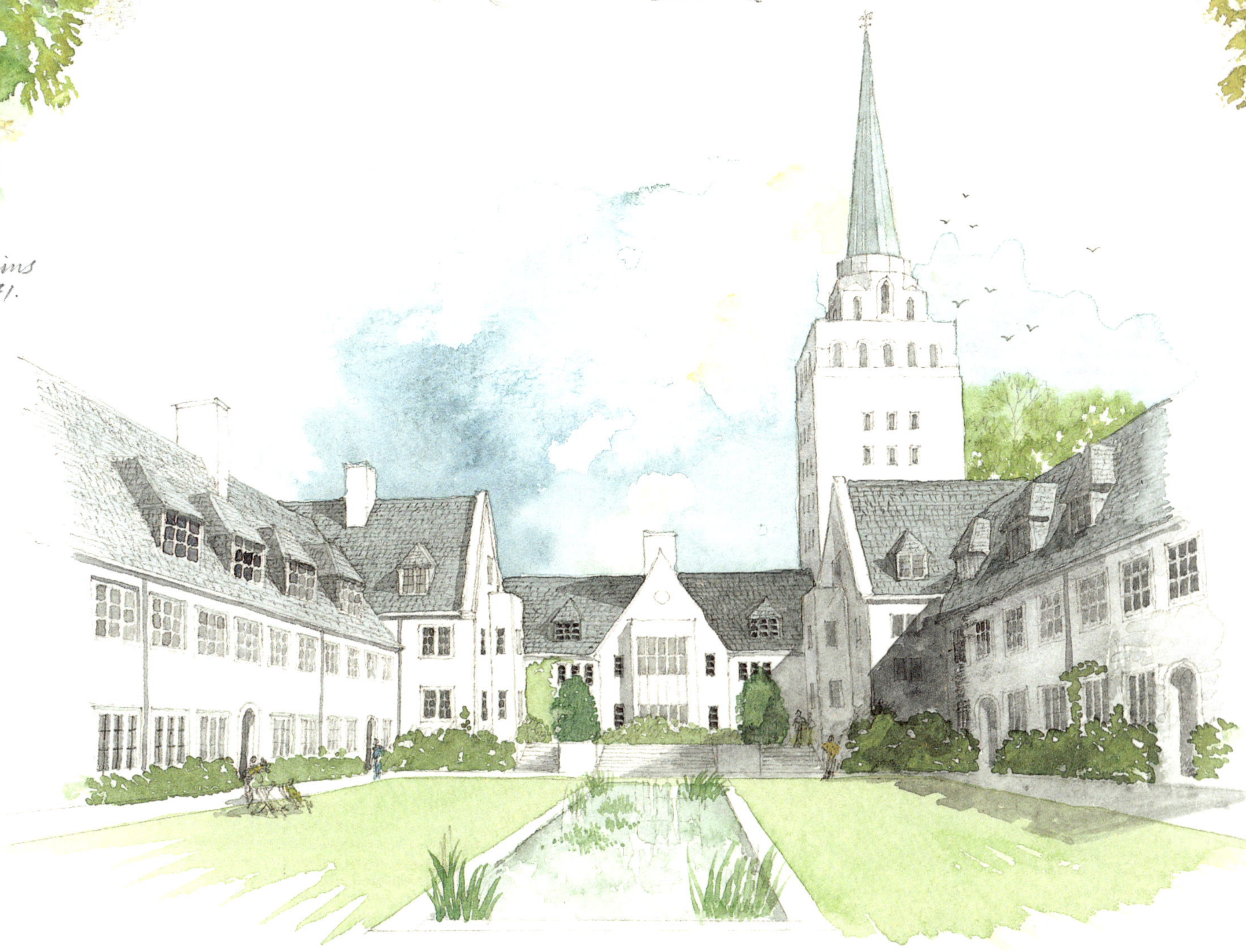

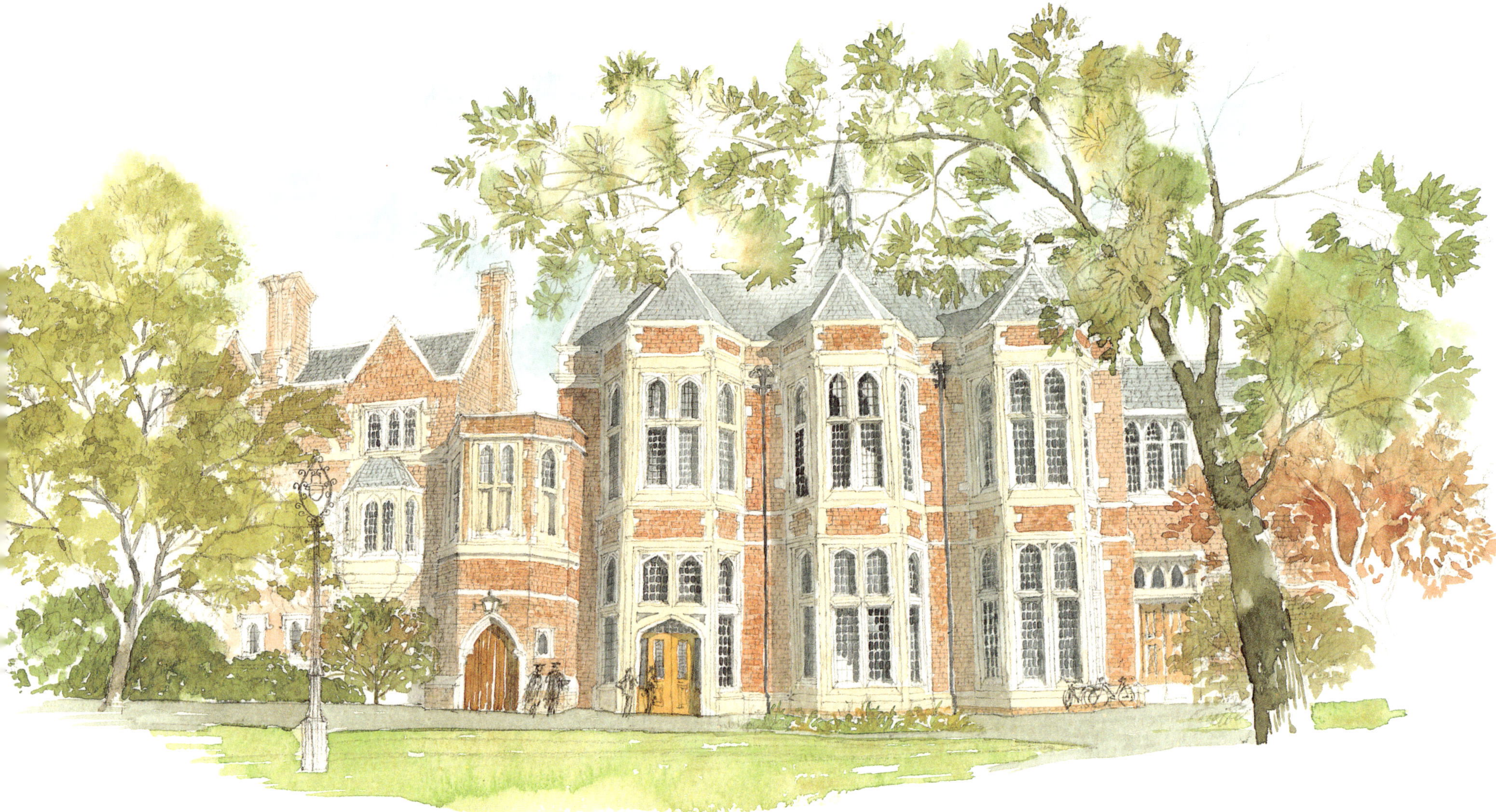

The Victorian buildings of the Oxford Union provide a setting in which generations of aspiring politicians have honed their debating skills.

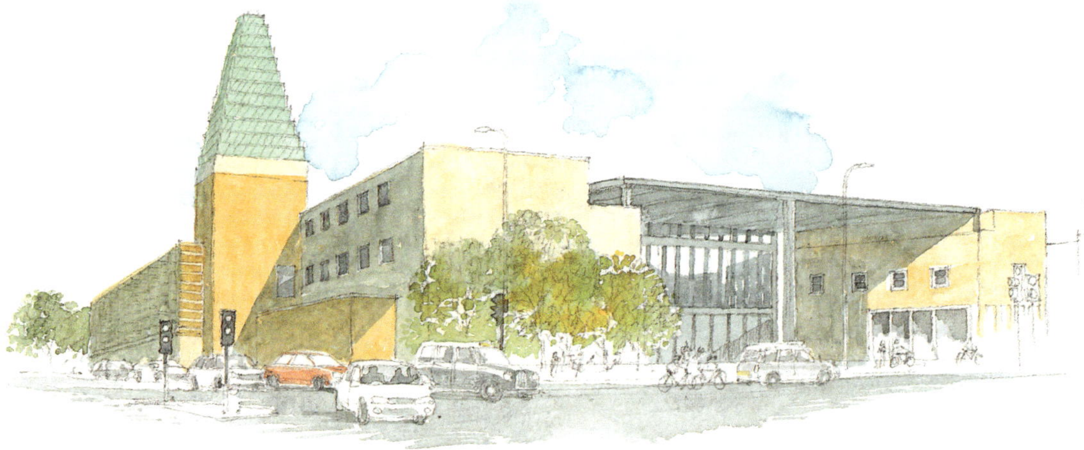

One of Oxford's most prominent new buildings is the Saïd Business School, built opposite the railway station in 2001 to the design of the architect Sir Jeremy Dixon.

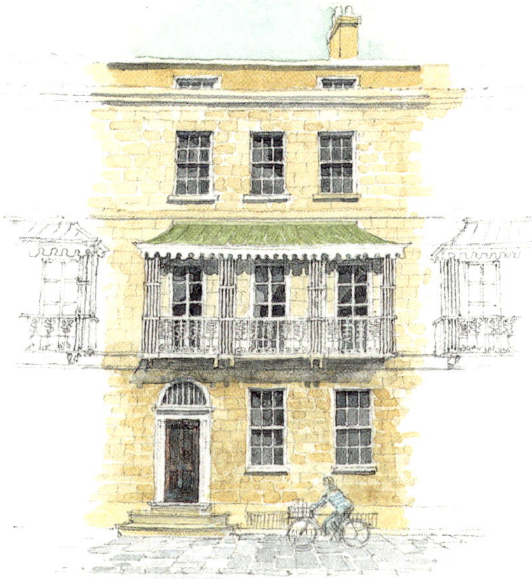

The late-Georgian terrace houses on Beaumont Street feature fine decorated iron verandahs.

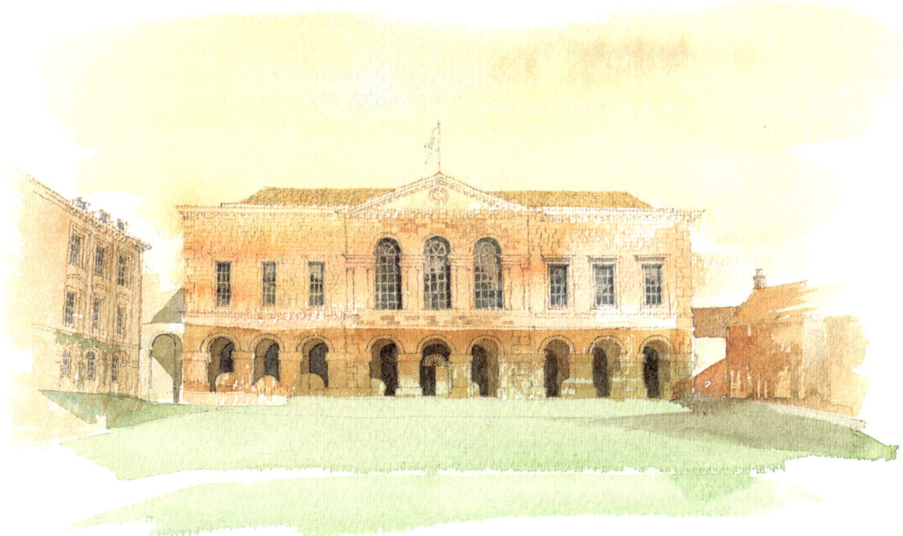

The library at Worcester College houses an internationally important collection of architectural drawings.

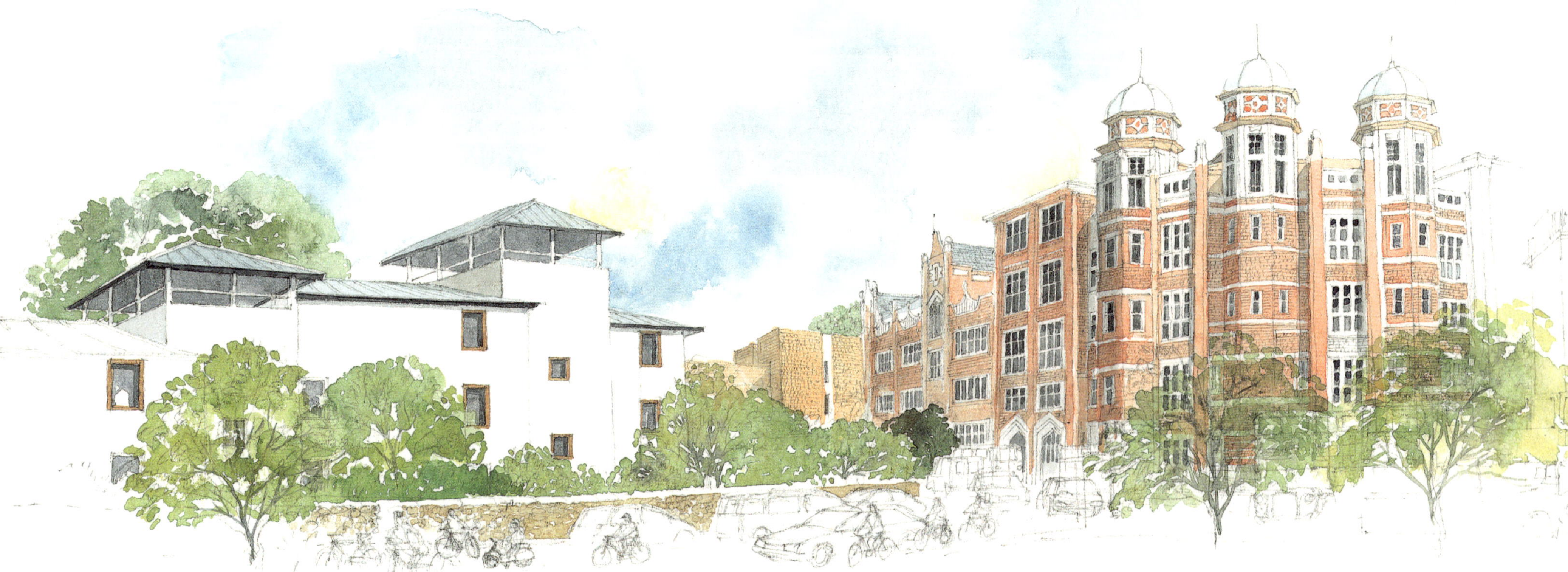

At the western approach to the city centre, austere recent additions to Worcester College contrast with the jolly Gloucester Green development of 1987-90.

The spikily Gothic Randolph Hotel confronts the majestic Greek Revival Ashmolean across Beaumont Street.

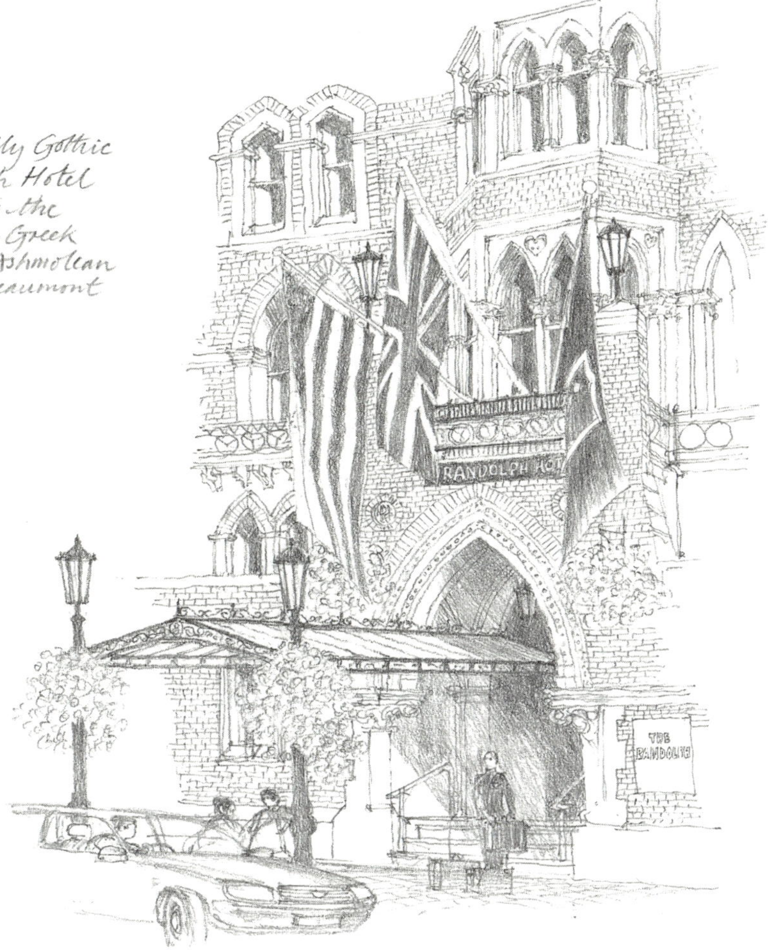

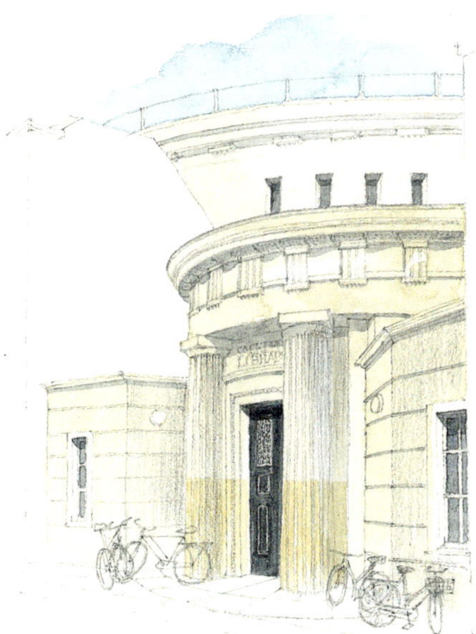

The Ashmolean is one of Britain's outstanding provincial museums. It has developed around the original nucleus collected in the 17th century by Elias Ashmole, and now encompasses Roman and Greek sculpture, the celebrated 'Alfred Jewel' made for Alfred the Great, and superb Renaissance and Old Master paintings.

The new Sackler Library is tucked in behind the Ashmolean Museum.

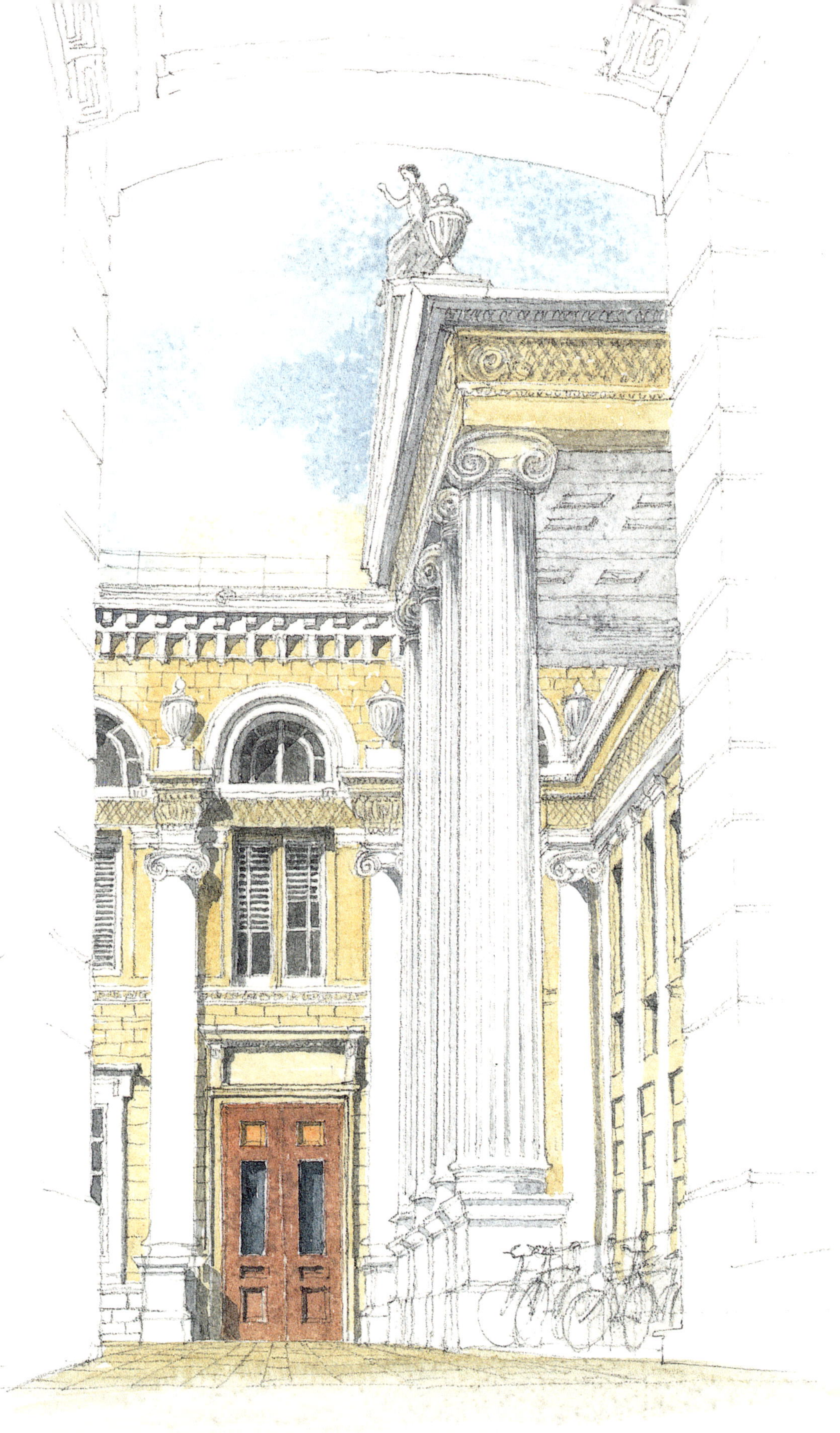

Going North

There is no doubt that from a visual point of view the best routes into Oxford are from the north. Both the Woodstock Road and the Banbury Road are blessedly free of real ugliness, and they converge, like streams coalescing to form a broad river, in the tree-lined St Giles, the city's most beautiful street after The High. The houses that range along the west side of St Giles are a happy text-book mix of medieval, Tudor, Georgian and Victorian, while most of the east side is taken up with the buildings of St John's College, which originated as the 15th-century suburban monastic foundation of St Bernard's. Much of the superior Victorian residential suburb to the north of here was developed on St John's land in a period when for the first time the university's hitherto celibate dons were being allowed to marry and raise families. Its leafy streets are lined with substantial detached and semi-detached villas, interspersed now with women's and postgraduate colleges. Here too, separated from North Oxford proper by the University Parks, is the less attractive science area, where the university has committed some of its worst architectural sins of recent decades, and those resolutely - one might say aggressively - High Victorian monuments, Keble College and the University Museum. Away to the east, its grounds running down to the River Cherwell, is St Catherine's College, a correspondingly emphatic statement of Modernism; while the land between St Giles and the canal to the west was developed as another Victorian suburb, this time the meaner workers' housing of Jericho, which has survived to become newly fashionable and bohemian. Juxtaposed with its humble terraces are the occasional monuments to the academic grandeur of past centuries, notably the neoclassical Radcliffe Observatory (out in the fields when it was begun in 1773 and now part of a new college) and the pompous frontage of the Oxford University Press.

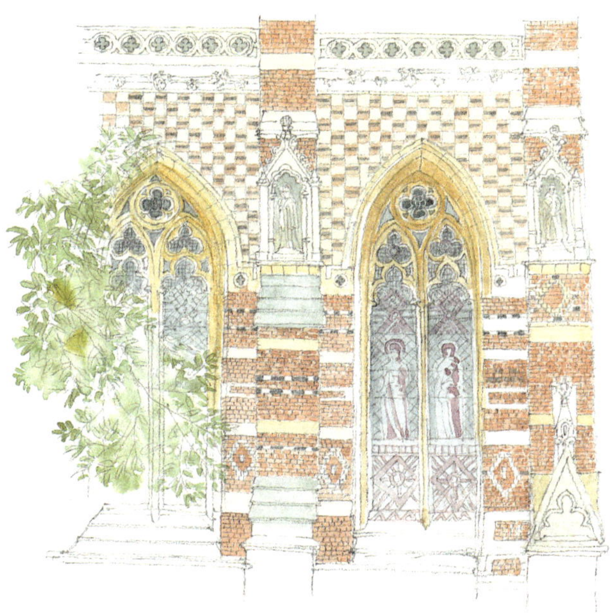

The richly patterned Victorian brickwork of Keble College, designed by William Butterfield, has been likened to a Fair Isle sweater.

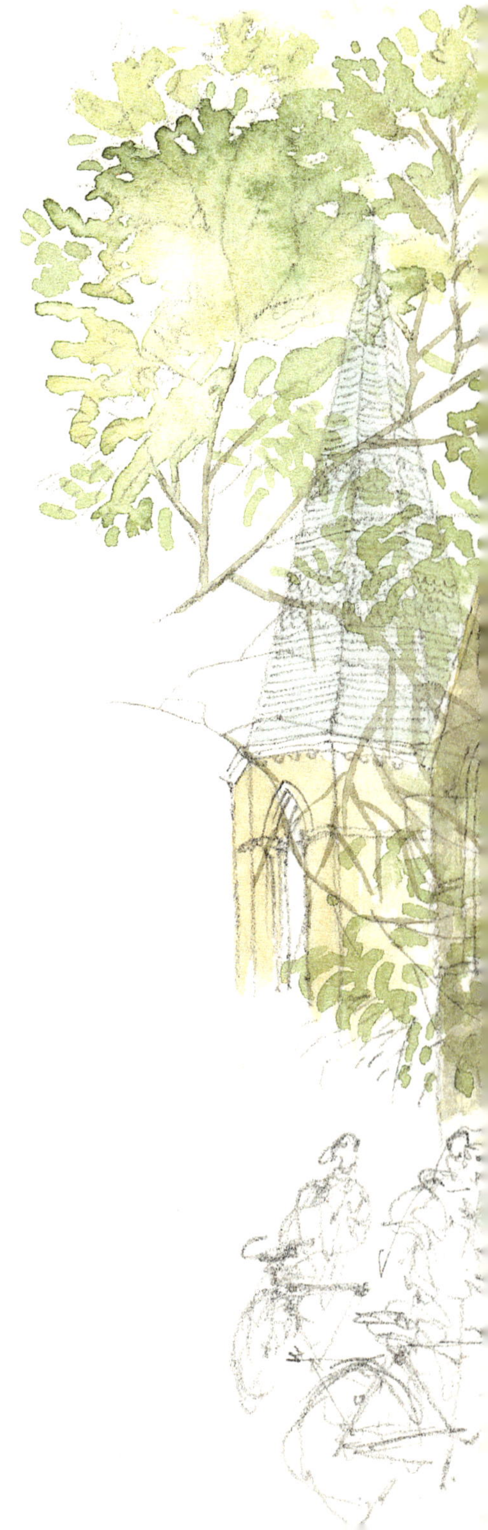

The Venetian Gothic University Museum opposite Keble was begun in 1855 to display and explain the wonders of the natural world.

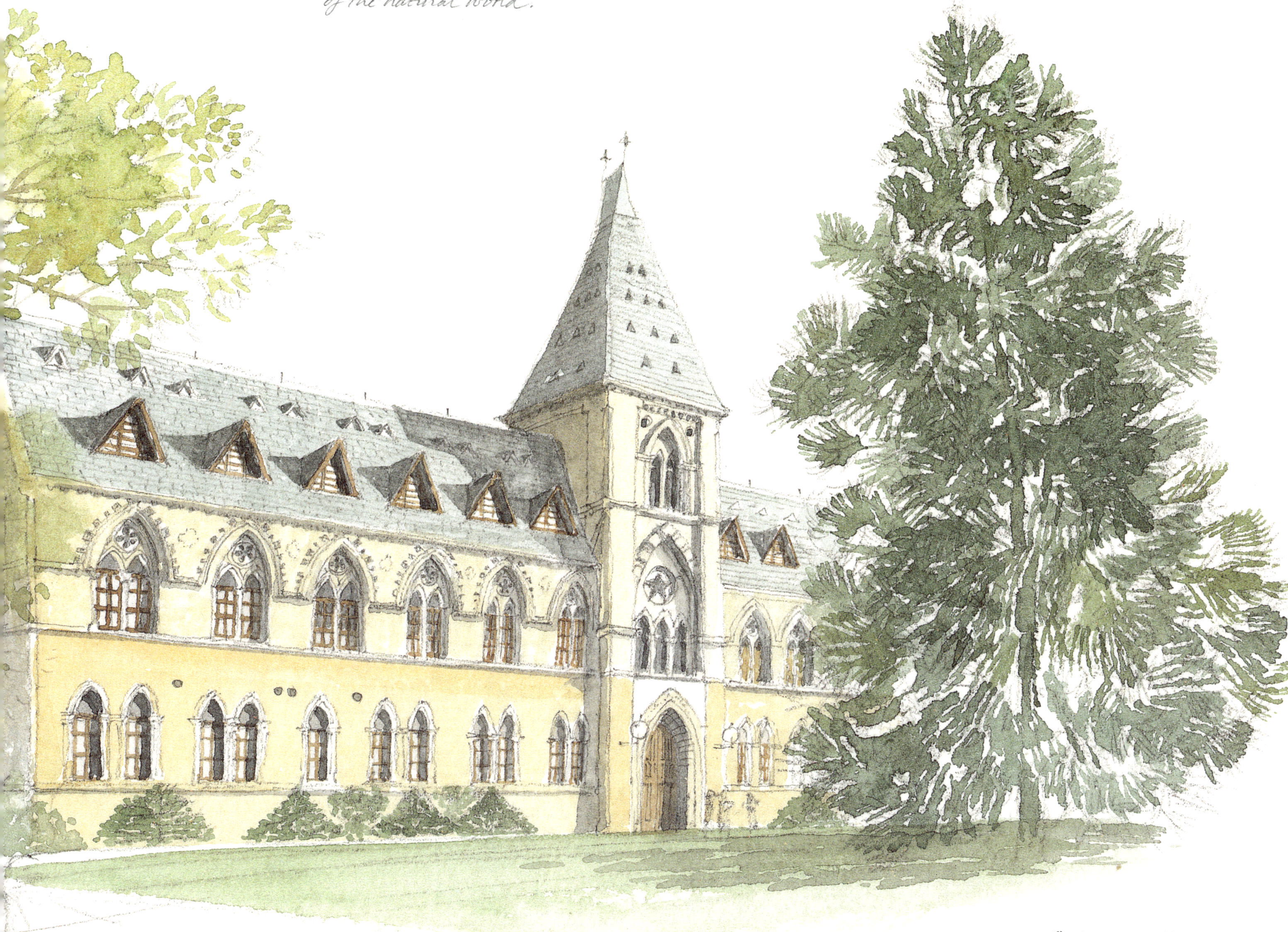

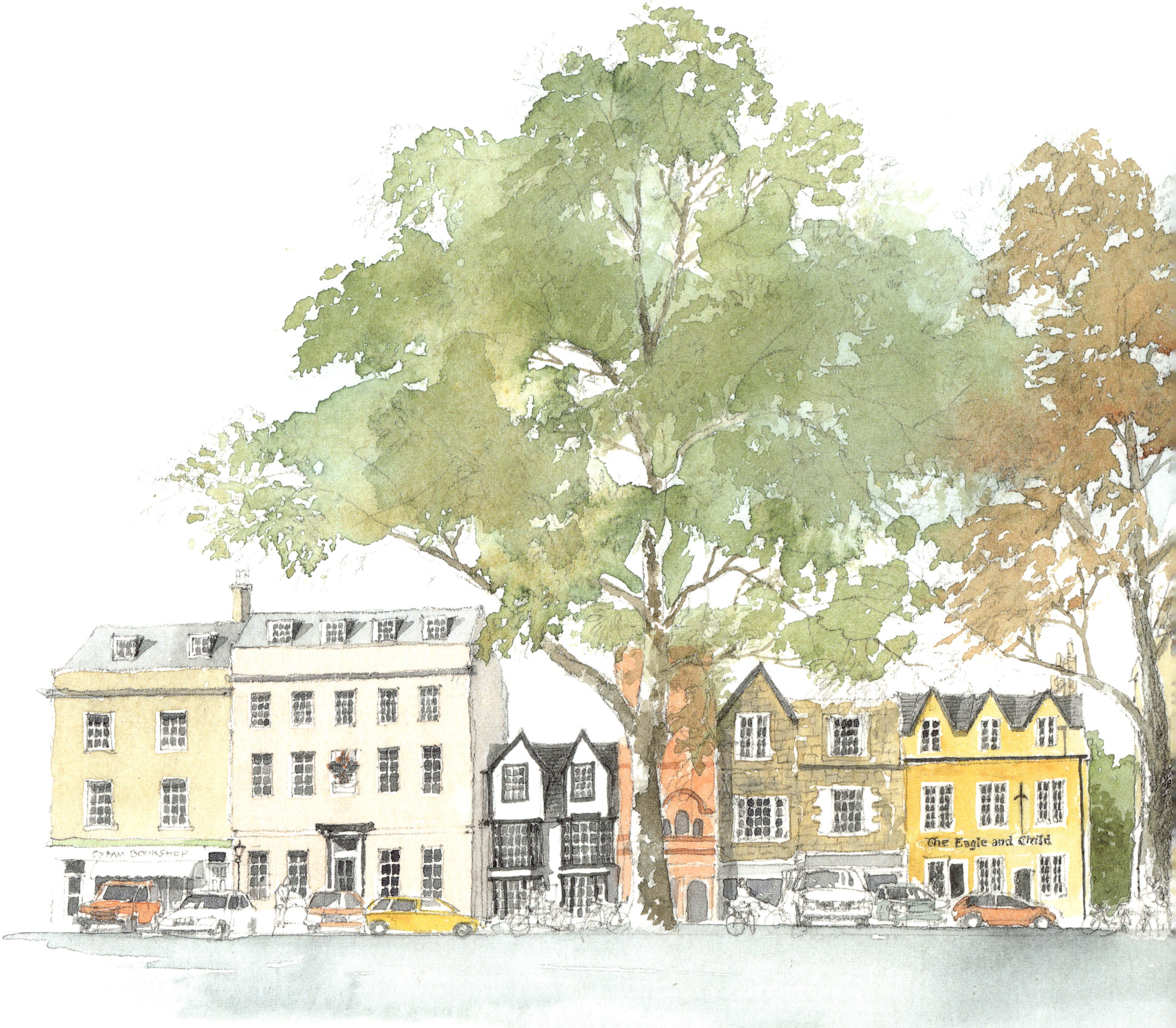
OXFAM BOOKSHOP
The Eagle and Child

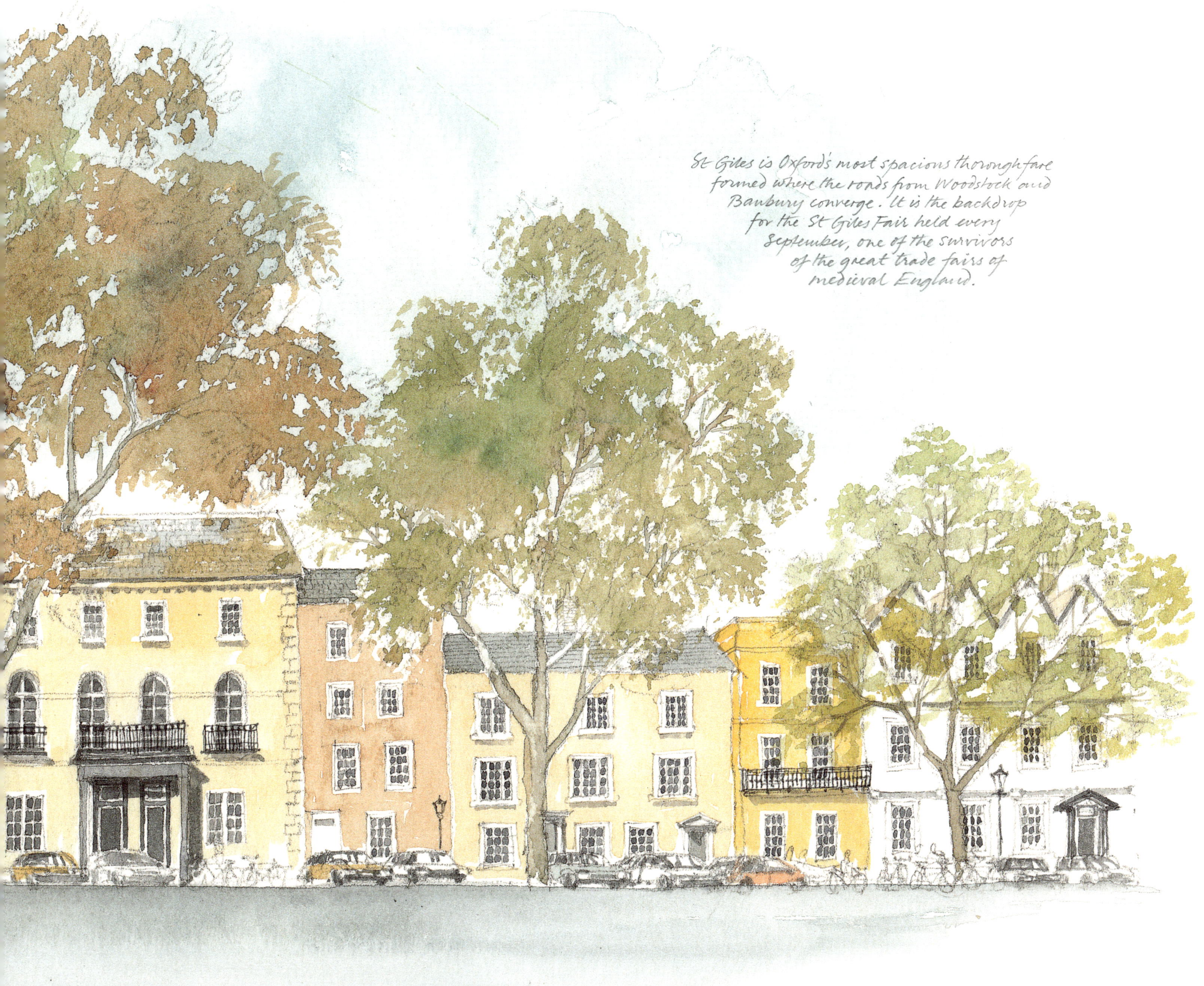
St Giles is Oxford's most spacious thoroughfare
formed where the roads from Woodstock and
Banbury converge. It is the backdrop
for the St Giles Fair held every
September, one of the survivors
of the great trade fairs of
medieval England.

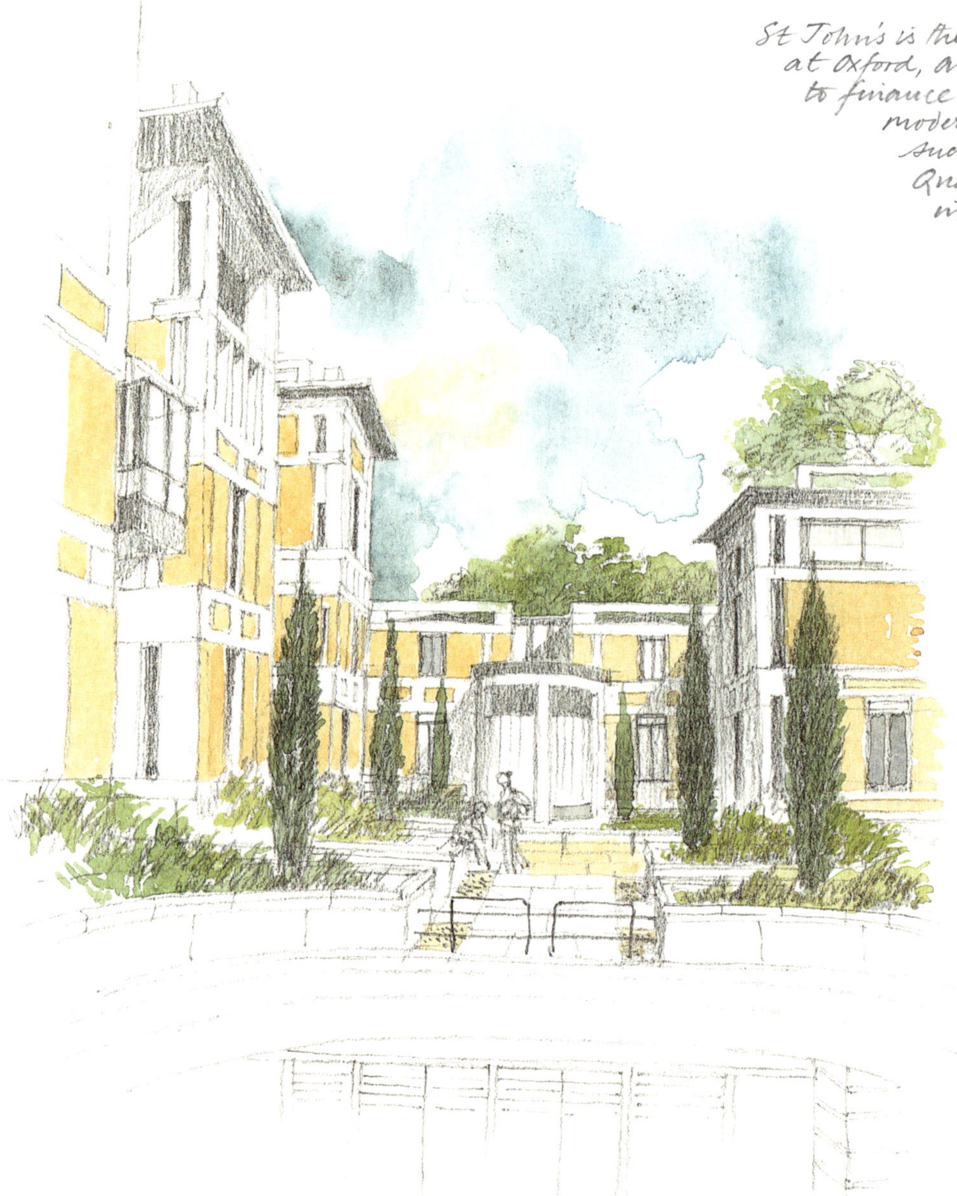

St John's is the richest college at Oxford, and has been able to finance outstanding modern extensions such as the Garden Quad, finished in 1994.

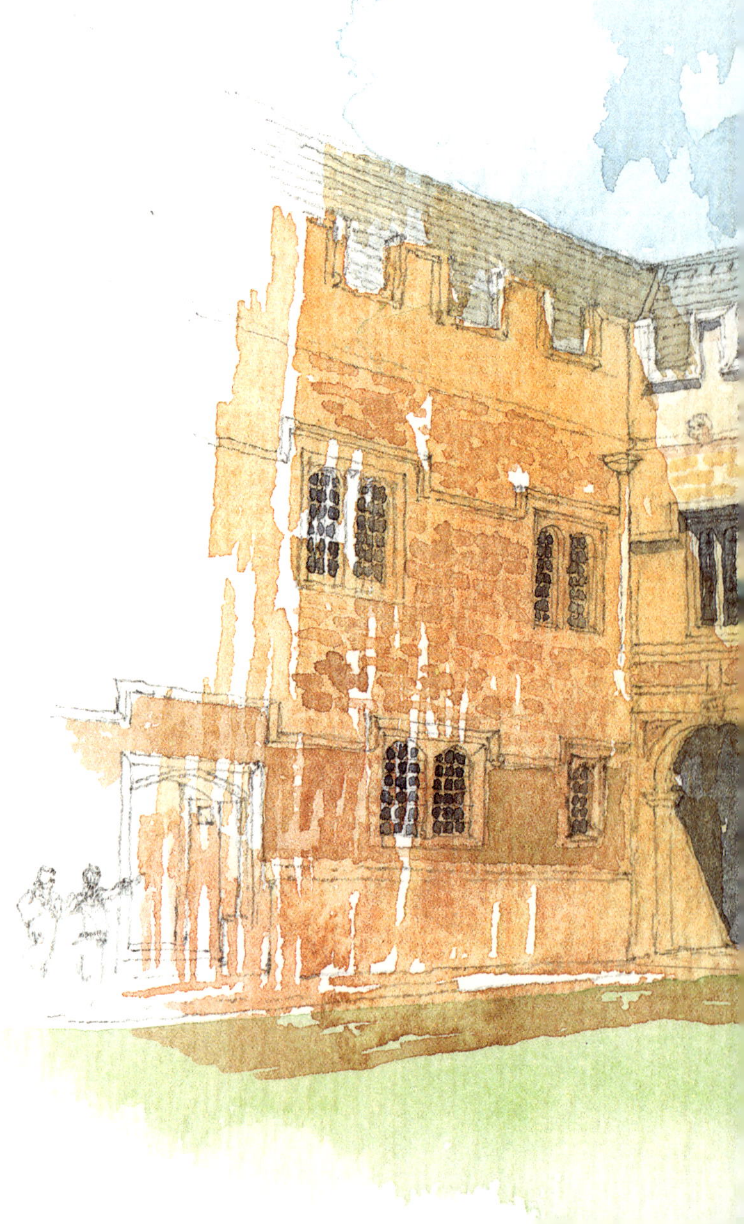

Canterbury Quad at St John's, built at the expense of Archbishop Laud of Canterbury in the 1630s, is one of Oxford's most beautiful spaces.

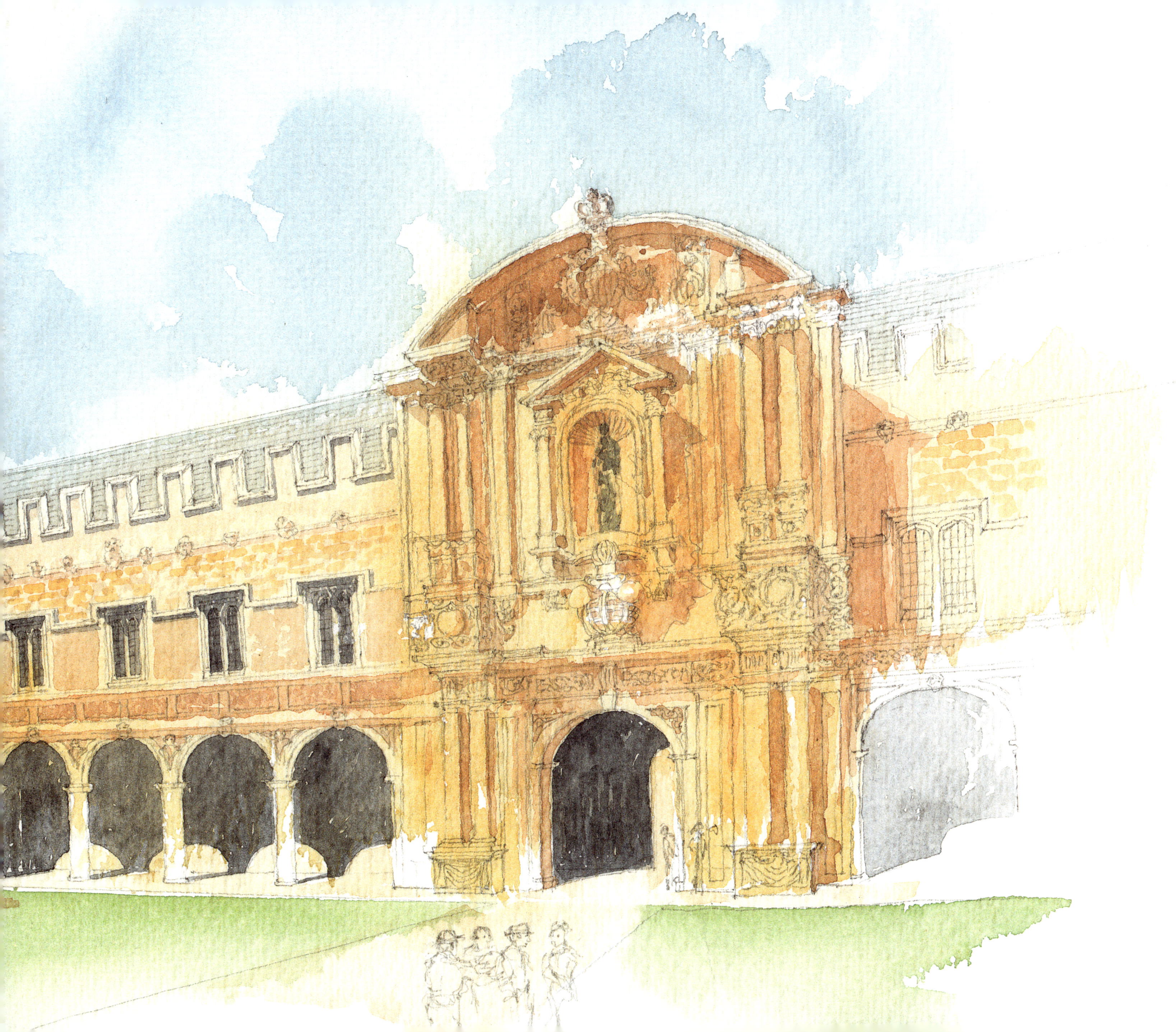

The Talbot Building at Lady Margaret Hall, the first women's college to be founded at Oxford. Since 1979 it has been mixed. Its 12 acres of grounds run down to the river.

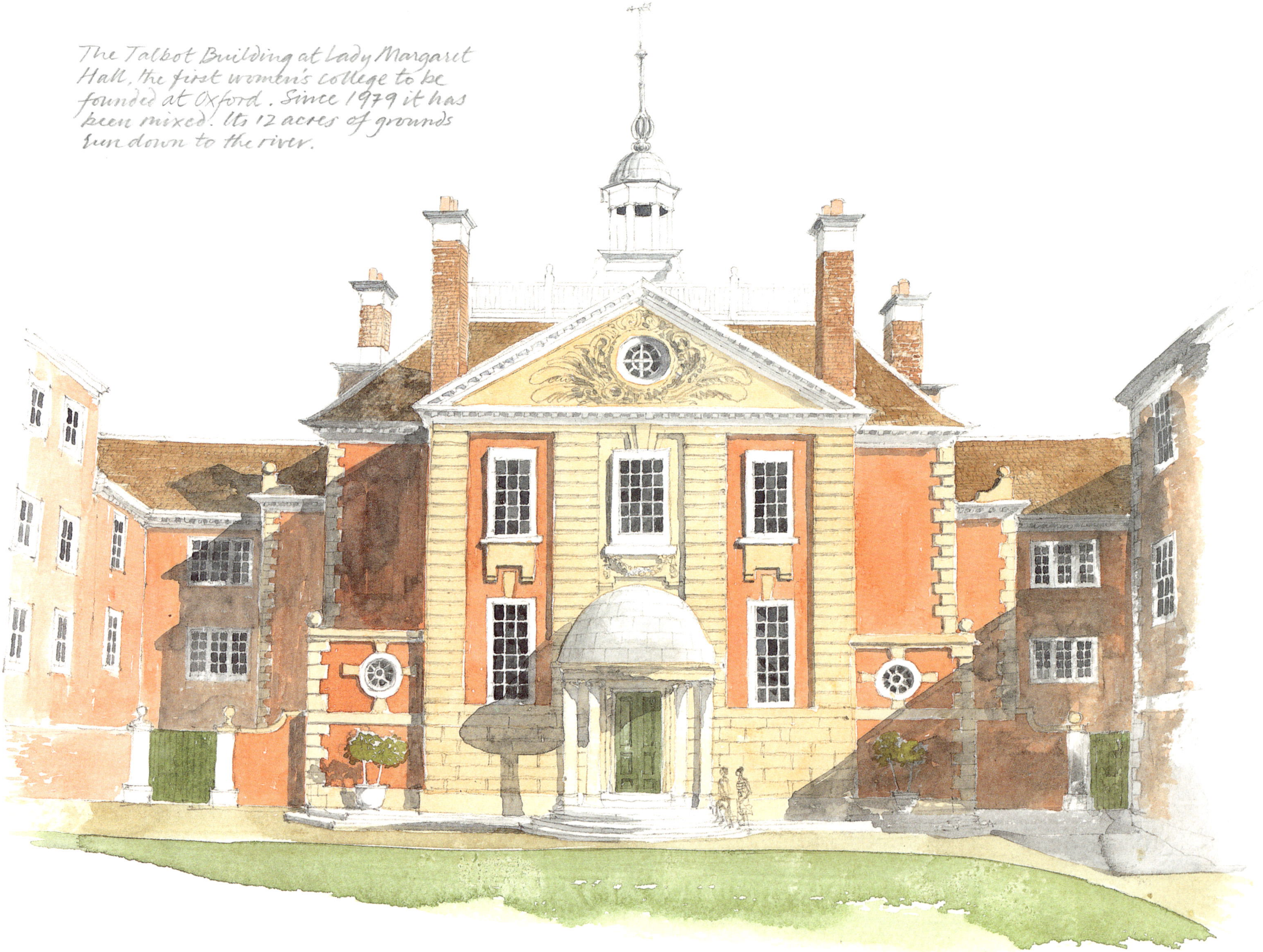

Wolfson College, a postgraduate foundation of the 1960s, occupies a spacious site on the banks of the Cherwell in North Oxford.

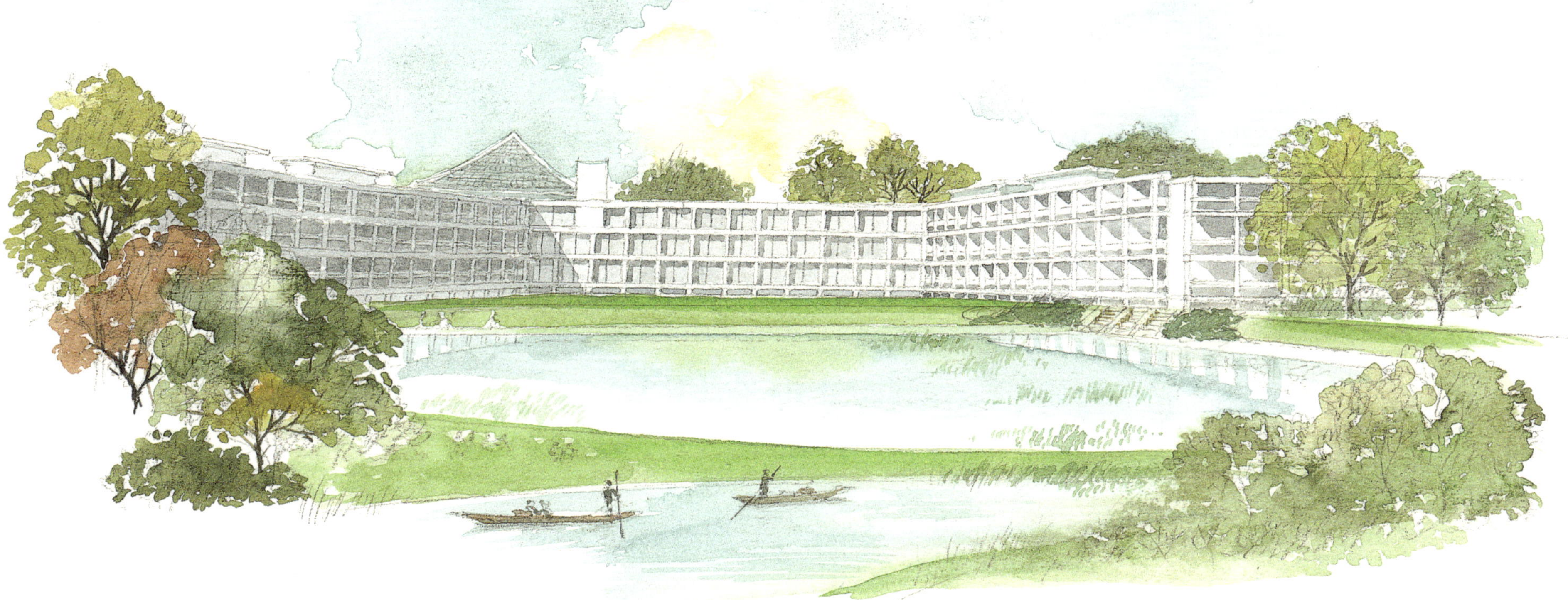

The stark modern buildings of St Catherine's College tend to provoke strong reactions, whether positive or otherwise.

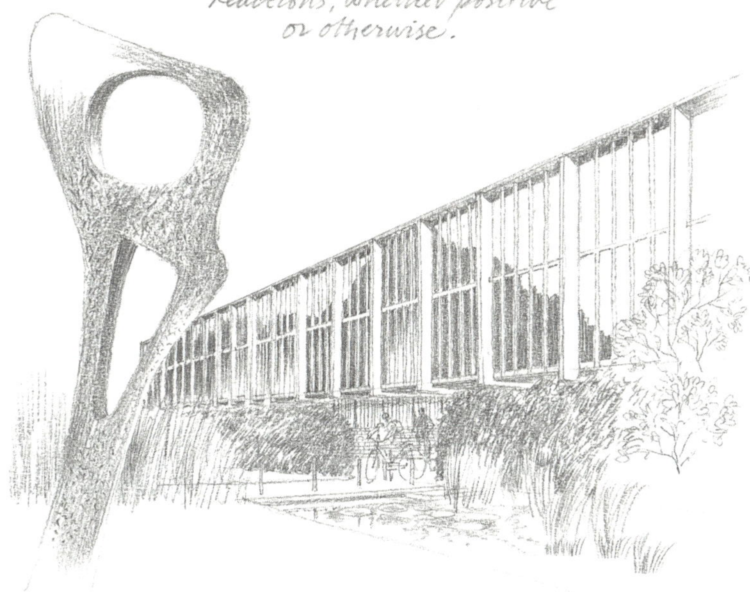

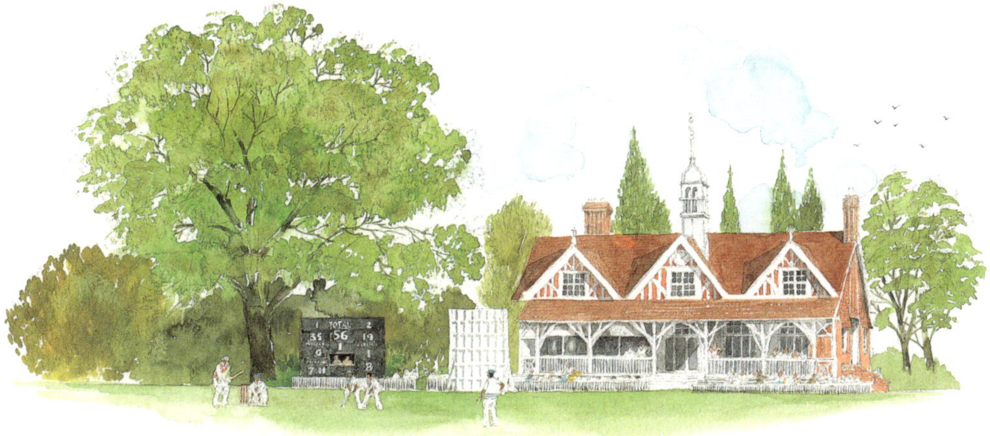

This beautiful cricket ground is situated in the University Parks. Many University cricketers who have later represented their countries have walked down the steps of the old pavilion which in 1880 was designed by Sir Thomas Jackson.

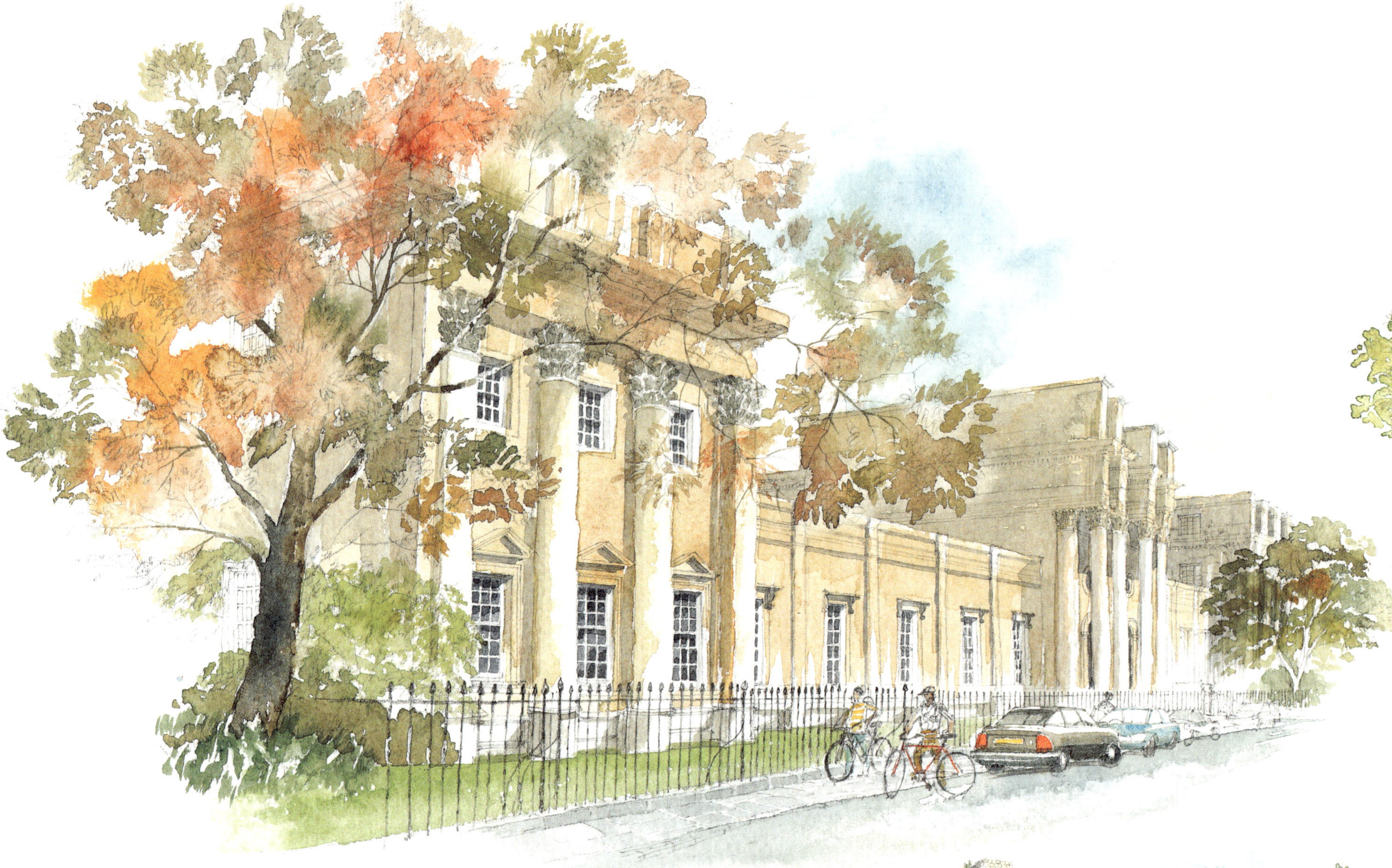

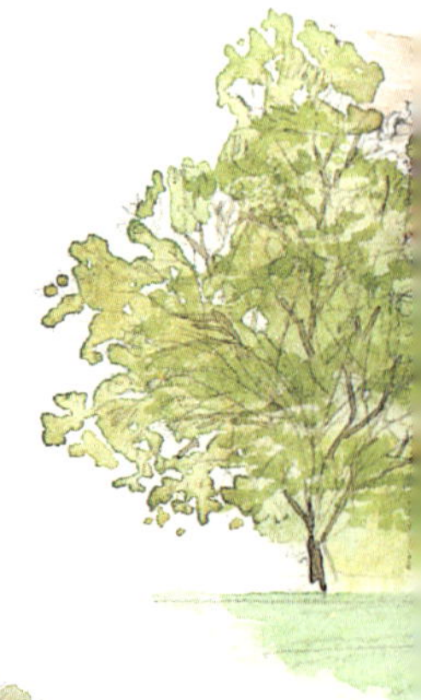

The grandiose Oxford University Press buildings of the 1820s inject a note of architectural pomp into an otherwise humdrum street.

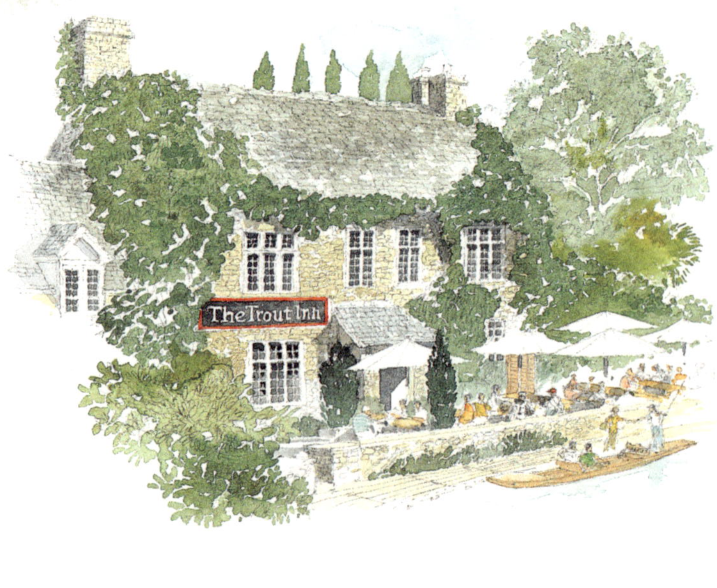

The Trout Inn on the Thames at Godstow is a popular destination for a walk across Port Meadow, or to stop in a boat.

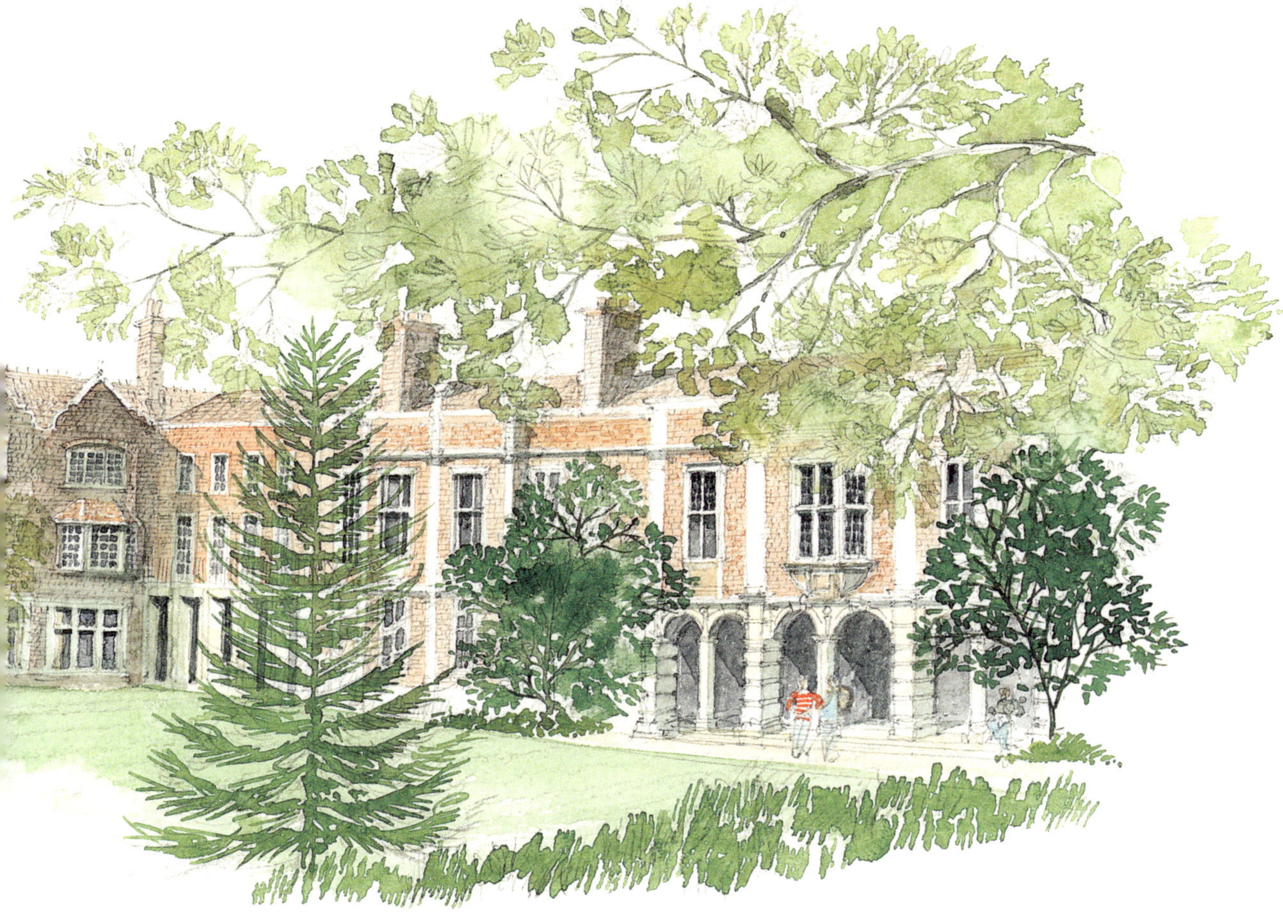

Somerville College's library range of 1902-3 faces a beautiful garden; this was one of the first women's colleges.

Two Victorian North Oxford churches in contrasting styles: St Philip and St James in the Woodstock Road (bottom left) and St Barnabas in Jericho (right)

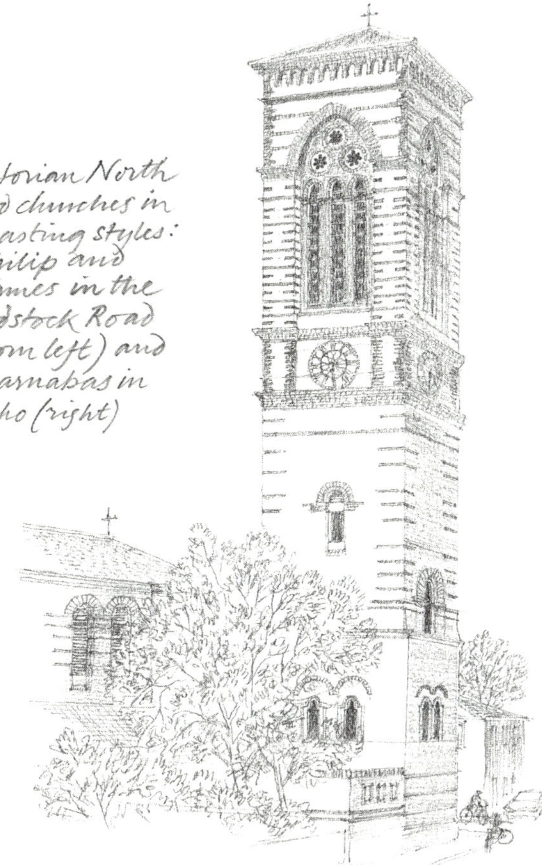

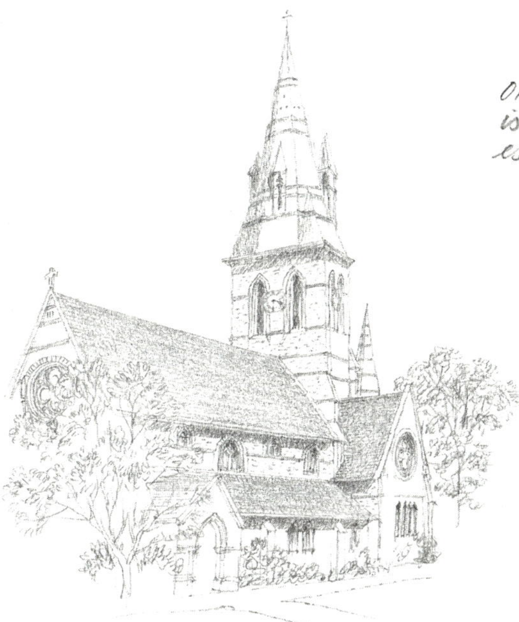

The neoclassical Radcliffe Observatory, begun in 1773, is now part of the recently established Green College.

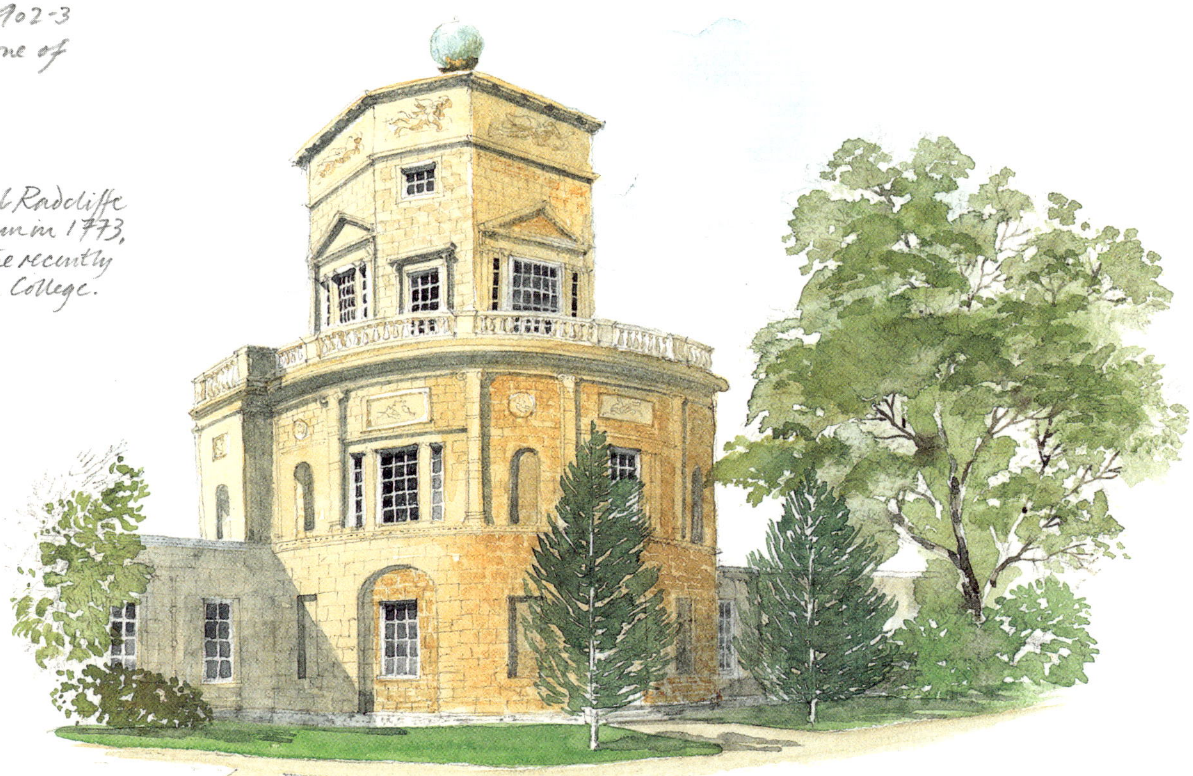

Two examples of Victorian Gothic villas in Norham Gardens, part of the North Oxford suburb laid out by William Wilkinson on land owned by St John's College.

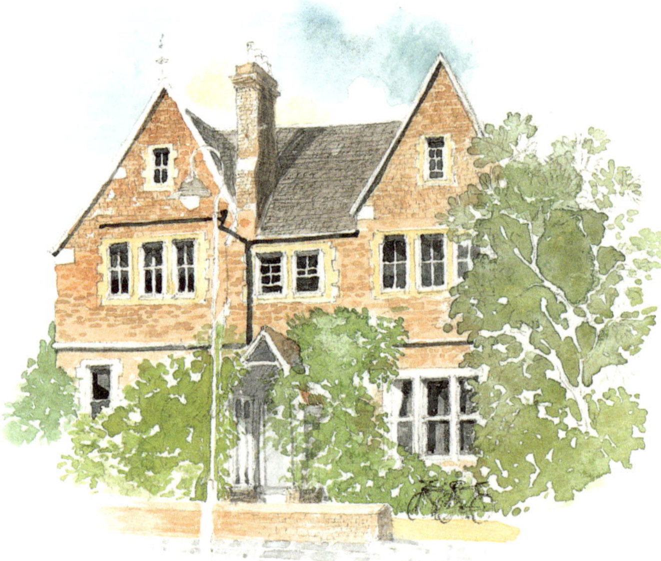

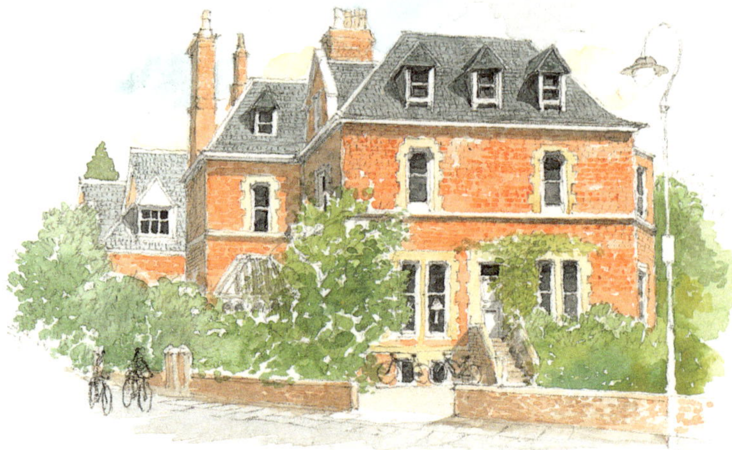

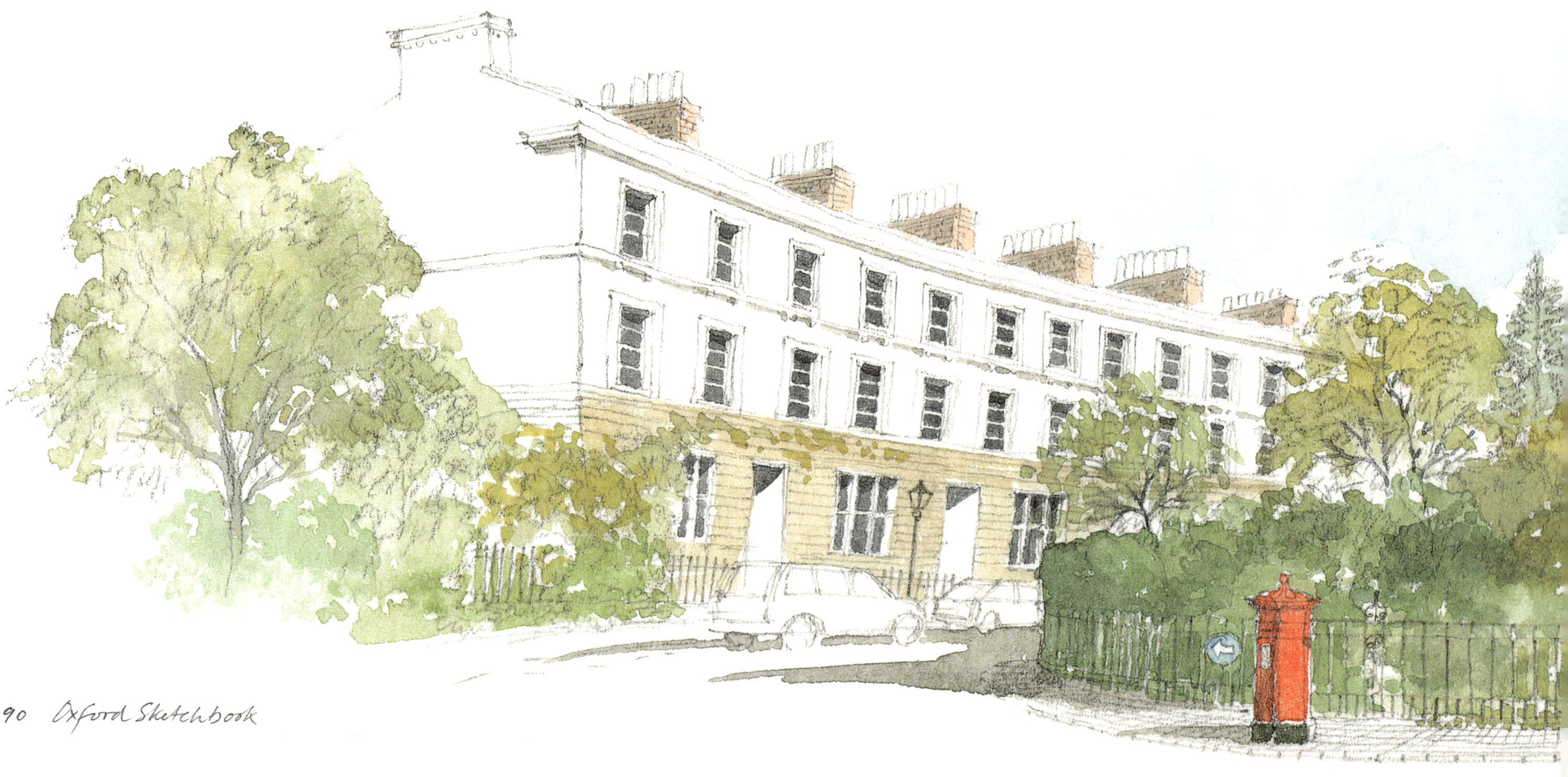

The humble punt was used in the 19th century as a commercial craft. As river transport declined, the Victorians modified the punt to the slender shape that we know today. Cherwell Boat House is a delightful spot from which to hire one and to enjoy one of Oxford's traditions of punting on the river.

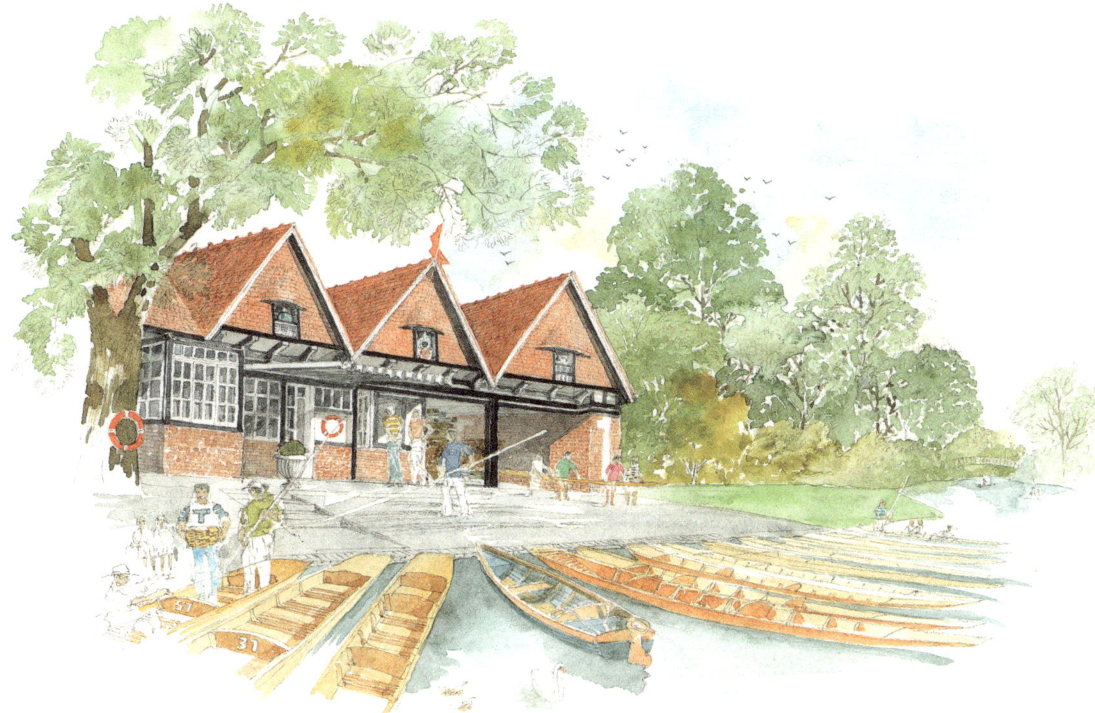

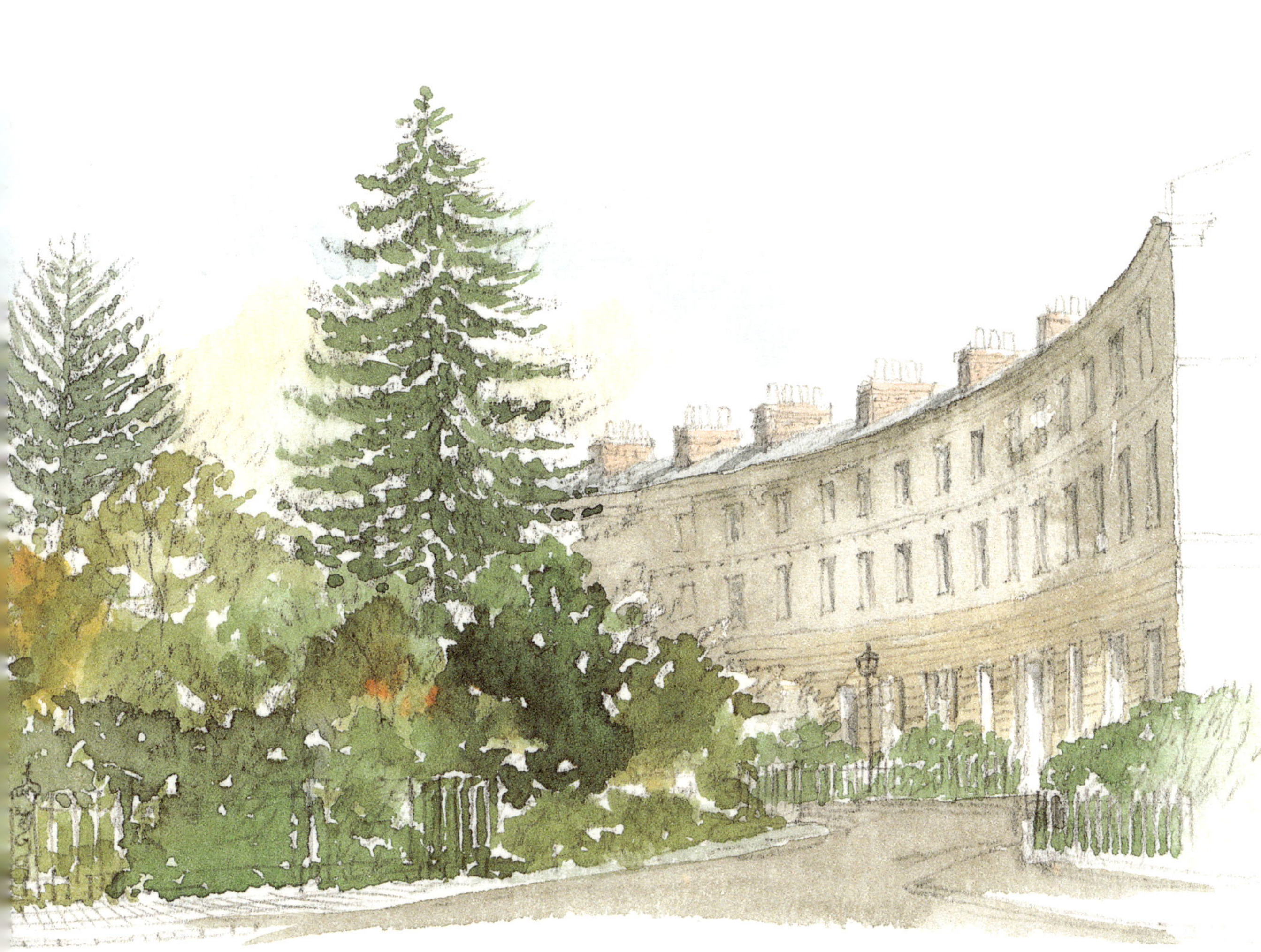

Park Town, an elegant residential enclave off the Banbury Road, was developed in the 1850s, still in the architectural traditions of Bath and Cheltenham.

Gazetteer

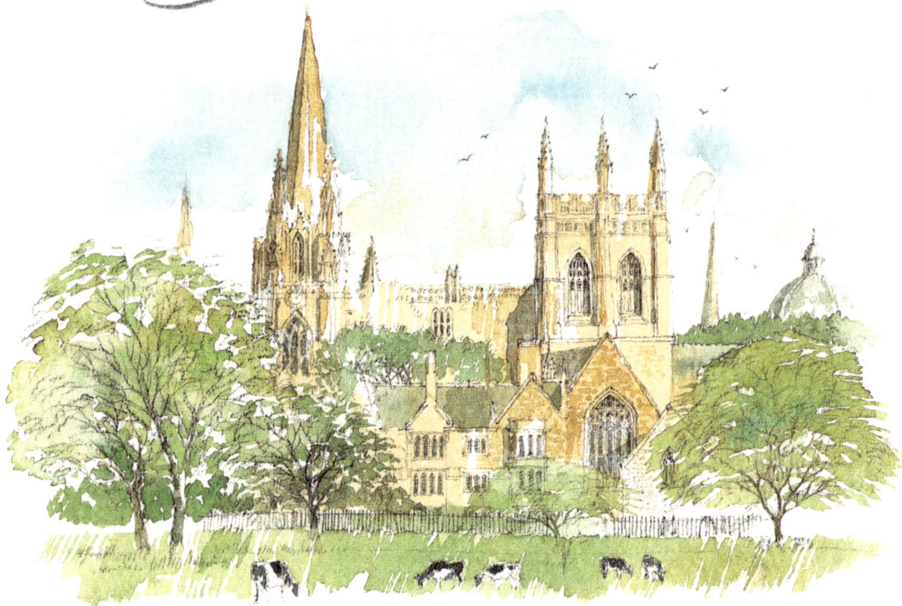

Page 7
Tom Tower, Christ Church
The great gate tower of Christ Church was left unfinished at Cardinal Wolsey's fall from grace in 1529. In 1681, the head of the college at the time, Dean Fell, commissioned Sir Christopher Wren to design an upper stage which would contain Great Tom, the huge medieval bell brought from Oseney Abbey after the Reformation. The Dean expected something classical, but Wren decided to continue Wolsey's Tudor-Gothic style in simplified form, turning the plan from square to octagonal, and capping the design with an ogee dome. In doing so he gave Oxford its first 'Gothick' building, a landmark in the early Gothic Revival. (See also pages 10, 44–45, 61–63.)

Page 10
St Frideswide
What is now England's smallest ancient cathedral, and doubles as the chapel of Christ Church College, was originally built as the church of a nunnery traditionally said to have been founded in the early 8th century by St Frideswide. It was probably begun in the 1160s to a rather strange design, in which an attempt was made to incorporate the triforium (the intermediate gallery stage) of the normal three-storey Norman elevation within the main arcade. In about 1500, the choir was given a wonderful new stone vault with elaborate fans of ribs and dangling pendants. The architect was probably William Orchard, the designer of the earlier Divinity School vault, who was buried in the nunnery precincts after his death in 1504. Cardinal Wolsey demolished part of the nave to make way for his great quadrangle, and had he not fallen from grace, the rest would have followed in favour of a vast new chapel. King Henry VIII economised by making St Frideswide both the college chapel and (in 1546) the cathedral of a new diocese. (See also pages 61–63.)

Page 11
Jesus College
Jesus College was officially founded in 1571 by Queen Elizabeth I, following a petition from Dr Hugh Price, the Treasurer of St David's Cathedral in Wales; consequently, it has a strong tradition of admitting Welsh students. It is a small college on a cramped site, but its two quadrangles offer a charming mixture of styles and building dates, from the 16th to the 19th centuries. Work on the second quadrangle began in 1639, was interrupted by the Civil War, and not finally completed until 1713; it is extremely conservative in style, still very much Tudor-Gothic except for the curvaceous gables.

Page 12
The Emperors' Heads
The Broad Street railings that follow the curve of the Sheldonian Theatre are punctuated by stone piers topped by the so-called Emperors' Heads—really statues inspired by ancient Roman boundary posts. The original heads were replaced in 1868 and again in 1972, having become unattractively blackened and decayed with age.

Page 13
St Mary's Church, Iffley
One of the finest Norman village churches in England, St Mary's is thought to have been built in the 1170s and is remarkable for the encrustation of carved detail on both exterior (particularly the west front and south door) and interior. In recent years the church has been enriched by a Nativity window, made by the great English artist John Piper in 1982 and installed here in his memory after his death in 1992.

Page 15
Lincoln College
Founded in 1427 by Richard Fleming, Bishop of Lincoln, its Front Quad is still basically 15th-century. This is the period of the Hall's open timber roof, though the panelling was inserted in about 1700. The chapel is of 1629–31, with important stained glass of that date by Bernard van Linge. (See also pages 27, 50–51.)

Page 17
Martyrs' Memorial (1841–43)
The Memorial was commissioned by a Low Church group to commemorate the Protestant martyrs, Archbishop Cranmer and Bishops Latimer and Ridley, who were burnt at the stake in Broad Street in 1556, and was intended as a challenge to the members of the High Church Oxford Movement. A competition, which stipulated that the monument should be based on the late 13th century Eleanor Cross at Waltham Abbey in Hertfordshire, was won by George Gilbert Scott, one of the most prolific Victorian architects. (See also page 56.)

Page 20
Radcliffe Square
The church of St Mary the Virgin was rebuilt on a grand scale at the University's expense in the 15th century and was the earliest focus for University activity. Academic ceremonies were held here from the 14th century until the building of the Sheldonian Theatre in the 1660s. The University was governed from the Convocation House attached to its north side, and the University's collection of books was kept here until the late 15th century. It was Nicholas Hawksmoor's idea to create a public square—a 'Forum Universitatis'—between the church and the Bodleian Library, and to place in it the new library for which Dr John Radcliffe left £40,000 in his will in 1714. Hawksmoor produced a succession of very fine designs for the library, and eventually in 1734 proposed a great domed rotunda, free-standing in the centre of the square. He died in 1736 before work could begin, and it was instead built (1737–49) in a modified version by James Gibbs. Arguably Oxford's finest building, it became part of the Bodleian Library in 1862, and since then has been known as the Radcliffe Camera. (See also pages 16, 26, 44–45.)

Page 21
The High Street
The High Street runs in a gentle curve from Carfax (the central crossroads of historic Oxford) in the west to Magdalen Bridge in the east. The grand buildings of the University and colleges—St Mary the Virgin, Brasenose, All Souls, Queen's, University College, the Examination Schools and Magdalen—alternate with more modest houses and shops in a completely fortuitous but very happy sequence.

Pages 22–25
Magdalen College
Magdalen was founded in 1458 by William Waynflete, Bishop of Winchester, on an exceptionally spacious site between the city's East Gate and the River Cherwell. Its original nucleus, begun in 1474, was an enclosed cloister with the chapel and hall along its south side. The magnificent bell tower was added in 1492–1505. In the early 18th century it was proposed to demolish much of the medieval complex and replace it with a very large new quadrangle in a sober Palladian style; in the event only one range of this (erected to Edward Holdsworth's design in 1733–35 and since known as the New Building) was ever built, and the cloister quadrangle was happily spared. After 150 years of indecision and abandoned schemes, the college expanded again in the 1880s with St Swithun's Quad (designed by Bodley and Garner), which characteristically was left incomplete until extended by Sir Giles Gilbert Scott in 1928–30. The very conservative nature of Magdalen's architecture has been confirmed in recent years by the Grove Buildings, which were designed in a Tudor-Gothic idiom by the Greek architect Demetri Porphyrios and built in the 1990s. To the north of the college buildings is Oxford's only deer park, and to the east the Magdalen College Walks, essentially a water meadow surrounded by tree-lined walks which in the Spring is celebrated for its profusion of purple fritillaries.

Page 26
Carfax Tower
The crossroads known as Carfax has always been the civic focus of Oxford, just as the Radcliffe Square area has always been the university's. Proposals by Nicholas Hawksmoor in the early 18th century to remodel it as a kind of Roman forum came to nothing, and in 1787, the spectacular Jacobean conduit was removed as a traffic obstacle. In the 1890s, the area was further opened out by the demolition of most of the church of St Martin, leaving only its 14th-century tower.

St Mary the Virgin, south porch

Added as the High Street entrance to the church in 1637, the porch is a splendid piece of Mannerist architecture (although it has a Gothic fan vault within); it demonstrated the High Church sympathies of the University by incorporating a statue of the Virgin Mary. It was traditionally ascribed to the mason-sculptor-architect Nicholas Stone, but now seems to have been designed by the mason John Jackson.

The Mitre

The Mitre, formerly one of Oxford's many coaching inns, is largely of 17th and 18th century date, but it stands on vaulted medieval cellars.

Page 27

All Saints Church and the south side of the High

The impressive baroque church of All Saints was built in 1701–10 to designs by Dean Henry Aldrich of Christ Church, but the fine steeple was not completed until 1720, with probable input from Nicholas Hawksmoor. Since the 1970s it has been the library of Lincoln College (see also page 50). A group of modest stuccoed houses separates the church from the High Street frontage of Brasenose, designed by Sir Thomas Jackson and built 1881–1911.

Pages 28–29

The Queen's College

Although the college was founded as long ago as 1340 (by Robert Eglesfield, chaplain to Queen Philippa after whom it is named), this early foundation is now not at all apparent in the architecture. Work began on a new North Quad in 1671, when the Williamson Building was designed by Christopher Wren, and continued with the addition of a magnificent library in 1693–96 (architect unknown). In 1708–9 Hawksmoor offered no less than seven schemes for replacing the medieval Front Quad in a very grand manner, and work began in 1710 on a scheme much modified by Dr George Clarke (the University's architectural pundit) and William Townesend (the most prominent local mason-architect). The main front, with its domed gatehouse, is one of the High's most impressive features. As the site is quite constricted, the college's most recent addition had to be built beyond Magdalen Bridge; this is James Stirling's Florey Building of 1968–70, an extremely striking structure sheathed in glass and bright red tile, which has proved functionally highly problematic.

Pages 30–31

St Edmund Hall

Until it became a full college in 1957, St Edmund Hall was the last surviving example of the University's once numerous Halls or hostels. It takes its name from St Edmund of Abingdon, who lectured at Oxford in the early 13th century and is thought to have lived on this site. As it now stands, Front Quad is a picturesque composite of various dates from the 15th century onwards. The only part of it with any architectural pretension is the building containing the chapel and former library, which was built in the 1680s according to designs by William Byrd. In 1968–70, an overly large new building (containing a dining hall with accommodations above) was shoehorned into the space to the east, with a concrete stair tower that rears uncomfortably in long views of the High. The college has also expanded its area northwards by converting the extremely interesting medieval church of St Peter-in-the-East into its library.

Pages 32–35

New College

The college was founded in 1379 by William of Wykeham, Bishop of Winchester, on a spacious site within the northeast angle of the city walls that had been depopulated by the Black Death. As Chancellor of England, Wykeham was a very rich man, and his college (he also founded a sister college at Winchester) was much the biggest at Oxford or Cambridge at that date. For the first time, the various component parts of the college—hall, chapel, library and accommodations—were conceived as an integrated whole, arranged around a single Great Quadrangle with an additional cloister attached to the chapel. The architect was almost certainly William Wynford, who was later to rebuild the nave of Winchester Cathedral. Although new ranges were added to the north along Holywell Street in the late 19th century, the original approach to the college down New College Lane is still essentially as it was in the late 14th century, with a gate tower adorned with statues of the Founder and an angel kneeling to either side of the Virgin Mary. The chapel is one of Oxford's largest and finest, despite alterations in the 18th and 19th centuries. To the east of the medieval buildings is the open-ended Garden Quad of 1682–1707, which is separated by a beautiful wrought iron screen from one of Oxford's loveliest gardens.

Pages 36–37

Hertford College

The history of the college is complex, for it began in the 13th century as Hart Hall, changed its name in 1740 to Hertford College, was taken over and rebuilt for Magdalen Hall in 1820, and was finally refounded in 1874 as Hertford College. The long classical façade facing the Bodleian comprises a centrepiece designed by Sir Thomas Jackson in the 1880s (it contains the dining hall on its upper floor), sandwiched between blocks of 1820–22. Jackson was responsible for pulling the complex together visually, adding new buildings in a variety of styles, including the so-called Bridge of Sighs, which was built in 1913–14 to link the main quad with North Quad across New College Lane.

Pages 38–39

Holywell Street

This gently curving street is one of Oxford's most picturesque, lined with a happy medley of domestic buildings and marred only by the gloomy Victorian ranges of New College which loom over its eastern end. Its west end is framed by the King's Arms pub and the former Indian Institute, a jolly 'Free Style' building of the 1880s (architect Basil Champneys) which was intended for the training of future Indian civil servants. A little further along is the Music Room, built originally in 1748 as one of Europe's first purpose-designed public concert halls.

Pages 40–41

All Souls College

All Souls was co-founded in 1438 by Archbishop Chichele of Canterbury and King Henry VI; it was intended for a Warden and forty Fellows, and has never had undergraduates. The Front Quad, facing the High, was built immediately and remains essentially as completed in 1443. The chapel, which occupies the north side, adopts the T-plan popularised at New College and has a west façade towards what later became Radcliffe Square. In the early 18th century one of the Fellows, Dr George Clarke, encouraged the college to think of expanding northwards over the site of the medieval cloister, and his friend Nicholas Hawksmoor began producing designs. When in 1710 All Souls received a major legacy from Christopher Codrington (a West Indies sugar planter) to finance the building of a new library, Hawksmoor revised his plans and proposed a vast new quadrangle with the library along its north side. His scheme, in 'contextual' Gothic to harmonise with the medieval buildings and also designed to present its main elevation to the new Radcliffe Square, was begun in 1715. In the Codrington Library he gave Oxford one of its finest interiors, while the lofty twin towers of the Common Room block contributed memorably to the city skyline. (See also pages 44–45.)

Page 42

Mansfield College

This began as a training college for Congregationalist ministers, with pleasant Tudor-Gothic buildings erected in 1887–89 to designs by Basil Champneys. There is a handsome Arts and Crafts library, whose projecting oriel window is echoed in modern form by the adjoining Rothermere American Centre (by the American firm of Kohn Pedersen Fox, completed 2001).

Rhodes House

The diamond magnate and empire-builder Cecil Rhodes left money in his will to establish an institution where nominated scholars from America, the British Empire and Germany could get together. The architect chosen was Sir Herbert Baker, who had worked with Rhodes in South Africa, and his design was executed in 1926–29. A domed classical pantheon serves as entrance hall, and is embraced by ranges that recall Cotswold manor houses. The main material is squared rubble, which started an unfortunate fashion in inter-war Oxford buildings.

Page 43

Wadham College

The college is named after its founders, Nicholas and Dorothy Wadham, who were wealthy Somerset landowners and whose statues stand in niches over the entrance to the Hall, below that of King James I. This is the only ancient college which was built all at one go, in 1610–13, and the main quadrangle has remained unchanged ever since. The designer was the West Country master mason William Arnold. The chapel has retained many of its original fittings, including a colourful east window signed by Bernard van Linge and made in 1622. The most famous alumnus was probably Christopher Wren, an undergraduate here in the early 1650, and Sir Thomas Jackson, the architect who contributed so much to the appearance of late 19th century Oxford, was also here. In the 1970s a new Brutalist library in yellow concrete was built to the designs of Gillespie, Kidd & Coia, followed in 1990–2 by more picturesque ranges of student rooms designed by Richard MacCormac.

Page 46

Bodleian Library

In the 1420s, the University embarked on the building of a large and imposing room for theology lectures, to be called the Divinity School. Work proceeded very slowly, and in 1444 the design was radically altered when it was decided to add an extra floor to contain the University's collection of books, especially the library which Duke Humphrey of Gloucester had just donated. Shortage of funds delayed completion until the 1480s, when the Divinity School was given a magnificently ornate vault (probably designed by William Orchard) and the library above it a much simpler wooden roof. This remained the University's library until 1610 when lack of space necessitated expansion by the addition of a quadrangle. This is known as the Schools Quadrangle, on account of the inclusion of lecture rooms for the different subjects or 'schools', while the library as a whole is named the Bodleian after Sir Thomas Bodley who masterminded its enlargement. The quadrangle, executed by masons from Halifax, was given a lofty gate tower with the five orders of classical architecture and a statue of James I donating his collected writings to a figure representing the University. Continued pressure on space eventually necessitated that a large extension to the library—the New Bodleian—be built on the other side of the Broad in 1937–40. Designed by Sir Giles Gilbert Scott, it is lumpish and rubble-faced, and replaced an attractive group of vernacular houses.

Page 47
Sheldonian Theatre
The Sheldonian, which is basically a hall for the University's ceremonies, takes its name from Archbishop Sheldon of Canterbury who gave a large donation to the building fund. It was one of the first architectural commissions awarded to the brilliant young scientist and mathematician Christopher Wren, and was completed in 1669. He based the D-plan design on an ancient Roman theatre, spanning the 70-foot width of the auditorium with an ingenious timber roof that greatly impressed contemporaries. This is concealed from within by a vast illusionistic ceiling celebrating the triumph of Religion and Learning, painted by Robert Streater.

Clarendon Building
In 1702–4 the University Press published Clarendon's History of the Great Rebellion, (i.e. the Civil War) and the proceeds from the sales financed the erection of a new building for the Press in 1712–13. At the prompting of Dr George Clarke the commission went to Nicholas Hawksmoor, whose powerful baroque design has a grand Doric portico framing the central arch into the Bodleian precincts. The presses (which had previously been housed in the roof space of the Sheldonian) occupied the rooms to either side until 1830, when they moved to more spacious premises in Walton Street. (See also page 88.)

Pages 48–49
Brasenose College
Founded in 1509, the college took over the site and the name of Brasenose Hall, which in turn seems to have owed its strange name to an ancient brass door knocker. Old Quad dates from soon after the foundation, and was extended in 1656–63 by the addition of a range containing the library and chapel. Designed by the mason John Jackson, this is a curious but appealing mélange of Gothic and classical motifs which presents its main elevation to what is now Radcliffe Square. Hawksmoor's proposal to rebuild the college in a grandiose baroque manner remained unbuilt, and the next expansion came in 1881–1911 with the addition in stages of New Quad, designed in Gothic with Arts and Crafts touches by Sir Thomas Jackson. In 1959 the college commissioned an ingenious infill of its cramped site, designed by Powell & Moya, which set a new standard for modern additions in sensitive historic settings.

Pages 52–53
Exeter College
Founded originally as Stapledon Hall in 1314, Exeter takes its name from Bishop Stapledon of Exeter. Though one of the oldest colleges, nothing remains from before the 15th century. Most of the earlier work was rebuilt in the 17th and 18th centuries, while the most striking feature, the chapel, was added by Sir George Gilbert Scott in 1854–60 in the style of the Sainte-Chapelle in Paris. The chapel interior represents High Victorian at its most lavish and is very fine in its way. The tapestry behind the altar is by William Morris and Edward Burne-Jones, who were both undergraduates at the college.

Page 54
St Michael's Church, Cornmarket
The tower, the earliest surviving structure in the city, probably dates from the first half of the 11th century and was intended as a semi-fortified structure linked to the North Gate (demolished in 1771). The rest of the church mostly dates from the 13th and 14th centuries.

Page 55
Covered Market
In 1773–74 a new covered market building was erected in order to remove the open-air stalls which clogged the area around Carfax. It was rebuilt and enlarged in 1886–97, and still performs its original function.

Page 58
Trinity College
Durham College, established in the late 13th century by the Benedictines of Durham Cathedral, was one of several monastic colleges set up outside the town walls. It was suppressed in 1544 and refounded as Trinity College in 1544 by Sir Thomas Pope, a civil servant. Although a 15th-century range from the monastic buildings survives in Durham Quad, nothing else escaped the rebuilding which began in 1665–68 with a new residential block designed by the youthful Christopher Wren. This eventually developed into an open-ended Garden Quad, facing east across spacious gardens to a very handsome set of gate piers and wrought-iron gates on Parks Road. Next came the rebuilding of the chapel, completed in 1694, which has one of the finest ecclesiastical interiors of its period in the country, combining sumptuous plasterwork, woodwork and carving almost certainly by Grinling Gibbons. These older buildings are set well back from Broad Street, where imposing 18th-century entrance gates are juxtaposed with a little group of 17th-century houses. Sir Thomas Jackson added a neo-Elizabethan range along the right-hand side of this Front Quad in the 1880s.

Page 59
Balliol College
Balliol received its charter in 1282 from the widow of John of Balliol, as a penance for the fact that in 1255 he had kidnapped the Bishop of Durham. Despite this early foundation, and the survival of a hall and library from the 15th century, the appearance of the college is now predominantly of the Victorian era, when it established itself as Oxford's intellectual powerhouse.The stripey stone chapel designed by William Butterfield (1856–57) introduced 'constructional polychromy' to Oxford and was immediately unpopular. Alfred Waterhouse supplied the rather forbidding range along Broad Street (1867–68) and the hall (1873–77), of which the latter is now framed by somewhat Brutalist buildings by the Oxford Architects' Partnership of the 1960s.

Page 60
Town Hall
In 1893, at a time when cities all over the country were building ambitious new town halls to symbolise municipal pride, Oxford's Palladian town hall was demolished and replaced on a much larger scale. The architect responsible was H. T. Hare, and the style that was adopted was a lavish version of the neo-Jacobean which Sir Thomas Jackson had already popularised.

Pages 61–63
Christ Church
The over-mighty Cardinal Wolsey suppressed the ancient nunnery of St Frideswide in 1525 in order to found a college that he hoped would outdo all others at Oxford and Cambridge in both size and splendour. When he fell from favour in 1529, however, Cardinal College was only partially complete. The foundation was adopted by Wolsey's ungrateful master King Henry VIII, who renamed the college 'Christ Church' and abandoned the idea of building a vast new chapel in favour of taking over what remained of the nunnery church. The cloister which Wolsey intended was therefore never built, but construction of the college resumed in 1638 with the addition of a spectacular fan-vaulted staircase leading up to the hall. After the Civil War (when Christ Church served as the headquarters of Charles I) the great quadrangle was completed and Sir Christopher Wren was commissioned by Dean Fell to complete the gatehouse with Tom Tower (see page 7). Fell's successor Dean Aldrich was a talented amateur architect who designed a second quad (Peckwater Quad, 1707–14) in a precocious Palladian style. Its fourth side was subsequently filled with Oxford's most grandiose college library, which was begun in 1717 but not finally completed until the 1750s, when the upper room was decorated with lavish rococo plasterwork. In the 1770s James Wyatt designed the elegantly neo-classical Canterbury Quad, with a triumphal arch leading out into Merton Street. The next major addition, Meadow Buildings, was constructed in the 1860s according to a rather joyless design by the Irish architect Thomas Deane. It was followed in 1876–98 by the much more enjoyable bell tower at the southeast corner of Tom Quad, designed by Bodley and Garner. The most recent additions of significance, built in the 1960s, were undertaken by the firm of Powell & Moya: a picture gallery and Blue Boar Quad. (See also pages 7, 10.)

Page 65
Oriel College
Oriel received its charter from King Edward II in 1326, but all its medieval buildings were swept away in the 1620s to make way for a new Front Quad. The unknown architect copied Wadham College in placing the hall and chapel together in the range opposite the entrance, but the overall effect is made less austere by adding curvaceous gables all along the roofline instead of battlements. The central porch is surmounted by statues of two unidentified kings (possibly Edward II and Charles I) and of the Virgin Mary. Back Quad is dominated by the handsome neoclassical library, designed by James Wyatt and begun in 1788. Beyond this is St Mary's Quad, formerly the separate St Mary Hall. Its north range, which fronts the High, is the Rhodes Building of 1908–11, designed by Basil Champneys and paid for by Cecil Rhodes.

Page 66
Corpus Christi College
The intimately scaled Front Quad is one of Oxford's best-preserved early Tudor buildings, being substantially unchanged since the college's foundation by Bishop Fox of Winchester in 1517. At its centre is the pillar sundial of 1581, crowned by a pelican, to which an ingenious perpetual calendar was added in the 17th century. The hall has a fine hammerbeam roof by Humphrey Coke, chief carpenter to Henry VIII, and early 18th century panelling. In 1706–12 Oxford's ubiquitous architect-contractor of the period, William Townesend, created the tiny Fellows' Quad, enclosed by a loggia and a new Fellows' Building. With no further room for expansion on its original site, in the 1960s the college commissioned Powell & Moya to design an infill building across Merton Street in Magpie Lane. (See also page 68.)

Page 67
Merton College
Despite the claims of University College, Merton is probably Oxford's oldest college, founded in 1264 by Walter de Merton, who was then Chancellor of England. As there was no architectural blueprint for such a college, it developed piecemeal, starting with the dining hall (which was largely rebuilt in the 1870s). This was followed by the chapel, whose splendid choir is of the 1290s (still complete with most of its contemporary stained glass), and the 14th-century Mob Quad—Oxford's first complete quadrangle. The original intention was to build a large cruciform church, but the aisled nave was abandoned as unnecessary, resulting in what was the first of Oxford's T-plan chapels; the stately tower was added in the mid-15th century. Nothing more of significance was done in the college until the beginning of the 17th century, when the large Fellows' Quad was constructed, carried out (like the Schools Quadrangle at the Bodleian Library) by

masons from Halifax. A further quad, known as St Albans, was added to the college in 1904–10, designed in an attractive 'free Tudor' style by architect Basil Champneys.

Page 68
University College
Although William of Durham left money in 1249 for the purchase of property to maintain theology students, the foundation document for the college was not drawn up until 1280, and the chapel was not built until a century later. None of the existing buildings is earlier than 1634, when the Front Quad was started. It is still in a conservative Tudor-Gothic style, except for its cresting of shaped gables, and was not finished until the 1670s. When a second quadrangle was added at the expense of Dr John Radcliffe in 1716–19 its design copied the earlier quad closely, to the extent of still having a fan-vaulted entrance. The chapel, rebuilt in the 1660s, retains its 17th-century woodwork and a complete set of stained glass windows by Abraham van Linge, dated 1641. George Gilbert Scott added a new library in medieval Gothic style in 1861, while in 1893 Basil Champneys designed a small domed building to contain the white marble monument to the drowned poet Shelley, a former member of the college.

Page 69
Examination Schools
With the reform of the University in the mid-19th century, there was a need for more space for examinations and lectures, and in 1876–82, a large new building was erected on the south side of the High Street. It was designed by Thomas Jackson and launched him on a career as the most prolific Oxford architects of his generation. The neo-Elizabethan style of the building, with its lavish and eclectic ornamentation, was quite unlike the medieval Gothic style of the previous generation, and was later dubbed 'Anglo-Jackson'.

Pages 70–71
Botanic Garden
The University Botanic Garden, or Physic Garden, was founded and endowed in 1621 by the Earl of Danby. It was intended not as a pleasure garden but as a tool of scientific research. In 1632–33 the mason-sculptor Nicholas Stone built the three imposing classical gateways which are set into the high enclosing wall. The main gate, facing Magdalen College, is lavishly rusticated in the manner of the Italian Renaissance architect Serlio. Other buildings associated with the work of the garden were added in the 18th, 19th and 20th centuries.

Pages 74–75
Pembroke College
The college was nominally founded by King James I in 1624, and was named after the then Chancellor of the University, the Earl of Pembroke. It incorporates a range of almshouses facing Christ Church, begun by Cardinal Wolsey circa 1525 and now converted into the Master's Lodgings, while Old Quad was built abutting the city wall over an extended period in the 17th century and refaced in the early 19th. The much larger Chapel Quad has a simple classical chapel of circa 1730 and an ambitiously large Tudor-Gothic hall of 1848.

Page 76
Oxford Castle
A Norman knight, Robert d'Oilly, built a motte-and-bailey castle in 1071 alongside a branch of the Thames, just outside the west gate of the Saxon town. The main survivals nowadays are the artificial earth mound, the Romanesque crypt of the castle chapel, and St George's Tower, plain but massive. Much of the site was later taken up with the 19th-century gaol and the neo-Norman county hall and assize court (which looks like a gaol).

Nuffield College
Lord Nuffield (the founder of the Morris car firm) founded the college in 1937 on a site across the road from the castle and gaol. It was to be a graduate college focussing on social, political and economic studies. The University chose a classical scheme by Austen Harrison, but at Nuffield's insistence it was redesigned in a stripped Cotswold Tudor idiom, and finally built in 1949–60. Its most striking feature is the blocky tower with its sharply pointed spire, which actually functions as the library book-stack. The chapel contains stained glass by John Piper and Patrick Reyntiens.

Page 77
Oxford Union Society
In 1856–57 Benjamin Woodward (architect of the University Museum) designed a debating hall in polychromatic brick, whose interior was then decorated in Pre-Raphaelite style by William Morris, Edward Burn-Jones, Dante Gabriel Rossetti and others. The room was converted into a library when a larger debating hall was built in 1878 to designs by Alfred Waterhouse.

Said Business School
After considerable debate the University's first business school went up in 1999–2001 on a prominent site at the western approach to the historic centre. The design, by Sir Jeremy Dixon and Edward Jones, is generally bland, with the exception of the stripey brick façade and zigguratical tower facing the railway station.

Page 78
Beaumont Street
Beaumont and St John Streets were built in 1822–33 to meet a demand for houses for the city's professional classes.

Worcester College
In 1714, Sir Thomas Cookes, a Worcestershire landowner, gave money to refound and rebuild what had been the monastic Gloucester College, which was originally established in the late 13th century. A 15th-century range survives, made up of separate units for the different Benedictine monasteries that had sent monks to the college. Dr George Clarke of All Souls College provided the basic plan for the rebuilding, which was then worked up by Nicholas Hawksmoor and carried out with considerable modifications by William Townesend. The three main elements of chapel, library and hall are combined into a U-plan. Construction began in 1720, but the work proceeded very slowly; the library, to which Dr George Clarke bequeathed his outstanding collection of architectural drawings, was completed in 1736, but the hall and chapel had to wait until 1784 and 1791 respectively. They were decorated by James Wyatt in a restrained neo-classical style, which in the 1860s and 1870s William Burges (of Cardiff Castle fame) did his best to submerge beneath a richly unrestrained polychromatic overlay. The chapel looks today as Burges left it, but the hall was re-classicised in 1966. A residential range was built in the 1750s, to which Provost's Lodgings were added according to Henry Keene's designs in 1773–76. Worcester College has unusually extensive grounds, which have made it possible to absorb a number of recent additions: a disappointing block of 1961 by Sir Hugh Casson, the more interesting Sainsbury Building of 1983 by Richard MacCormac, and the Linbury Building of 1991 by the firm of Maguire and Murray.

Gloucester Green
The site has successively contained the city gaol, a cattle market, and the main bus station. It was redeveloped in 1987–90 to include a jolly brick and stone range (architects Kendrick Associates) that harks back to the 'Free Style' of the Edwardian period.

Page 79
Ashmolean Museum
One of Oxford's finest buildings, the Ashmolean was built in 1841–45 to house the University's art collection, whose nucleus was the collection formed in the 17th century by Elias Ashmole. The museum also incorporates the Taylorian Institution, which was endowed in 1788 under the will of the architect Sir Robert Taylor, for the purpose of teaching modern languages. The architect of the new Museum was C. R. Cockerell, who drew on his prior experience of excavating ancient Greek buildings such as the Temple of Apollo at Bassae. The Sackler classics library, which is tucked into the St John Street flank of the museum and completed in 2002 (the architect was Robert Adam), follows Cockerell's lead in going back to ancient Greece for inspiration.

Randolph Hotel
Breaking with the long tradition of picturesque coaching inns, the Randolph was built according to the designs of William Wilkinson in 1863–66 in the same aggressively spiky Gothic idiom that was then being adopted for houses in North Oxford.

Page 80
Keble College
Built in 1868–82 in memory of John Keble, the founder of the High Church Oxford Movement, this college was designed by William Butterfield in polychromatic patterned brick of a kind that was new and shocking in a stone-built city. This reaches its apogee in the richly decorated chapel, which was paid for by the guano-based fortune of the Gibbs family from Bristol. Keble College broke with tradition in several ways, having forward-facing pews in the chapel and corridors rather than staircases. For the first major additions since Butterfield, the firm of Ahrends Burton & Koralek opted in 1973–77 for yellow brick, but in further additions of 1995 architect Rick Mather reverted to red brick.

Page 81
University Museum
The idea of a new scientific museum was promoted by Dr Henry Acland who, under the influence of his friend John Ruskin, chose a Gothic design by the young Irish architect Benjamin Woodward. This was built in 1855–60. To the right of the long patterned stone façade is a former chemistry laboratory, designed like a monastic kitchen, and behind it the enormous hall for exhibits, with a glass roof supported on iron Gothic columns.

Pages 82–83
St Giles
A spacious and tree-lined street, St Giles runs between the Martyrs' Memorial at its southern end to the church of St Giles at the northern end, where the Woodstock and Banbury Roads diverge. Much of the eastern side is taken up with St John's College and its buildings, such as the handsome former Judge's Lodgings (1702) that are now owned by the college. The west side of the street is lined with a pleasing mixture of Town and Gown—the houses and pubs of different dates, shapes and sizes juxtaposed with two 20th-century theological institutions, Blackfriars and Pusey House.

Pages 84–85
St John's College
Archbishop Chichele of Canterbury (see also All Souls College) founded the monastic college of St Bernard in 1437; this was dissolved during the Reformation and then founded anew in 1555 by Sir Thomas White, a London merchant. Beyond the undemonstrative Front Quad lies Canterbury Quad, built at the instigation

of Archbishop Laud in 1631–36, and one of Oxford's most beautiful. It combines old-fashioned Tudor-Gothic elevations with elegant Renaissance arcades and pedimented Mannerist centrepieces. The latter have bronze statues of King Charles I and Queen Henrietta Maria. The architect responsible is unknown, but the mason was the Londoner John Jackson. The college subsequently expanded northwards along St Giles, where there are ranges of 17th, 19th and early 20th-century date, all of which are more or less in Tudor-Gothic style. In 1958, it was decided to abandon traditional caution, and the Architects' Co-Partnership was commissioned to design the so-called 'Beehive' building, Oxford's first college building in an uncompromisingly modernist style. This addition was followed in 1970–75 by the Sir Thomas White Building, designed by Philip Dowson of Arup Associates, and then by Richard MacCormac's monumental Garden Quad (completed in 1994), which makes reference to sources as varied as Hardwick Hall, Sir John Soane, and Japanese temple architecture.

Page 86

Lady Margaret Hall

Although founded in 1878 for girls to be prepared for examinations, Lady Margaret Hall did not achieve full college status until 1960. The original building was a characteristic Norham Gardens house in yellow brick, which was progressively augmented over an extended period by new buildings. These are by such architects as Basil Champneys (1881–83), Sir Reginald Blomfield (1896, 1909–10, 1915), Sir Giles Gilbert Scott (1931), and Raymond Erith (1957–61), and the styles adopted are predominantly late 17th- to early 18th-century domestic. The exception is Scott's chapel in Byzantine style. On the whole the architectural quality is higher than at Somerville, and the buildings are greatly helped by the attractive riverside setting.

Page 87

Wolfson College

Founded as Iffley College in 1964, it was renamed after Lord Wolfson, a major donor, and the new buildings for science graduates went up on the banks of the River Cherwell in 1969–74. The architects were Powell & Moya, who had previously made their name in Oxford with tactful infills to colleges in the historic centre. The rather monotonous ranges of concrete and glass are humanised by the informal planning and leafy riverside setting.

University Cricket Pavilion

This was built in 1880–81 by Sir Thomas Jackson, in a half-timbered idiom that was also adopted for college boat houses of the period. The University Parks in which it stands were laid out in the 1860s.

St Catherine's College

The existing St Catherine's Society for Non-Collegiate Students was rehoused in 1964 in a completely new college built on the water meadows to the north of Magdalen Walks. The architect who designed it was Arne Jacobsen from Denmark, who had been chosen after a tour of recent Continental buildings by University luminaries. As Oxford's most extended essay to date in flat-roofed modernism, with long minimalist blocks running parallel to each other without ever forming a quadrangle in the traditional sense, this design was considered refreshing and forward-looking by some, bleak and charmless by others.

Page 88

Oxford University Press

By the early 19th century, pressure of space rendered the Clarendon Building inadequate for the growing needs of the University's press, so a much larger building was erected on Walton Street in 1826–30, with a noble classical frontage designed by Daniel Robertson. The southern half of the building was intended to house the lucrative Bible press, and the northern the 'learned' press.

Page 89

Somerville College

One of the University's first two women's colleges, Somerville was founded in 1879 and named after the mathematician Mary Somerville. To the original nucleus of Walton Hall, a succession of architects made piecemeal additions in a variety of styles and materials, beginning with Sir Thomas Jackson in 1881, followed by Basil Champneys' library range in 1902–3, and continuing on and off through the 20th century. None of the component parts is particularly distinguished.

St Barnabas, Jericho

St Barnabas church was intended to bring Anglo-Catholicism to the working class inhabitants of the Jericho quarter. It was constructed from rendered brick in 1869–72 and financed by Thomas Combe, Printer to the University and an early patron of the Pre-Raphaelite painters. The architect who designed the building was Arthur Blomfield, and its form evokes that of an Early Christian basilica such as those of Ravenna or Torcello.

St Philip & St James, Woodstock Road

In contrast to St Barnabas, St Philip & St James church was built to minister to the well-to-do residents of the new North Oxford suburb. Stone-built and erected according to the designs of G. E. Street in 1860–65, it adopts a powerful and muscular version of the French 13th-century Gothic style. Unfortunately, most of the original fittings were removed when it became the Oxford Centre for Mission Studies in 1983.

Radcliffe Observatory

Work on the University's observatory, financed by the trustees of Dr Radcliffe (see also Radcliffe Camera and University College), began in 1773 to the designs of Henry Keene. These however were soon modified by the rising star of English classicism, James Wyatt, who took over after Keene died in 1776 and effectively made the building his own. It rises to a central octagonal tower loosely modelled on the Tower of the Winds in Athens, within which is the handsome domed observatory room. The exterior is embellished with carved reliefs of the Winds by John Bacon, and with Coade stone plaques of the Zodiac. The building now stands within the precincts of the recently established Green College.

Page 90–91

Norham Gardens

The Norham Manor Estate was developed by St John's College according to a plan prepared in about 1860 by William Wilkinson. Its leafy roads were gradually built up with substantial detached villas by various architects, mostly in varieties of Gothic.

Park Town

This residential enclave off the Banbury Road was built in 1853–55, in a style and layout consciously emulating the Regency developments of Cheltenham and Leamington Spa. The architect was the City Surveyor, Samuel Lipscomb Seckham.

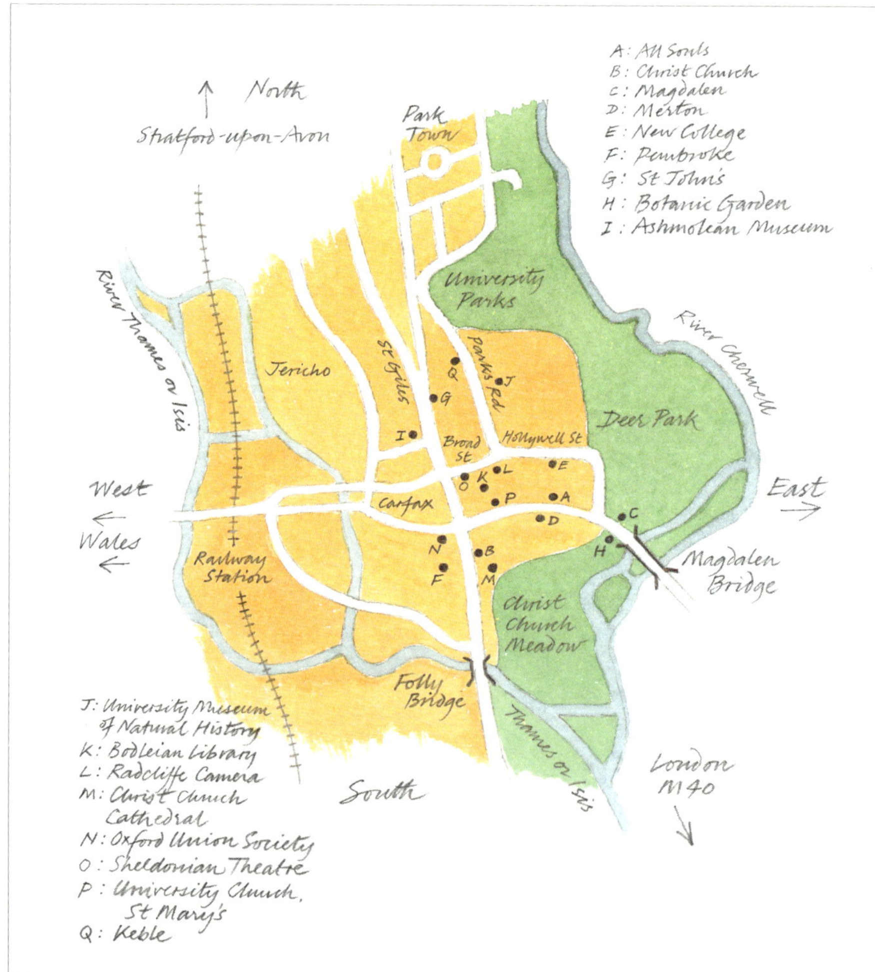

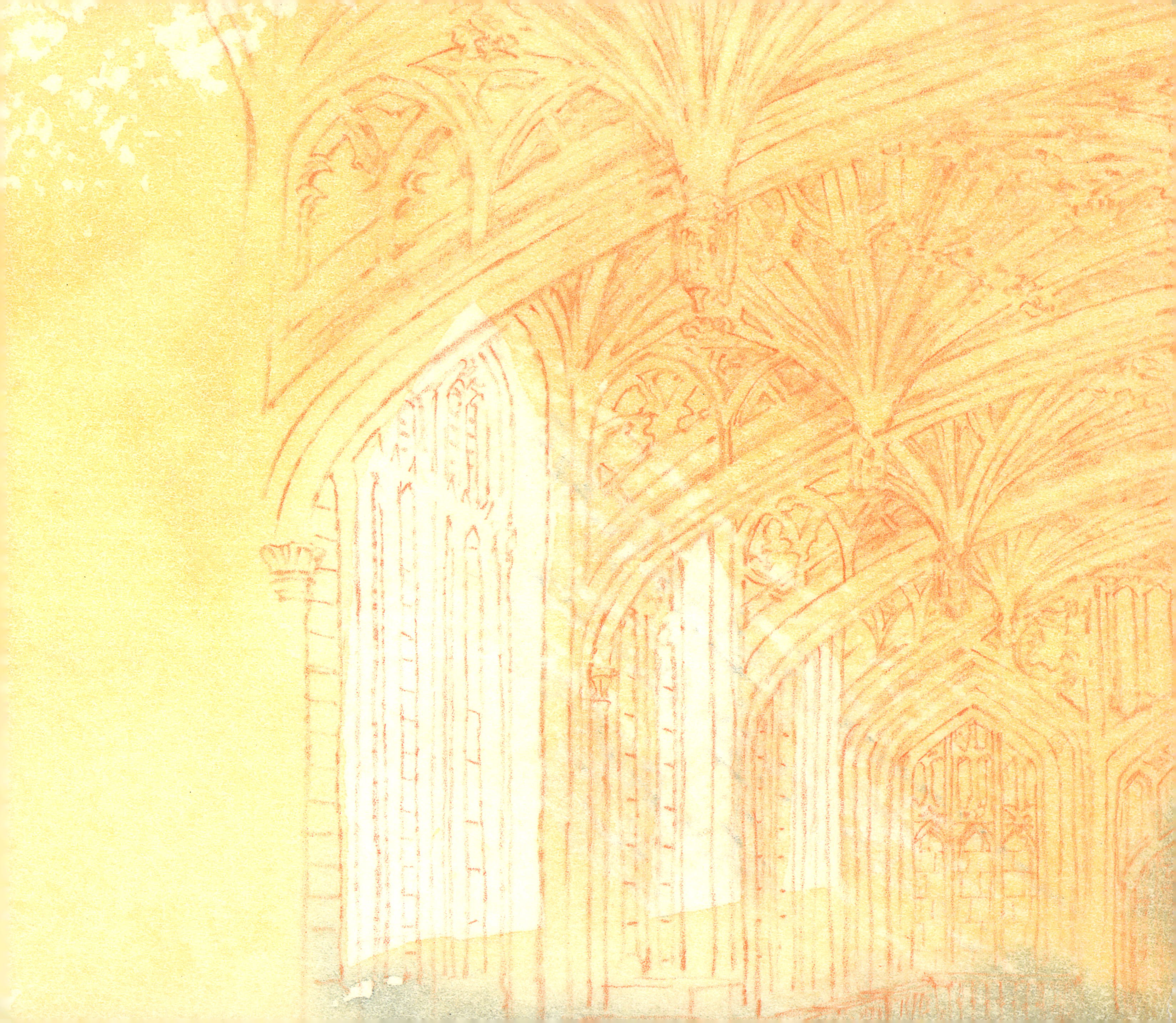